A Practical Manual of
BEEKEEPING

Visit our How To website at **www.howto.co.uk**

At **www.howto.co.uk** you can engage in conversation with our authors – all of whom have 'been there and done that' in their specialist fields. You can get access to special offers and additional content but most imporantly you will be able to engage with, and become a part of, a wide and growing community of people just like yourself.

At **www.howto.co.uk** you'll be able to talk and share tips with people who have similar interests and are facing similar challenges in their lives. People who, just like you, have the desire to change their lives for the better – be it through moving to a new country, starting a new business, growing their own vegetables, or writing a novel.

At **www.howto.co.uk** you'll find the support and encouragement you need to help make your aspirations a reality.

You can go direct to **www.practical-manual-of-beekeeping.co.uk** which is part of the main How To site.

How To Books strives to present authentic, inspiring, practical information in their books. Now, when you buy a title from **How To Books**, you get even more than just words on a page.

A Practical Manual of
BEEKEEPING

How to keep bees and develop your full potential as an apiarist

David Cramp

Spring Hill

Published by Spring Hill

Spring Hill is an imprint of How To Books Ltd,
Spring Hill House, Spring Hill Road,
Begbroke, Oxford OX5 1RX, United Kingdom.
Tel: (01865) 375794, Fax: (01865) 379162
info@howtobooks.co.uk
www.howtobooks.co.uk

How To Books greatly reduce the carbon footprint of their books by sourcing their
typesetting and printing in the UK.

First edition 2008
Reprinted 2009
Reprinted 2010

British Library Cataloguing in Publication Data
A catalogue record for this book is available from the British Library.

ISBN 978 1 90586 223 8

Cover design by Baseline Arts Ltd, Oxford
Produced for How To Books by Deer Park Productions, Tavistock
Typeset by Kestrel Data, Exeter, Devon
Printed and bound by Bell & Bain Ltd, Glasgow

NOTE: The material contained in this book is set out in good faith for general guidance and
no liability can be accepted for loss or expense incurred as a result of relying in particular
circumstances on statements made in the book. Laws and regulations are complex and
liable to change, and readers should check the current position with the relevant
authorities before making personal arrangements.

Contents

List of illustrations and tables

Illustrations

Tables

List of photographs

(between pages 144 and 145)

Introduction

Many readers will ask themselves whether another book on beekeeping can really add anything new to the beekeeping scene. The answer to this question is yes. Although much contained in this book may be known already, information about beekeeping is spread throughout many manuals, specialist books and scientific papers that, even though interesting to search out and read, are not readily accessible to those beginning in beekeeping. This book's aims, therefore, are to gather this knowledge together, to ensure it is presented practically and free from myths, to add to it my wide experience of beekeeping in various parts of the world and to show that anyone can learn how to keep bees, at whatever level they wish.

Beekeepers vary from those who aspire to be hobbyists, who simply enjoy a fascinating pastime; to jobbing beekeepers, moving from hemisphere to hemisphere; managers of their own beekeeping businesses; or researchers, undertaking cutting-edge work into bee flight in space, for example. All this is possible if you are prepared to regard beekeeping not as a quaint, rustic pastime pursued by old, white-haired gentlemen with pipes or by dotty old dears in horn-rimmed glasses but as a vital, multi-billion pound global industry that can offer you the world – if you are prepared to commit yourself to it.

Knowing nothing about bees and beekeeping, I first grasped the opportunity to become a beekeeper when I was given a swarm of bees in a duvet cover as a gift. Suddenly I found that the world was my oyster. I wish only that I had taken this step earlier in my life.

This book will help you to start and continue to be a beekeeper. It offers advice in a very practical manner, with step-by-step guidance at each stage of the way. The advice and information it contains are based on general beekeeping knowledge, my own experiences, my successes in beekeeping and, more importantly, my frequent early failings.

No book on beekeeping can cover everything about such a vast subject, and so a decision was taken to steer the reader towards the practical rather than the theoretical side of the subject. It is hoped that, by doing so, this book should help to get you started. You can pick up the more theoretical aspects from specialist books and beekeeping journals and papers – the important thing now is to begin to explore the exciting world of beekeeping.

Acknowledgements

In writing this book, I gratefully acknowledge two important occurrences; firstly, the unusual birthday present of a swarm of bees in a duvet cover given to me by my wife 18 years ago which started me out on the utterly fascinating route to being a beekeeper; and secondly, 18 years of valuable input from the global community of beekeepers which saved me from the ditch many times and convinced me beyond all doubt that beekeeping really is the finest of professions.

Photo credits

Photos 1, 3, 10	The International Bee Research Association (IBRA)
Photo 4	Ray Williamson, BBKA Collection
Photos 17, 18, 19	National Bee Unit, Central Science Laboratory UK
Photos 20, 21, 22	Colin Eastham
Figure 32	Courtesy of Mark and Thien Gretchen, Seguin, Texas, USA

Chapter 1

Honey-bees and human beings

UNDERSTANDING THE RELATIONSHIP BETWEEN BEES AND POLLINATION

You have just started to read a book about how to enter an exciting, multi-billion pound/dollar, global industry that is not only of vital and strategic interest to governments but is also one that can offer you a fascinating hobby or career that could make you money and take you all over the world.

The honey-bee is one of our best known insects, whose relationship with humans can be traced back to the dawn of humankind when early people 'stole' honey from wild bee nests. Cave paintings in Spain from as long ago as 6000 BC show our ancestors taking honey from bees, which surely indicates that beekeeping is at least as old as the other two oldest professions!

By the time humans did come on the scene, the honey-bee had already been around for about 40–50 million years or more – it had evolved from its hunting-wasp ancestors and had become a strict vegetarian. Bees and flowering plants then evolved with each other in a truly remarkable relationship that changed and coloured the world we live in. This evolutionary symbiotic relationship is probably the most important reason why our world looks like it does today, and still the vital work of bees goes on. It is a sobering thought that, if all humans were to be wiped out, the world would probably revert to the rich, ecologically balanced state that existed some 10,000 years ago. On the other hand, if bees and other pollinating insects were to be wiped out, humans and other animals would not last for long.

Bees pollinate plants so that plants can reproduce, and that really is the bottom line. That is what bees are all about. That is why we need bees and that is why hundreds of millions of dollars, pounds and euros are spent annually by governments around the globe in protecting bees, in bee research and in beekeeping subsidies of one type or another.

Because of their pollinating activities, honey-bees are the most economically important insects on earth, and certainly the most studied. Honey production is essentially a side issue. The honey-bee's role – and thus the beekeeper's role – in this becomes more important and valuable by the day as our farming and other practices dramatically eradicate the habitats of other types of bees and pollinating insects. Some insects can exist only by eating the pollen of certain plants. If those plants were removed so that more crops could be planted, bees and other pollinating insects would die out. What, then, would pollinate our huge areas of mono-crops? The answer would be to truck in honey-bees by the million.

Pollination can be achieved only by using large numbers of honey-bees. In this way, our crops and wildflowers are pollinated, and the beekeeper can obtain a pollination fee and honey for sale. As a reward for pollination, and as an enticement to the bee, most plants offer food – nectar – in return. The bees take this, alter it through the addition of enzymes, reduce its moisture content and store it as honey so that they and their colony may survive winter periods or other periods of dearth. In this way they differ from wasps, bumble-bees and other types of bee, whose colonies die out on the approach of winter, with only the newly mated queens hibernating until the spring when they will start new colonies.

PROFITING FROM A GOLD MINE

Food for free?

If you look at fields full of flowering crops or wild flowers in the countryside, or at garden and park flowers in the cities, you are not only looking at beauty but also at gold – thousands of tons of valuable honey. Liquid gold sitting there, all for you! If you don't go and get it, the flowers will die at the end of the season and all those tons of honey will go to waste. All that money will simply have dried up in front of your eyes. If, on the other hand, you have bees, they will go and get it for you for free, and you can then either eat it or sell it or both.

Bees are probably the only livestock that use other people's land without permission – and those landowners welcome them. It is a win-win situation for the bee and for everyone else. Your bees are happy carrying out their work; you can enjoy your hobby or business, and if you want to you can make a profit; the farmers get their crops pollinated and so they make a profit; the shops obtain food to sell and they make a profit; the general public have food to eat; and the government is happy that its agricultural and environmental sectors are running smoothly and that somewhere along the line they will be able to raise some tax.

Bees and the economy

Don't forget that governments regard the whole set-up as so important that they are willing to spend millions on ensuring that the status quo does not change and that nothing happens to harm it. Recent research in the USA has valued crops that require pollination by honey-bees at an estimated $24 billion annually, and the value of commercial bee pollination on contracts at around $10 billion annually. These are huge figures by any standard and they show that bees are big business.

Using honey in medicine

Honey sale value, on the other hand, is much less, at $285 million annually in the USA. However, now that hard clinical trials are showing that certain types of honey can provide antibiotic wound treatments more effectively and with fewer side-effects than conventional treatments, this non-pollination side of beekeeping has become a rapidly growing industry. Active manuka honey has been shown to beat the MRSA super-bug with no side-effects to the patient and is used in burn dressings. Buckwheat honey has been found in clinical trials to be more effective as a cough treatment than many over-the-counter cough medicines. Honey is no longer old Gran's remedy for colds or an 'alternative' therapy. It is now a mainstream medicine available on national health systems and used in hospitals in the UK, the USA and other countries.

COPING WITH BEE STINGS

But bees sting, don't they? And that hurts, doesn't it? Other than producing honey, bees are best known for their tendency to sting on sight. In fact, it is not in a bee's interest to sting for the sake of it because they die in the process and they will avoid doing so unless in defence of their nest, which of course is why beekeepers are stung. All beekeepers will be stung during their beekeeping careers. This is a fact and it is also a fact that it is painful. But it is not very painful and the pain doesn't last for long.

Bee sting 'cures' rely on this fact. By the time you apply the patented bee-sting cure bought from the snake oil stall at the market (which, technically, can't cure anything unless it's an anaesthetic), the pain would be just about to disappear anyway.

Most beekeepers will tell you that bee stings are more or less of no concern to them and that, if you are well clothed and use calm bees, stings will be few and far between. For a very few, however, there is a danger. Allergy to insect venom does exist and can be fatal if the person stung goes into anaphylactic shock. This is extremely rare, however, and one statistic indicates that you are more likely to die from a horse falling on you than from a bee sting. Because there is a very remote possibility of suffering a fatal allergic reaction, many beekeepers carry with them an epi-pen injector for emergency use. This requires a prescription in most countries.

MAKING A HOBBY OF BEEKEEPING

Beekeeping, though, is more than just a profit-making activity: it can also be a fascinating, environmentally sound hobby that can totally absorb you. Beekeeping in many countries is predominantly a hobby activity. The numbers of commercial beekeepers who 'farm' bees are comparatively few and, in some countries such as the UK and many other European countries, they are a tiny proportion of the whole, and the 'whole' is but a tiny proportion of the population.

Why, then, are governments interested in this small group of people and their hobby? The answer is that, whether beekeepers are hobbyists or commercial operators, they have bees, and the national agricultural sector and the countryside commissions rely totally on these bees. The fewer the commercial beekeepers there are, the more hobbyists are needed to keep these vital sectors going.

BEES AND LEARNING

Honey-bees are not domestic animals. They are wild and, unlike horses and cows and other livestock, they don't recognize beekeepers as their 'owners'. Having said that, recent research has shown that, despite the small size of its brain, a bee can recognize human faces if trained to do so and can remember them for two days. Scientists hope that, by studying this amazing ability further, they will be able to develop better face-recognition computer software. It is unlikely, however, that the average beekeeper will find their bees flocking to them on sight.

Bees (like other insects) are assumed to act on instinct alone. However, they can also 'learn' – and not only learn a primary task but they can also learn and remember a secondary task resulting from the first. Like most other life forms, their daily life involves family (colony) survival and the propagation of their species.

MASTER CHEMISTS

To accomplish this, bees manufacture wax as a building material and honey as an energy food. They also collect pollen as a protein food. They produce propolis to use as a glue, a gap filler and an antibiotic and anti-viral varnish for the nest. They manufacture a highly complex venom to deter predators, including beekeepers, and complex arrays of pheromones that regulate life in the hive. Finally, they produce royal jelly – a highly nutritious substance with which to feed their brood, and they even produce silk to cocoon themselves in during their larval/pupal development. In short, they are master chemists, able to manufacture or collect and alter everything needed for their survival.

RESEARCHING HONEY-BEES

Honey-bees can navigate using the position of the sun, polarized light and landmarks. They can 'tell' other bees about the distance and bearing to sources of food using a well developed symbolic language based on movement and sound. They can also regulate the temperature of the nest to an exact degree using heating and cooling systems of immense complexity. As long as it has water and food, a colony placed on the sides of a volcano or iceberg will maintain its brood nest at 34° C (93° F).

It is these facets of the honey-bee's ability that have caused it to be one of the most researched insects on earth, and all countries maintain at least one institute devoted to bee research, and many universities have bee research departments.

So, could you manage to keep these highly complex creatures? The answer is yes, you could – if you knew how to, and that can be learnt from this book. It is not difficult at all, as long as you know what you are doing.

BECOMING A BEEKEEPER

A beekeeper, then, is someone who is not only engaged in a hobby or business but also someone who (by design or not) is taking an active part in protecting the future of the planet. This sounds dramatic but in fact is true, as you will find out if you continue.

Spending your time beekeeping

Unlike other livestock, bees do not need constant attention. They will go out each day and get on with it whether you are there or not. If you devote one day in ten to them with occasional bursts of more attention when required and during the harvest, you would be able to keep bees satisfactorily, and this is, in the main, for only part of the year. During the winter months you can leave them alone completely unless something dramatic happens, such as flooding or lightning strikes.

Hobby beekeepers usually increase the number of beehives they keep, and some may expand their activity into selling part of their honey crop at local markets and in shops. Most will join their local beekeeping associations that, in some countries such as the UK, are very social institutions holding shows, dinners and drinks parties, lectures and advice sessions, and some of the most cut-throat competitions where skulduggery reigns supreme (they would never admit to this, though).

Specializing

Most commercial beekeepers who make their living from bees started out as hobbyists. Some specialize in honey production, others in pollination services to farmers; others specialize in rearing queen bees for sale; and yet others specialize in other hive products, such as beeswax, pollen, propolis or royal jelly. There is even a large and profitable market in bee venom. Some graduate into apitherapy – a very effective alternative type of healing that is fast becoming mainstream medicine. Mead, honey or propolis soap, face creams and so on are all side-lines for the imaginative beekeeper.

Other beekeepers devote their efforts to breeding the 'perfect' bee: a calm, gentle, disease-resistant, productive creature. Despite the fact that a male bee or drone has no father (which complicates the issue), breeding success is often claimed to be at hand. And then there are the professional itinerant beekeepers who make a living by hiring themselves out to large commercial outfits all over the world. These young men and women travel the world moving from one hemisphere to the other according to the seasons, using their beekeeping skills to pick up the many jobs available in commercial beekeeping.

These people start as basic beekeepers and move on to become team leaders, head beekeepers and managers. They lead a physically hard life of travel and excitement. They pick up a huge range of skills, from heavy-truck driving, to landowner dispute mediation, plant biology and chemistry, to disease problem-solving and everything in between, and they come from all over the world. They need a huge amount of practical ability so that they can exist for weeks on end in often very remote areas, and they are known as the world's last cowboys. In one beekeeping firm in New Zealand I worked with Peruvians, Canadians, Australians, Philippinos and Brits. Just down the road another similar firm employed Bulgarians and Peruvians. At the end of the season, most of them moved on to the Northern Hemisphere. But they would be back. And when on a night out, these young men tell the pretty young woman in the local pub that they are beekeepers, that young lady always wants to find out more (or the other way round, of course)!

Destressing yourself

You can even adopt a Zen approach to beekeeping – go with the seasons and be part of nature. Remember that bees are probably the most 'natural' of all humanity's livestock. They are totally wild creatures. There is nothing domesticated about them at all, and so nature and the seasons mean everything to them – and to you, if you follow them. All the clues to success with this approach are in front of you.

Finally, while still on the subject of beekeepers, I know of two very highly placed executives who each have two hives and who just like to destress themselves after a busy week in the office by sitting in the sun with a glass of wine and watching the bees coming and going from the hives. They leave all the honey to the bees and carry out only minimal essential tasks to ensure their bees' survival. What more could you ask for?

THE WORLD IS YOUR OYSTER

So what type of beekeeper will you be? There is a huge choice but, whatever you choose to do, you will need some essential instruction and guidance, and it is the aim of this book to start you off and to provide essential information clearly and accurately. By following the information in this book you will soon be enjoying yourself as a beekeeper, with a whole new world of possibilities opening up in front of you. If you are a beekeeper, the world is your oyster.

Chapter 2

Understanding the honey-bee colony

CONSIDERING THE COLONY AS A SINGLE ORGANISM

A single honey-bee cannot live for very long on its own. There would be no point in doing so. A worker bee cannot reproduce; a queen bee cannot construct comb, collect food or even feed herself; and a drone bee is able to accomplish only one task and that is to mate. All three castes of honey-bee that live in a colony of bees – the queen, the worker and the drone – therefore can live only as part of a colony. The colony is in effect the organism, with the individual bees acting as the cells that make up that organism. In order to keep bees successfully, the beekeeper has to understand that organism: how and why it works and what it needs for its survival. Only then can the beekeeper work with bees, adapting his or her requirements to theirs. You can't direct bees, but you can encourage them to work your way – to a certain extent.

When you first look into a hive and see thousands of bees apparently moving around at random and flying off the comb in all directions, the colony appears to be a place of chaos. But it isn't. All this movement has a purpose and, within a short time in beekeeping, you will begin to see this purpose for what it is, and that is a highly organized society going about its business. You will also begin to notice when things aren't going right in the colony and, with more experience, you will be able to look at each comb and, almost instantly, will be able to picture clearly in your mind the state of the colony. Is it healthy? Is there a queen? Is the queen laying well? Are the bees building up in numbers as you would expect? Will they survive the winter? Do they need feeding? It is like reading a book with clearly drawn diagrams. First, however, you should gain an understanding of the development of the three inhabitants of the hive – the queen, the worker and the drone (see Figure 1).

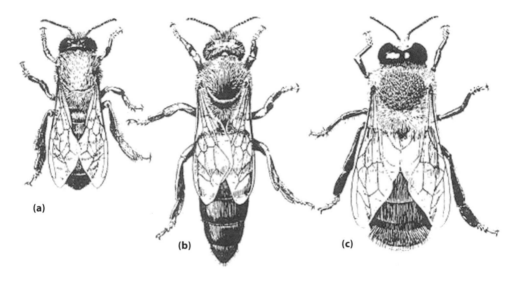

(a)

(b)

(c)

Fig. 1. The inhabitants of the hive: (a) worker, (b) queen and (c) drone.

BEE DEVELOPMENT

Each type of bee begins life as a small egg laid by the queen in the base of a wax cell in the comb. After three days, the egg hatches and the bee begins its larval phase in an open cell, being fed by nurse bees first on royal jelly and then on a mixture of pollen and honey (unless they are destined to be a queen bee, when royal jelly will be fed continuously). After another five days, (six for a drone bee), the workers cap the cell, and the larva spins a cocoon around itself and begins its pupal stage during which it gradually changes into an adult bee. The bee then chews through the capping of wax and emerges as an adult. This means, of course, that every bee you see is an adult.

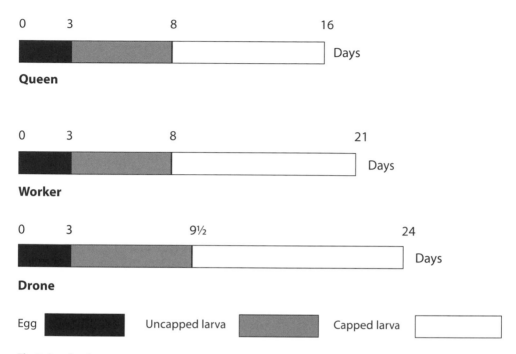

Fig. 2. Bee development

Figure 2 shows this development and how long it takes. While it is important to remember the timings of this development, which we look at in more detail in later chapters of this book, the following are some notes about what each type of bee does after emerging:

- **Queen:** if climatic conditions permit, the queen will make a mating flight around five or six days after emergence. She will start to lay eggs 36 hours or more after a successful mating flight, usually more after three days.

- **Drones:** these are fed by workers until around seven days old. They remain in the hive until approximately 12–13 days old (when they are sexually mature). Thereafter, they undertake mating flights during the afternoons. They are removed from the hive during the autumn or during times of dearth.

■ **Workers:** this is a complex subject we can only touch on here. A worker's lifespan will vary according to the time of year. During the summer, the average life span is 15–38 days; during the winter it can be 140 days or more. This depends very much on the prevailing conditions.

Note: the number of days until emergence can vary considerably (e.g. for a queen, 14–17 days; for a worker, 16–24 days; and for a drone, 20–28 days). This variability may be due to environmental factors (especially temperature) and nutrition.

QUEEN BEES

There is generally one queen bee in any colony. The queen is a complete female in that she can mate and lay eggs, and those, essentially, are her only tasks in life – to mate and lay eggs. She isn't much bigger than a worker, especially before she has mated, and, in a very populous hive, can be difficult to find but, with experience, most beekeepers can find her easily enough. Finding the queen is an important part of beekeeping management, and tips on queen-finding are given in Chapter 6.

On emergence from her cell as an adult virgin, the queen mates within a few days. With worker bee encouragement she leaves the hive and flies some distance to what is known as a drone congregation area (DCA), where she mates on the wing with up to 20–30 drone bees, but usually fewer. Her pheromones attract the waiting drones which, one after another, fly up to her, grasp her from behind, evert their internal genitals and literally explode into the queen, ripping themselves apart in the process and dying on the spot. Then the next drone takes over.

As soon as the queen has stored enough sperm in her sperm sac or spermatheca, she returns to the hive and starts life as the queen bee of the colony. Her time outside the hive is dangerous because of predators, such as birds, and also as a result of bad weather, and so all is usually accomplished in this one flight. She meets drones from many different colonies, thus helping to maintain genetic diversity and preventing inbreeding. It is perhaps a point worth making that only the fastest and strongest drones reach her before she goes home, which may help in propagating only the best of the species.

DCAs are mysterious affairs, and much scientific research has gone into trying to find out why they are where they are and exactly what their boundaries are. There is a DCA over Selborne Common in Hampshire that was first described by the Rev. Gilbert White in the 1700s. It still reappears in the same place each year and can easily be heard on a fine summer's day. In these DCAs, drones mate with a queen. If they pass an invisible boundary inches away, they won't. Why not? How do drones, which are new each year, know where they are? How do virgin queens know where they are? This is a subject ripe for further investigation, the results of which would aid commercial beekeepers immensely, and this is another opportunity for those interested in beekeeping – research on the subject. Why not combine your hobby with a career as a scientist?

Participating in multiple sex

Research has shown that worker bees back in the colony will pay more attention to a queen that has mated with a large number of drones than to one that has mated with fewer, and that they will more readily accept her. The multiple-mated queen and the queen mated fewer times have been found to have pheromonal differences, behavioural differences and queen/worker interaction differences. In other words, the more matings the better. If a beekeeper is introducing an expensively purchased queen to a colony, this is an important matter, and scientists therefore hope to devise a test so that beekeepers can know the quality of the queen they buy from a queen rearer.

Once the queen returns to her nest, she will have enough stored sperm in her spermatheca to last her for her lifetime, and she will become an egg-laying machine able to lay up to 2,000 eggs a day in her prime. During her 'reign' she will exude chemical messages called pheromones that are passed around the colony by bee-to-bee contact. Worker bees of a certain age groom, clean and feed the queen, who is unable to carry out these tasks herself, and it is these attendants that initiate the passing around of queen pheromones. The most important of these pheromones tell the bees that the queen is there; that she is fit and healthy and is laying eggs. These pheromones also inhibit the enlargement of worker bee ovaries.

Swarming

The fast and effective passage of these pheromones around the colony is essential to colony stability. If the queen is ageing or has other problems and the strength of her pheromones diminishes, or if the colony becomes so crowded that the message takes longer to get around, then the workers may sense this and start to build new queen cells in preparation for queen renewal. Unless the beekeeper acts decisively, this may lead to swarming, where the old queen and up to half the workers and a few drones depart the colony and start another one elsewhere while the workers in the original colony raise a new queen. Thus where there was one colony there will now be two, with the new young queen getting the best of the deal by retaining the existing nest, stores and brood.

This is in effect colony reproduction and is an entirely natural state of affairs, but it does mean that half the beekeeper's honey-producing livestock flies off and, in all likelihood, becomes someone else's honey-producing livestock. (Most beekeepers collect swarms that are, in effect, free additions to their livestock numbers.) We deal with swarms and swarm control in more detail in Chapter 6.

Attributes and role

The queen can sting, but her sting lacks an effective barb and its base is well anchored so that she can usually withdraw it safely. She uses her sting only to kill rival queens and would rarely, if ever, sting a human.

The queen bee can live for around four years (10 times longer than a worker) unless replaced earlier by the bees or the beekeeper (queen replacement is discussed in Chapter 6). She will not fly out of the hive again unless she leads a swarm in search of a new home, or unless you drop her, when she may fly off never to be seen again.

Considering that she comes from the same genome as a worker bee, her long life is surprising, especially as most organisms trade long life for not reproducing. Yet the queen has it both ways. She can lay up to around 2,000 eggs a day and still live for a long time.

Research shows that a substance called vitellogenin – a yoke protein important to reproduction – is in higher concentrations in queens than in workers, especially as they age. This substance has been shown to reduce oxidative stress in honey-bees by scavenging free radicals that can lead to ageing or illness – a little like drinking green tea and taking vitamin E pills.

As she lays her eggs, the queen measures the size of the cells with her antennae before laying one egg at the base of the cell. If the cell is a 'worker'-size cell, then the queen will fertilize the egg as it passes out of her and, around 21 days later, one of the most interesting and complex creatures on earth, a worker bee, inheriting genes from both her father and mother, will emerge from the cell.

WORKER BEES

Duties

The worker is an incomplete female in that she can't mate and reproduce, but she does do just about everything else and, if you see a honey-bee collecting nectar and pollen from flowers, it will be a worker. Worker bees pass through various task-related phases as they age. Unlike ants, for example, which have task-related castes (such as soldier ants for defence and so on), honey-bee workers engage in defence or other duties at certain ages (see Figure 3).

On emerging from her cell as an adult bee, the worker begins work by cleaning out brood cells and then by capping brood with wax as they enter their pupal stage. She then tends the brood and feeds them and, after that, she engages in such duties as tending the queen. As the worker becomes older (during the summer months we are talking of an average 15–38 day lifespan), she receives nectar from incoming foragers and places this in storage cells. She also engages in housework, such as hive-cleaning duties that include, for some, undertaker bee duties or the removal of dead bees.

She then engages in ventilation and fanning duties, and produces wax. Workers can synthesize the sugars in nectar and honey into beeswax, which they extrude through glands underneath their abdomens. Each worker has four 'wax mirrors' from which wax is extruded. Wax is employed to build comb that is used as a nursery for brood, as a store for pollen, a store for honey and as a surface on which to live in the hive. In other

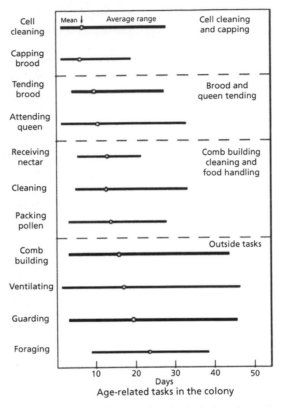

Fig. 3. A worker bee's age-related tasks in the colony

words, wax is central to the bees' existence. Without it, no food can be stored, no eggs could be laid and no brood reared. The colony would soon die out.

Finally, the worker begins guard and defence duties at the entrance to the hive and will readily launch herself at the beekeeper or strange bees. This guarding stage may last for only a day or two, after which she will fly off and forage for nectar, pollen, propolis or water. Therefore as her various glands develop and then atrophy, her duties change, and she finally works herself to death as a forager if she hasn't previously died in combat, from disease or from having been eaten by a predator.

Regulating the duties

The colony can, however, alter this progression of duties if it needs to. If, for example, the colony's forager bees are killed by pesticides, then younger bees will become foragers sooner and may miss out an intervening stage. On the other hand, if all the younger nurse bees who feed the brood are removed, older forager bees will revert to being nurse bees, and this is no mean feat: their food-producing glands have atrophied by the time they become foragers and have to become active again in order for them to produce brood food.

One of the pheromone chemicals that regulates this progression of work is ethyl oleate. Possibly spread around the colony by mouth-to-mouth contact, this pheromone slows down the development of younger bees. Older forager bees carry some 30 times as much of this chemical as younger bees do so, if there are plenty of foragers bringing in the honey, there will be plenty of ethyl oleate in the hive, and this will keep younger bees from developing into foragers. However, should the colony run low on mature foragers (for example, due to spray poisoning), the supply of this grow-slow pheromone will dwindle, and young bees will mature rapidly to fill in the ranks. When foragers again abound, a new abundance of the pheromone will slow the replacement process.

Living in a state of dynamic equilibrium

The whole colony, therefore, lives in a state of dynamic equilibrium, ready to alter or amend its priorities and population ratios at any given time, but only and always for the colony's benefit and survival. The beekeeper can't change any of this but can work with the flow by helping to ensure that external factors, such as lack of shelter, starvation, disease, queen failure and so on, are minimized and remedied swiftly if they do occur.

The worker bee, then, is an immensely complex creature that has given up her right to reproduce in exchange for furthering the cause of her genetic propagation via a single laying queen. This evolutionary trait, however, is apparently not yet complete. If the queen dies and colony attempts to raise another queen fail, then the ovaries of certain of the workers will enlarge and they will begin to lay eggs. However, the colony is doomed because, as workers have no apparatus for mating, the eggs will result in unfertilized drone brood laid in small worker cells.

Competition from other laying workers is intense, and a clear sign of this laying-worker syndrome is the sight of several eggs in a cell. These eggs will often be placed halfway down the cell due to the shorter length of the worker's abdomen. If at this stage another queen bee is introduced to the colony, the laying workers will invariably kill her (dealing with this problem is examined in Chapter 8).

The 'waggle dance'

Bees are such efficient pollinators because, as forager bees, they can communicate the source of food to each other. Immediately on setting up as a colony, scout bees are out looking for the nearest and best sources of nectar and pollen. When they find these, they return to the nest with samples and tell the other foragers about the location and how to get there using a highly symbolic dance language based on movement and sound.

Performing the 'waggle dance'

What is known as the 'waggle dance' has been studied by scientists for decades, and it is generally believed to be the method by which bees tell one another of the location of food and potential new nest sites. The dance takes the form of a figure of eight and is performed by worker bees on the vertical surface of a comb (see Figure 4). The worker moves along a straight line in the figure of eight and waggles from side to side. When this waggle phase is complete, the bee circles to one side and returns to the starting point. This sequence is then often repeated over 100 times, with the direction of the return phase circling alternating each time.

The duration of the waggle phase is correlated to the distance of the food source and the number of cycles performed is correlated to the size of the food supply. The further the foraging site, therefore, the longer the duration of the waggle, and the bigger the food source the greater the number of dance cycles. The angle of the straight line from the vertical (vertical comb) is equal to the angle between the food source and the sun upon departure from the hive, and the vigour with which the waggle is performed is an indication of how much food is present at the site.

While carrying out this dance routine, the bee will often stop and give out small samples of nectar to those attending the dance. The attending bees gather a great deal of information from this dance, such as how far away the nectar is, the direction of

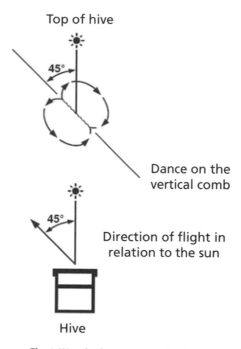

Top of hive

45°

Dance on the
vertical comb

45°

Direction of flight in
relation to the sun

Hive

Fig. 4. Waggle-dance communication

flight to take and the value of the source, and they also gain a taste of the nectar, which can give them an odour cue.

Another dance consists of the bee performing a circular movement. This is believed to tell attending bees that there is nectar near to the hive and to go out and look in the surrounding area.

Understanding the waggle dance

The significance of this dance was really discovered by professor Karl von Frisch in Germany in the 1960s. His books, *The Dancing Bees* and *Bees: Their Chemical Senses and Language*, describe the experiments he used and they are worth reading. The latter was in fact the first book I ever read on bees, and the only reason I bought it was that I love books and here was a hardback for only £6.95. How it changed things!

Over the succeeding decades, however, von Frisch's theories were constantly challenged by scientists who believed that the bees found the food by flying downwind of the odour plume and that all that the returning forager imparted was the odour. What was questioned about the Frisch theory was whether bees could decode the dance because scientists did not believe observing bees with such small brains could actually follow the instructions.

New tests carried out at Rothamsted in the UK, however, have shown that von Frisch was right all along. Radar has helped to resolve this long-standing controversy, and the scientists found that the famous waggle dance contains information about the whereabouts of nectar, just as was originally proposed in the 1960s.

Radar tracking effectively proved the bees do follow waggle-dance instructions. The scientists fixed radar transponders to bees who had watched the waggle dance to track their route to the food source, and it was found they flew straight there. To double check, bee recruits were taken to release sites 250 m (820 ft) away from the hive. These bees flew to where the feeding site should have been had they not been displaced, showing they were following the dance instructions accurately. The scientists found that this was very strong supporting evidence for the von Frisch hypothesis because, in this case, there was no possibility the bees were following regular routes or any odours the dancer might have left in the air.

The worker's lifespan

All in all, a worker bee's lifespan varies according to the time of the year. During summer, the average lifespan is 15–38 days whereas, during winter, it can be 140 days or more. This variation is probably due to environmental factors – she will work hard during the summer weather – and also to nutrition. During the winter months she will not work much and will live off stores in the hive and body fat built up prior to the winter period.

Worker bee genetic variation

The worker bee, therefore, changes her duties according to a time schedule, but the situation is more complex than this. For example, at a given stage in their development, not all workers will be needed as undertaker bees, removing dead bees from the hive. So who decides which workers will do this and which ones won't? This is probably where genetic variation comes into play: some workers will be more genetically disposed to carrying out this task than others.

Why is this? Remember that the queen mates with many drones, and so one group of workers will be super-sisters derived from one father, all with a particular genetic make-up, while other workers will be from the same queen but another father with a different genetic make-up. Workers from the different genetic groups will have different genetically driven dispositions to carry out the myriad tasks in the colony. There may be many different subfamilies in the colony, and this depends on the number of drones the queen mated with. All the workers therefore will have the same mother, but not necessarily the same father. Research has shown that this genetic variation is vital for the efficient working of the hive and is another reason for the queen to mate with so many drones.

The number of worker bees in a colony will vary throughout the year but, during the height of the active season, will number around 60,000–80,000 or more bees.

DRONE BEES

If on measuring the size of the cell a queen bee finds that it is a larger drone cell, she will not fertilize the egg as it passes out and, around 24 days later, a drone bee will emerge. Resulting from an unfertilized egg by a process known as parthenogenesis, the drone bee is, in effect, a flying gamete, having converted the genetic content of an unfertilized egg from one female into sperm and having carried this to another female.

Recognizing drones

The drone is a very specialized animal indeed. He is a big, burly bee, and most novice beekeepers mistake drones for the queen. He is easily distinguished, however, because of his blunt abdomen and huge eyes, which cover most of his head. He has no sting and can be handled safely. This fact often leads even mature beekeepers to show off in front of non-beekeepers, and small children have been known to trick their teachers by presenting them with a handful of buzzing drones.

Drones and mating

The drone is optimized for mating and, to do this to best effect, he needs to be able to fly extremely fast (his flight muscles and wing size are larger than worker bees'), to have extremely sharp vision and an extraordinary array of sense organs designed to respond to queen and other drone pheromones over large distances. For example, a queen bee has around 3,000–4,000 eye facets in her compound eye; a worker bee has up to 6,900; but a drone has up to 8,600. A queen bee has some 1,600 antennal plate organs (sensory organs); the worker has around 3,000, and the drone has an amazing 30,000. And it is these receptors that have been studied closely to find out how a drone finds a queen in the air and, sure enough, a research team in the USA has recently identified an odorant receptor that allows male drones to find a queen in flight. The receptor on the male antennae can detect an available queen up to 60 m (195 ft) away. The drone detects the queen substance pheromone, and this is the first time an odorant receptor has been linked to a specific pheromone in honey-bees.

Queen substance pheromone

The 'queen substance' (or 'queen retinue pheromone') was first identified decades ago, but scientists have only recently begun to understand its structure and role in the hive. This pheromone is a primary source of the queen's ability to influence behaviour in the hive. It is made up of eight components, one of which – 9-oxo-2-decenoic acid (9-ODA) – attracts the drones during mating flights. (It also draws workers to the queen and retards their reproductive growth, which means that the lack of a queen can lead to the presence of laying workers; we deal with this problem in Chapter 8.)

After mating

In the sense that the drone is a vital link in the reproductive chain, the colony could not do without him, but he has few if any other tasks. During the autumn and winter periods or other periods of dearth when mating cannot take place or other survival factors take priority for the colony, the workers will therefore destroy drone brood and drag out drones and kill them or refuse their readmittance to the hive.

The number of drones in a colony at the height of the season will be in the hundreds only, perhaps at most around a thousand. The drone is fed by workers until he is around seven days old, and he remains in the hive until around 12–13 days old when he is sexually mature. He takes mating flights during afternoon periods. Usually drones are pushed out of the hive when there is little forage or when winter approaches and they have no further purpose. Some may survive: I have found drones in hives in mid-winter and I think that those who say that all drones are kicked out as winter approaches have never looked in a hive over this period – for very good reasons.

THE POLITICS OF THE HIVE, OR 'WHO TELLS WHOM WHAT TO DO?'

So who actually controls what goes on in the hive? Which of the three castes of bees gives direction to the whole? Who decides when to send out foragers to concentrate on water collection rather than nectar, for example? Who is the boss?

Decision-making in the colony

For thousands of years decision-making in the colony was thought to be the mandate of the king bee, and the politics of the bee kingdom has been discussed in books and by bee masters for centuries. This bee – which could be seen easily – was thought to direct the total effort by sending out foragers for certain products and sending out his armies for defence when required. In 1609, Charles Butler in England produced his book on bees called *The Feminine Monarchie* (see Figure 5), in which he recognized that the king was in fact a female and so should be called a queen.

Even Butler, however, believed that the bees obeyed this monarch in all things and that the 'queen' kept order in the hive by using a whole hierarchy of the nobility and other officials – princes, dukes, colonels, captains and so on – each with its own distinguishing marks, hair tufts and tassels. The Romans even added magistrates to the hierarchy! More recently, as we have begun to understand the dynamics of the hive better, new research has shown that, although the queen is the mother of all the bees in the colony and also their surrogate father (she holds the sperm in her spermatheca), we can see that major colony activities are initiated by the cumulative group actions of the colony's older workers and not by the queen's individual decision. For example, scientists discovered that older workers give signals to the queen and to the rest of the colony that it is time to swarm and leave the hive. They also initiate her swarm flight by piping to her and telling her to fly (we look at swarming in more detail in Chapter 6).

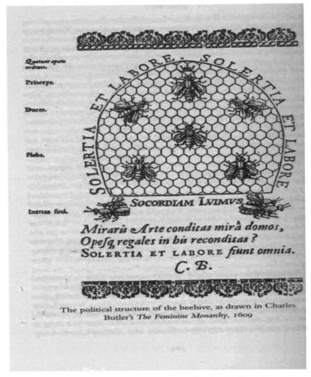

Fig. 5. *The Feminine Monarchie* by Charles Butler, often regarded as the father of English beekeeping.

We have also seen the example of ethyl oleate mentioned earlier in this chapter. Again, this is a worker-inspired instruction.

Decentralized control

The bee colony is not, therefore, a dominance hierarchy – which is unusual from a human perspective –but it is, in fact, very decentralized. Like humans, bees live in large, organized groups where social behaviours co-ordinate the efforts of thousands of individuals in order to accomplish complex activities, such as food provision, defence, household maintenance, brood rearing and so on. But unlike humans, although the colony is centred around the queen for the obvious reason that she is the propagator of the species, she doesn't rule. She doesn't control. The colony appears to be controlled by what has been called 'the anonymous consensus of the colony's workers'. These recent findings could well be of importance to our understanding of the dynamics of all social animals, including ourselves.

THE BIRTH OF A QUEEN

Preparing for the birth

When the colony requires a new queen – if, for example, the old one dies or becomes old and ineffective in her laying, or for other reasons that will become clear later on in the book – the workers begin to construct queen cups, which are cells on the surface of the comb but facing vertically downwards. If they proceed with the plan, the queen lays fertilized eggs into the cups (the same as worker eggs), and the creation of a new queen begins. After 16 days, a queen bee emerges from her very distinctive cell.

If allowed to by the worker bees, the new queen kills off potential rival queens still in sealed cells by stinging them through the cell wall, and then she fights any other virgin queens in the hive that have emerged – again, if allowed to by the workers. Worker bees occasionally keep another virgin in readiness in case the first fails to mate, and they will protect this virgin until they have a mated queen.

Queen bee development

The difference between a worker bee and a queen is due solely to the quality and quantity of the food fed to the larvae. The queen larvae receive a much larger percentage of royal jelly over a longer period than do worker larvae. Royal jelly contains a much higher proportion of worker mandibular gland secretions, and the difference is very marked. Royal jelly has up to 10 times more pantothenic acid and 18 times more biopterin than food fed to worker larvae, but quantity is also important, and queen larvae must consume far more food than workers.

For the first two or three days of larval development, the respiratory and growth rates of queens and workers are similar. The queen rates accelerate, however, during the last few days so, although the development of workers and queens is based on nutrition, the effects of the different feeding patterns are not expressed until the larvae are at least three days old.

This whole subject is immensely complex, and this chapter is designed as an introduction only. What you need to remember, though, is that worker and queen bees start out exactly the same and that different nutritional regimes cause them to differ markedly. In effect, all fertilized eggs start out as potential queens. After three days of development a change in diet for the majority of them forms the worker bees. The others remain as queens.

Researching royal jelly

Recent research at the Australian National University may explain why eating royal jelly causes honey-bee larvae to become queens instead of workers. Scientists from the Research School of Biological Sciences at the university have discovered that a copious diet of royal jelly flicks a genetic switch in young bees that determines whether they'll become a queen or live a life of drudgery. They found that royal jelly seems to modify chemically the bee's genome by a process called DNA methylation and disrupts the expression of genes that turn young bees into workers.

When they 'silenced' a gene controlling DNA methylation without recourse to royal jelly, they discovered that the larvae began to develop as queens with the associated fertility, rather than as infertile workers. They believe this is the first time that DNA methylation has been functionally implicated in insects. This molecular process is common in vertebrates – including humans.

Replacing a queen

If the queen suddenly dies or is removed, there will be no eggs in queen cups to develop into queens. The workers will then choose young larvae under three days old in worker cells that already exist, draw out the cells, feed them as for queens and so produce emergency queens.

There is much debate and research on how effective these queens are compared with planned ones, but it is evident that the bees do not always choose the best larvae and that some of these emergency queens are, at best, sufficient. This is something to remember, and in Chapter 11 we come back to it when we look at rearing queens. One thing is certain, though, and that is that each time a beekeeper looks into the hive, they should check on the existence of, and health of, the queen.

COLONY NEST REQUIREMENTS

Finding a new nesting site

The queen, worker and drone are, then, the residents in a healthy colony of bees. When a swarm of bees takes up residence at a site of their choosing, this site has been carefully chosen for certain characteristics. Occasionally, a swarm is unable to find a suitable home and so will end up out in the open where it may prosper for a while until succumbing to cold, wet weather in the winter months or to varroa. Generally, however, a cavity is looked for. This could be a hollow tree, an old chimney, a cavity wall or, on one occasion, the pannier of a motorcycle.

Inspection of bee nests has found that the average nest comprises a cavity of around 40 l (70 pt) capacity, with most being between 20 and 100 l (35 and 175 pt), and these can differ between the different races. Research has shown that the Italian bee prefers a cavity of around 30 l (50 pt), whereas the central European German bee prefers a cavity of 60 l (100 pt). Tropical honey-bees often choose sites outside cavities under branches or overhangs.

The colony will choose a site out of direct exposure to sun, wind and rain with south-facing entrances (in the Northern Hemisphere), and the preferred cavity has only one entrance. From this knowledge, humans have been able to design the best type of artificial cavity to make for their bees and have learnt the best places to put them. Modern beehives and their preferred locations have been based on these criteria.

Developing the colony

On arrival at a new nest site, the workers immediately start to synthesize the honey in their stomachs into wax and begin to build comb. Until they build comb, the queen cannot lay eggs and the foragers cannot store food. Other workers search for food, nectar and pollen and, very soon, the colony is established with the queen laying eggs, the foragers bringing in food and the house bees maintaining the nest.

The colony grows: the bees store food beyond their immediate needs for periods of dearth (such as winter) and, if they have chosen a good site, they will prosper until the varroa mite causes the colony's death. This is not true of all areas of the world, but in most areas where the western honey-bee lives, varroa will kill the colony if left untreated. They don't intend to because, if the colony dies, so do the mites, but the varroa mite evolved with the eastern honey-bee, *Apis cerana* which, having evolved with it, knows how to control it and they can live together. When the western honey-bee (which is hugely superior in honey production) was taken to the Far East and the mite jumped species, the western bee had no defence and, apart from some bees of Russian origin, still hasn't. So it can be seen that, in nature, until evolutionary pressures cause natural defence mechanisms to develop, the honey-bee cannot currently survive on its own. It needs a beekeeper.

THE BEEKEEPER'S ROLE

Now that you know that the honey-bee colony is a living, dynamic entity that can be looked upon as a unit of livestock and now that you have an understanding of what those bees are up to and why, it is easier to see where the beekeeper comes in and exactly what their role is when working with bees. Like any other livestock guardian – whether a hobbyist, a research scientist or a commercial farmer – a beekeeper has a responsibility to use their skill and knowledge to provide the bees with appropriate shelter from the elements; to place colonies in such a position that there is plenty of forage and water for the bees in the local area; to protect the colony from predators and disease; to feed the colony when required; to encourage it to produce honey by providing it with storage room; and to know how to increase the number of colonies available if required or to prevent this happening if increase is not wanted.

There is nothing more dismal for a beekeeper than finding an apiary of neglected hives containing dead or dying colonies that provide a reservoir of disease-bearing organisms.

The beekeeper's tasks outlined above are a summary of what you must be able to accomplish if you become a beekeeper. This is not difficult: it is enjoyable and, at the end of the day, seeing everything work out well is immensely satisfying.

But to do all this, the beekeeper needs certain items of equipment, knowledge and a plan, and that is just the beginning. Once you start in beekeeping, you will never stop learning.

This book will now show you exactly what you need to get started, what you need to know to keep bees successfully, and it will provide you with the plan.

SUMMARY

This chapter has discussed the following points:

- **The colony or beehive should contain a queen bee, worker bees and drone bees.**

- **The queen bee mates on the wing with up to 20 or more drone bees (the more the better) from a wide radius in order to maintain genetic diversity. She stores the sperm and uses it to fertilize eggs. She can lay up to 2,000 eggs a day. She is fed and groomed by worker bees and, in this way, spreads pheromones around the colony. She has a sting which she uses only to fight rival queens. After mating she won't fly again unless part of a swarm – which we look at in Chapter 6. There is usually only one queen in the hive. All fertilized eggs result in bees that have the potential to be a queen.**

- **The worker bee is an incomplete female who is unable to mate. She carries out all the other tasks inside and outside the hive, such as cleaning, caring for and feeding brood, foraging for food and colony defence. She has a sting and will use it in defence of the colony. The** colony may contain many thousands of workers – perhaps 60,000–80,000 or more in a good colony. Worker bees start off with the potential to be queens, but diet change causes them to veer from this course and they fail to develop as queens.

- The drone bee is a male bee optimized for mating with a virgin queen bee. He has no sting and is fed by workers. In times of lack of food, drones are often ejected from the hive by workers. There are usually a few hundred in a colony.

- A colony of bees requires a cavity in which to live and in which they construct wax combs for the storage of food (honey and pollen) and for the rearing of young brood. The cavity or beehive must be well sited in an area where forage and water are available and where it is protected from the elements.

- The beekeeper's role is to ensure that the bees' living requirements are met and that they are protected from disease and starvation.

Knowing these requirements and understanding the inhabitants of a colony of honeybees, we can now progress to adapting these requirements in the form of easily managed cavities (hives and other equipment) and to moving the bees more in the direction of our own choosing (hive and apiary management). It is really that simple. But, first of all, it is important to know exactly what these wonderful creatures produce and what they can do for us.

Chapter 3

Using the products of the hive and bees

This chapter addresses the question: 'Why keep bees?' I mentioned before that bees are master chemists. They produce and adapt for their own use a range of substances that will keep them and their colony fed, watered and disease free and that enables them to rear and look after their young. They also provide humans with some of the most important products on earth: honey, beeswax, pollen, propolis, venom and (perhaps for future investigation) silk. In some countries their brood is eaten, and so food can be added to this list. But they also provide us with pollination services without which some 75% of crops in some countries wouldn't exist. In the main, beekeepers start by producing honey and then perhaps move on to other products when they have more experience with bees.

This chapter outlines all that the honey-bee can produce and should give you some ideas to think about once you become more experienced. However, as most people associate honey-bees with honey, let's start with this 'liquid gold' and take a look at it in some detail.

PRODUCING HONEY

All beekeepers start beekeeping by wanting to produce honey, and this is probably the best way to begin. If given a shelter to live in, a colony of bees will produce honey without a beekeeper's intervention but, if you want them to produce it in abundance and in a manner that makes it easy to extract, then you need to learn more about beekeeping. But, in the meantime, what is this sweet substance and where does it come from?

Composition

Being a natural product, honey varies in composition enormously but, essentially, it is a fluid, viscous or crystallized substance, produced by bees from the nectar of blossoms that bees collect, transform or combine with substances of their own, which they then store and leave to mature. Its main components are water and sucrose. Sucrose is composed of glucose and fructose, and it is the glucose-to-fructose ratio that determines some of honey's most noticeable physical characteristics, such as how long it will take to crystallize, for example. Water is always present in honey, and the amount is critical to the beekeeper when processing or storing extracted honey. As we will see in Chapter 7, the beekeeper should always check their honey to ensure that this moisture/water presence is within bounds.

A more detailed definition of the composition of honey would be as follows:

■ Honey is composed mainly of sugars and water.

■ The average honey is 79.6% sugar and 17.2% water.

■ The main sugars are fructose (38.2%) and glucose (31.3%).

■ Other sugars include maltose (7.3%) and sucrose (1.3%).

■ Honey also contains acids (.57%), protein (.26%), a small amount of minerals (.17%) and a number of other minor components, including pigments, flavour and aroma substances, sugar alcohols, colloids and vitamins. This group of materials constitutes about 2.2% of the total composition.

Properties

Honey has many determinative properties but, for the average beekeeper who wants to sell honey, the important ones are as follows.

Hard or soft (liquid honey)

Most honeys eventually crystallize, but the rate of crystallization depends on the ratio of glucose to fructose in the honey, and that depends mainly on the floral source. Some honey, such as that from oilseed rape (canola), often crystallizes on the comb while still in the hive, making it very difficult for the bees to use as stores and difficult for the beekeeper to extract using standard equipment.

To the beekeeper, honey viscosity is very important, especially during extraction and packing, and larger companies will heat their honey so that it flows through their equipment more readily and can be packed in jars or drums easily. Some honeys may be thixotropic, which means they become jelly-like if left undisturbed. This is especially so of ling heather (*Calluna vulgaris*) and, again, this necessitates the use of special procedures for extracting it.

Taste

The taste of honey varies enormously. Try some clover honey and then some manuka honey and you will find a huge difference. Manuka isn't highly regarded for taste and used to be thrown away or fed back to the bees (but it is now highly priced and sought after due to its proven medicinal properties).

Colour

Colour shouldn't be an issue really but, in fact, in some countries such as the USA and Germany, for example, it is very much a determinant of price. The Americans prefer their honey 'water white', and dark honeys are referred to as 'bakers' honey' and command a lower price. In Germany, dark honey is preferred, and pale or white honeys are lower in price. I once produced some honeydew (see below) from the cork-oak forest aphids of southern Spain. It was a dense black and had a remarkably strong taste. A German who had bought one of my jars in a nearby bar hastened to my house and bought the entire year's harvest – or what there was left of it.

Antibacterial quality

Honey's 'hyper-osmotic' nature (due to the high concentration of solids and low moisture content) prevents the growth of bacteria and yeasts as this draws water out of the organisms, killing them by desiccation. It literally sucks them dry. Honey also has a high acidity, which plays an important role in the system that prevents bacterial growth. The pH of honeys may vary from approximately 3.2 to 4.5 (average pH = 3.9), making it inhospitable for attack by most, but not all, bacteria.

Honey also has its own antibacterial substance in its make-up. Bees add an enzyme called glucose oxidase to honey, and this enzyme reacts with glucose to produce hydrogen peroxide and gluconic acid, both of which have an antibacterial effect. This system is most active in dilute honey and probably helps preserve honey diluted for brood food use.

Like most products of the hive, honey is essentially a by-product of the all-important pollination process. The value of honey in the economy of the major honey-producing nations is far less than the value of pollination, but there is a huge global trade in honey and many beekeepers can make a very decent living by producing good honey either in bulk or packaged for sale.

Honeydew

Honeydew is a sugar-rich sticky substance, secreted by aphids and some scale insects as they feed on plant sap. Because the sap has little protein, the aphids need to take in large quantities of this high-pressure liquid and, when their mouth-part penetrates the phloem, the sugary liquid is forced out of the gut's terminal opening at the back end. Bees and ants feed on this liquid, which drips off the aphids onto the leaves and bark of the tree. Certain ants actively guard their aphids from predators and, in Germany where honeydew is highly prized, ant colonies are moved into certain forests for apicultural purposes. Honeydew is therefore still a plant-derived substance but it also has the addition of insect enzymes as well as bee enzymes and generally has a broader spectrum of sugars.

Honeydew is usually very dark in colour, often due to the sooty mould that can form on it. In times of drought, when aphid and other pests tend to increase in numbers, honeydew can be a very good crop for the beekeeper, and honeydew from the beech forests of New Zealand is a major export.

However, certain types of honeydew (for example, that excreted by leaf hoppers when feeding on the Tutu bush in New Zealand) are poisonous and have caused many problems in the past – which emphasizes the need for beekeepers to know which plants their bees are feeding on and at what time of the year.

COLLECTING POLLEN

Spreading pollen

Pollen is what bees are all about. Pollen is produced by the flower's anthers and, when the anthers dehisce or open, the pollen travels to the stigma of a receptive flower. How it 'travels' varies with the flower/plant. Grass pollen is mainly moved around by wind, and this is what causes hay fever in allergic individuals. Many pollens come into contact with and adhere to bees and other insects and, when the insect brushes against the stigma of a receptive flower, pollination occurs. Some flowers use both wind and insects for pollination, such as the olive, and, in this case, the bee assists in the pollination process.

The cucumber plant is a typical example of pollination. The male flowers have pollen and nectar. The bee is attracted to the nectar and, while taking it, pollen adheres to its body because the pollen grains have a tiny negative charge and the bee a tiny positive charge. Bees also have very hairy bodies with plumose or multi-branched hairs that can collect and hold pollen grains. The bee may then move to the female flowers on another cucumber plant attracted by the nectar it offers. While the bee is taking this nectar, the pollen comes into contact with the stigma of the plant sufficient for pollination to take place.

Harvesting the pollen

The bee in the above example is almost an accidental pollinator: its main target is the nectar. Bees, however, also use pollen as a protein-providing food for brood and young adult, maturing bees, and so a proportion of the foraging bees collect nectar and pollen while some collect just pollen. The bee 'combs' itself and, by doing so, cleans out the grains and packs them into what are called the corbiculae or pollen baskets on its hind legs. Have a look at the entrance to any beehive during the active season and you will easily see these pollen loads – they look like small round suitcases on the bees' legs.

Once in the hive the bee dumps the pollen into a cell. House bees pack down the pollen and cover it with a light cover of honey in order to preserve it. The pollen is stored near the brood nest and it disappears at a fast rate for use as food. It provides protein, starch, vitamins, minerals and fat in the bees' diet, and the availability of pollen – especially in the early spring for the brood – is something the beekeeper must ensure by the location of the hives. Get to know your early pollen plants, such as gorse, rock rose and willow. (Some nutritionists consider bee pollen to be a near perfect source of protein for humans.)

These small pollen grains can be removed from the bees' legs as they enter the hive and collected in what is known as a pollen trap. While pollen collection is dealt with in Chapter 12, suffice it to say that pollen has a market as a health food for humans and, as such, its collection is certainly worthy of the beekeeper's consideration. The market for pollen is mainly for human nutritional supplements, for feeding to bees and as an animal food. Pollen can be purchased in a variety of formats, including tablets, pollen granules, oral liquids, candy bars, tonics, etc. The manufacture of pollen products for human consumption has been growing at a rapid rate and, while the prices of pollen products vary, they can often yield high profits.

HARVESTING ROYAL JELLY

Royal jelly is a milky-white cream. It is strongly acid, and rich in protein, sugars, vitamins, RNA, DNA, and fatty acids. It is possibly the most valuable (in monetary terms) product of the hive and numerous, fabulous claims have been made about it. It is the food of queen bee larvae and, by feeding a worker bee larva this substance, she will develop into a queen rather than a worker. She will be a female bee that can mate – a totally different being from the worker, despite the fact that they start out exactly the same.

For humans, royal jelly can be used as a food supplement or as an addition to cosmetics to enhance their curative properties (and certainly to enhance their price!). There are numerous stories about the powers of royal jelly and the part it can play in human health, but most are anecdotal. In one of Roald Dahl's *Tales of the Unexpected*, a character turns his baby son into a bee (or at least a black-and-yellow striped, hairy baby who buzzed) by feeding him exclusively on royal jelly. Amazing stuff! The medicinal and curative properties of the substance lack much clinical research, but what we do know is that it contains the eight essential amino acids, the full vitamin B complex, acetylcholine (a powerful neurostimulant), testosterone, insulin-like peptides and an antibiotic component. And it can easily be produced by any beekeeper whether with one hive or a thousand.

Forming queen bees

What function does royal jelly have in the colony? Why is it produced? The basic answer to these questions is that royal jelly is all about queen production, an issue so vital to the propagation of the bee species that, in fact, all bees other than the drones (who don't have a father) are destined to become queens. At first!

One of the questions often asked by new beekeepers is: how is a queen formed? The nature of honey-bees turns this question on its head, and beekeepers should ask 'how is a worker bee formed?' because it is worth repeating that all female larvae are destined to be queens. Nurse bees interfere with the vast majority of these potential queens by limiting their royal jelly diet, thereby turning them into sterile female workers instead. It is simply this lack of royal jelly at a certain stage in their development that creates workers. Queens stay as queens because the continued feeding of royal jelly stimulates the correct hormone production to develop egg-producing organs.

Recent research in Brazil has looked at when and how these organs develop for queens but don't for workers. This research found that all female larvae start off with the same reproductive equipment (and are otherwise genetically the same as well). The pertinent parts are the egg-producing ovarioles – long, skinny subdivisions of the ovaries. To begin with, larval workers and queens have the same number of ovarioles. For the first 2½ to 3 days, this situation persists. While worker and queen larvae mature in different cells, this makes little difference to their development – the important thing is that both receive 100% royal jelly. So they stay the same and are on their way to queenhood.

On about day 3, the nurses stop giving larval workers 100% royal jelly food and give them instead a mixture of jelly, pollen and honey. The workers thus receive much less jelly than the queens, and, over the next few days, the number of worker ovarioles therefore dwindles.

On day 5, the workers and queens differ vastly in ovarioles count. It is then that both the worker and queen larvae spin cocoons and pupate (they undergo several changes to emerge as adult bees). The workers continue to reabsorb their ovarioles into their bodies through pupation. As emerging adults, workers have only about 10 ovarioles, whereas queens have over 100. With so few egg-producing ovarioles left, the larval workers largely lose the ability to reproduce.

The effects of royal jelly

Royal jelly creates queens through its effect on 'juvenile hormone'. This amazing hormone can, for example, keep caterpillars in the larval stage and so prevent them from developing into adults. It puts them into an 'eternal youth' state and keeps them there. It seems likely that lots of royal jelly changes the 'juvenile hormone' levels in maturing larvae so that females develop fully formed egg-producing organs: the workers (who don't receive enough jelly) fall into an 'eternal youth' state, but the queens (who receive plenty) don't and therefore mature.

The nurse bees are the royal-jelly producers and feeders as a normal part of all worker bee development. These nurse bees are young workers, usually around three to six days old. At this age, the worker bee has well developed glands that produce this brood food. The hypopharyngeal and mandibular glands, from which the main components of royal jelly are formed, are located in the worker bees' heads.

Harvesting royal jelly is not difficult and is dealt with in Chapter 12. Some beekeepers dedicate their production to royal jelly alone, and the demand for the product is huge. After all, it can make you young again!

PRODUCING BEESWAX

Bees produce beeswax by synthesizing the sugars in honey. The worker bee's four wax glands mature around her second week of life as an adult and are situated on her lower abdomen. The wax appears as a clear liquid, cools and turns white, forming a small wax scale or flake. The workers can produce this in very large quantities. I have seen bees that had been robbing a honey-extraction plant and that were unable to get out and, full of honey, formed clusters in the shed rafters, covering the floor below in wax scales. In the hive, they often link together into chains and clusters between the combs, which helps them to maintain a temperature of about 35° C (96° F) in order to produce wax. After clustering for around 24 hours, the small wax scales are secreted.

Uses

Wax is the bees' basic house-building unit. It is often mixed with some propolis (see below) for strength and, without it, a colony could not exist. It takes over 7 kg (15 lb) of honey to produce 1 kg (2 lb) of wax, and so you can see that, if you take away the beeswax at harvest time for sale as comb honey, the bees will need to use up a large amount of honey to replace it. It becomes a matter of working out what will make the most money for the beekeeper – selling honey alone and preserving the wax for a good harvest the next year or a second harvest in year one, or selling more expensive comb honey and letting the bees use up valuable honey in replacing it. It is estimated that a standard Langstroth frame of comb can hold up to 3.8 kg (8¼ lb) of honey. The wax necessary to hold this weighs only 100 g (3½ oz). Each wax scale produced by a honey-bee weighs about 1 mg, which means that nearly one million are needed to make 1 kg (2 lb) of wax, and approximately 9×10^5 of these little scales are needed to make sufficient wax for a normal bee colony. Work it out!

Composition

The composition of beeswax is complex, but it contains hydrocarbons, straight-chain monohydric alcohols, acids, hydroxy acids, oils and other substances. Its specific gravity is less than one, so it floats on water. It melts at 63–65° C (145–149° F) and solidifies at 60–63° C (140–145° F), depending on its purity.

Wax is normally a by-product for beekeepers and, as a guide, for each 60 kg (130 lb) of honey extracted from the hive, about 1 kg (2 lb) of beeswax is produced. This comes from the cappings of the honeycomb, which are removed during the honey-extraction process.

COLLECTING PROPOLIS

If you look on Google to find the composition of propolis, you will find many headings dealing with European propolis, American propolis, Indian propolis, South American propolis and so on and so on, which, of course, indicates that propolis composition varies enormously depending on its source. Some bees tend to produce more propolis than others, and its presence can cause the beekeeper problems. Because bees close gaps with it, they frequently stick the hive boxes together, which means using the hive tool to separate them. The same goes for the frames. Lids are another target and are frequently stuck down, especially if the lid undersurface is very close to the tops of the frames.

Defining propolis

In his 1998 paper, 'Review of the biological properties and toxicity of bee propolis (propolis)', G.A. Burdock describes propolis as a sticky, dark-coloured material that honey-bees collect from living plants, mix with wax and use in the construction and adaptation of their nests, mainly to fill out cracks in the beehive. It has been used in folk medicine since ancient times and is now known to be a natural medicine with antibacterial, anti-fungal, anti-tumoral, anti-oxidative, imunomodulatory and other beneficial properties.

Bees use propolis for small gaps (approximately 6.35 mm (¼ in) or less), while larger spaces are usually filled with beeswax. Its colour varies depending on its botanical source, the most common being dark brown. Propolis is sticky at and above room temperature. At lower temperatures it becomes hard and very brittle.

Bees' use of propolis

Research shows that bees collect and use propolis for the following tasks. To:

- prevent diseases and parasites from entering the hive;

- reinforce the structural stability of the hive;

- make the hive more defensible by sealing alternate entrances; and

■ mummify any large creature that dies in the hive (for example, a mouse or large insect they are unable to remove themselves). This prevents putrefaction and disease.

When bees collect propolis, they attach it to their corbiculae in just the same way as pollen, but they need the help of house bees to remove it when they enter the hive.

The bee colony is warm and moist and an ideal breeding ground for all manner of organisms, from fungi to bacteria. The bees tend to 'varnish' the inside of the hive with propolis which, with its anti-fungal and antibacterial properties, can minimize the effects of harmful organisms and prevent their worst effects.

Using propolis for humans

Beekeepers can spend much time scraping propolis off frames and other surfaces and many simply throw it away. However, propolis has a value and, if you want to make something of it, you should scrape it off carefully so that you don't lift off paint and wood. You should then store it until you have built up enough to sell.

Propolis is used for many purposes, such as medicinal ointments and tinctures, paints and varnishes. It is commonly found in chewing gum, cosmetics, creams, lozenges and ointments. Propolis has shown promise in dentistry for dental caries, as a natural sealant and enamel hardener, and many other uses have been found for it. There is a great deal of anecdotal evidence crediting propolis with many medicinal properties, but little clinical research has been carried out, so care must be taken in its use. What we do know is that some people are allergic to it and suffer skin problems if they touch it. One beekeeper I know of has allergic reactions even to the vapour of propolis and needs to wear a mask.

It is true to say, however, that in these days when increasing use is being made of natural products in the health industry, the value of propolis is rising, and so it has a good value as a secondary product of the hive. Clinical trials of propolis are bound to increase the value of the product further, just as clinical trials on manuka honey raised its value tremendously. In the meantime, one of the most extensively tested aspects of propolis is its antibacterial properties. Scientific tests have been conducted on a variety of bacteria, fungi, viruses and other micro-organisms, and many of these tests have demonstrated positive effects on such organisms using various extracts and concentrations of propolis. A synergistic effect has been reported for propolis extract when used with antibiotics. Whether propolis exhibits bactericidal or bacteriostatic characteristics often depends on its concentration in the applied extract. Sometimes, however, propolis extracts are more effective than commercially available drugs.

Don't ignore the possibilities of propolis, and see Chapter 12 for harvesting ideas.

PRODUCING VENOM

Protecting yourself against stings

Honey-bee venom has evolved as an effective defence mechanism over millions of years and is one of the reasons why everyone isn't a beekeeper. It isn't within the scope of this book to describe bee venom properly but, suffice it to say, it is a clear, odourless liquid comprising around 88% water and it has a very complex chemistry. At least 18 pharmacologically active components have been described, including various enzymes, peptides and amines. Of the small proteins, one called melittin constitutes about 50% of the venom's dry weight. This hydrolyzes cell membranes, causing changes in permeability, and is most responsible for the pain. Other components, however, act in concert with it, such as hyaluronidase, which causes changes in cell membranes and allows the venom to spread easily. Other components can cause anaphylactic shock in sting victims, and this is the cause of most fatalities from bee stings if they occur in hypersensitive individuals. Death is most often induced by a single sting and usually occurs within one hour of the sting.

It is for this reason that most sensible beekeepers take an epi pen with them to the apiary. This device, which contains epinephrine, can auto-inject this substance into your body and thus save your life. It is worth seeing your doctor about this aspect of beekeeping so that you can obtain a prescription for the epi pen, if required. Instead of the auto-injector, which is expensive, you can obtain a normal epinephrine-containing syringe, but with this you actually have to inject yourself – i.e. push the needle in!

Venom poisoning can be caused by large numbers of bees, and this can cause death in non-hypersensitive individuals. It has been estimated that it would take 500–1500 stings for this to occur.

Using venom for humans

Apitherapists claim that bee venom can be used for the treatment of the following:

- Chronic injuries, such as bursitis and tendonitis.

- Hypertension.

- Asthma.

- Scar tissue removal.

- Certain skin conditions, such as eczema.

- Hearing loss.

- Premenstrual syndrome (PMS).

However, there is no meaningful scientific evidence to indicate that bee venom is effective for any of these conditions but, as there is a value in the substance, it is worth considering it as a source of income. Equipment for its collection is necessarily specialized, but most can be purchased from reputable bee-supply companies. Chapter 12 looks at harvesting ideas.

HARVESTING SILK

The production of silk from honey-bee colonies is probably not economically viable, but honey-bee larvae produce silk to reinforce the wax cells in which they pupate. Researchers in Australia have now identified honey-bee silk genes and say that bees are among a group of insects that have evolved silks that are very tough and stable in comparison with classical silks.

SUMMARY

Bees can produce honey, honeydew, pollen, propolis, venom and silk, and all except silk (at the moment) can be a profitable commodity for beekeepers. With experience you will be able to decide just what you want your bees to produce for you and will learn the best ways of getting your bees to produce surplus.

There are other money-earning avenues for the experienced beekeeper, such as pollination services or producing queen bees for sale, and these activities are explained later in this book.

Chapter 4

Obtaining equipment and bees

Now that you know why you should keep bees and what beekeeping can do for you, it's time to move on to learning about how you can enter this fascinating and potentially lucrative sphere of activity. Getting started in beekeeping is not difficult and, to start off, you will need the following items:

- beehive(s)
- beekeeping tools
- suitable clothing
- bees
- beehive sites and, finally,
- somewhere to keep all your equipment.

ACQUIRING BEEHIVES

My advice is to start with two (or more) beehives. The reason for this is that, during the beekeeping year, much can go wrong with a colony of bees and, as you will learn, if one colony begins to fail due, for example, to a bad queen or if it becomes entirely queenless, you can use bees, larvae and eggs from the second colony to help out. If you have only one colony you will have no immediate source of help and the colony will die out. So my advice is to obtain two beehives initially.

Lid

Crown board

Honey super

Queen excluder

Brood chambers

Floor board

Fig. 6. The basic Langstroth hive. In the right-hand side of the figure, note the 'handles', or bars of wood for holding, on the supers and the scallop on the brood box. Handles make the whole business much easier

A modern beehive looks complicated to the beginner but is really just a simple series of boxes sitting on top of each other capped by a lid to keep the rain out. Inside the boxes, frames of beeswax hang down from a revetment along the inside edge of the hive. Hives usually have two sizes of box known as 'full' and '¾' boxes. These different sizes are in height only and they can be used for different purposes. Many beekeepers use just one size of box; others use the different sizes on one hive. Figure 6 shows the different parts of a hive.

Hive stands

Beehives should not be set directly on the ground. This is especially so if the floor (see below) is open mesh. The main reason is that damp will get into the hive, and this must not be allowed to happen. A hive stand, therefore, is anything that keeps the hive off the ground. Stands can be pallets (four hives to a pallet), concrete blocks, bricks,

Fig 7. A stainless-steel mesh floor

wooden rails or simple wooden stands that hold one hive. In the main it is far better to improvise than to buy a stand from a beekeeping supply company (it is better in that it is cheaper and just as effective).

Floors

On the hive stand sits the floor and, essentially, a hive sits on this hive 'floor', which is a simple stainless-steel mesh in a wooden frame with a ridge around the edge of three of its sides (see Figure 7). The brood box sits on this floor. Try to ensure that it has a stainless-steel mesh floor – many don't.

Many beekeepers recoil at the idea of an open floor, believing that this will cause draughts and cold in the beehive, thus chilling the delicate brood or even making the bees feel cold! This is, of course, nonsense for the most part. Bees keep the brood at the correct temperature for their survival even in winter (if there is any brood around at this time) – they don't try to heat the hive!

The mesh floor will aid the hive's ventilation, especially in hot weather when the bees do try to cool the hive. It will also aid in varroa control – if a varroa mite falls off a bee, it will fall through the mesh and will be unable to get back into the hive. Finally, any water that enters the hive will drain away immediately. Damp kills bees, not cold. My advice is always to use mesh floors.

Brood box (often called the brood chamber)

This first box is usually the larger size of box (full), and it is the box that holds the queen and where she will lay eggs and where the brood-rearing occurs. If the queen is a prolific layer and the colony builds up rapidly, overcrowding could cause swarming, and so many beekeepers place a second full box on top of the first and move the queen excluder (see below) up one. This gives the queen another box to lay in and can lower the chance of swarming.

The larger the colony, the bigger the honey crop, so it is advantageous to give a good queen plenty of room. A ¾ box could be used here instead of a full box as a second brood chamber and, in this case, the brood chamber is call a 'brood and a half'.

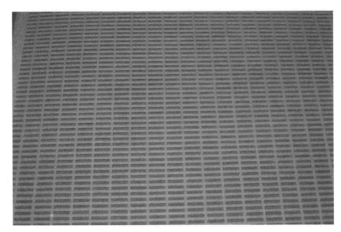

Fig. 8. A plastic queen excluder

Queen excluder

This is a flat grid of slotted zinc, plastic or wire that lies on top of the brood box (see Figure 8). Slotted zinc excluders can rip worker wings, so I prefer to use plastic excluders that are cheaper and less prone to warping/bending than metal ones. Worker bees can pass through the grid to the upper boxes to store honey, but the queen is unable to due to her larger size. This means that the upper boxes will contain only honeycomb and stored honey and will have no brood in them. This is important at harvest time because the beekeeper knows that any combs they are placing in their extractor will have only honey in them and that any bees they accidentally transfer to the honey room won't be the all-important queen.

The grids can easily be damaged and, if this happens, the queen will go up into the honey chambers and will start laying eggs all through the hive. As noted above, zinc excluders may have sharp edges that can damage wings and, if you accidentally bend the zinc (which is easily done when trying to lift it off after the bees have stuck it down with propolis), it stays bent and the slots may warp and widen. Wire excluders usually have a wooden frame around them that often warps, again exposing areas where the queen may slip through. Plastic excluders are tough, don't stay bent if knocked and are easy on the wings.

Many beekeepers don't use queen excluders (calling them honey excluders instead), but they make life much easier and, for the commercial beekeeper, ease means speed and therefore less hourly costs. My advice is to use them until *you* have worked out a reason why you shouldn't.

Supers

These boxes are so called because they are 'super' imposed on the brood chamber. They are often called 'honey supers'. Many beekeepers use ¾-sized boxes here for a variety of reasons, the main one being that when a full-sized box is full of honey, it is extremely heavy and difficult to move about. When full of honey, however, ¾ boxes are lighter and easier to handle. If the bees keep filling them up, you can place more on.

Some beekeepers, especially commercial operators, use full-sized boxes as supers (i.e. the same-sized boxes as the brood chamber). This has advantages in that all the boxes are interchangeable and you can swap the first super with the brood box (a method of limiting swarming, which we will discuss in detail in Chapter 6). My advice, however, is for beginners to use ¾ boxes as supers so there is no confusion. There will come a time when you will decide for yourself which boxes you want to use and where.

Frames

Inside the boxes hang frames. These comparatively cheap items are one of the most critical pieces of beekeeping equipment you will use. They can be good to work with or extremely irritating.

Frames may be wooden (currently more usual especially among hobbyists) or plastic. Wooden frames are literally just that – frames of wood in which a sheet of beeswax stamped with hexagonal shapes is held. The wax is kept in place with thin wire that crosses the frames. In the UK it is common to buy sheets of wax with wire already embedded in them. In most other countries, you have to embed the wires yourself. This is not difficult (see below). From this sheet of wax, bees will soon make more wax and will develop the hexagonal shapes into the cells that form their all-purpose furniture.

Plastic frames

Plastic frames are simply sheets of plastic moulded into a frame. The plastic is formed with the hexagons or cell bases, and many beekeepers dip these frames in molten wax that forms a thin cover over the plastic hexagons and gives the bees a start when building their cells. Because they are solid, plastic frames are strong and less easily damaged when extracting honey. They are also easy to clean and you don't have the hassle of embedding sheets of wax onto wires and replacing the wires when broken. The frame itself is less easily damaged when prising it up from the hive. My advice is, if you think you are going to go commercial, to use plastic frames.

Types of frame

Frames (whether plastic or wood) come in a variety of shapes and sizes and, obviously you must have ones that fit your hive. When frames hang in the box, there should be an even distance between them. When the bees draw out the honeycomb from the sheet of wax you've given them, they will always maintain a distance between one comb and another, and this distance is known as bee space.

The bee space is simply the crawling space a bee needs to pass easily between two structures (7.5 mm +/ 1.5 mm), thus allowing the bee to move around between frames. Frames placed too closely will be glued together with propolis, and those placed too far apart will have brace comb built between them. This applies to any part of the hive. Frames are kept apart in various ways. (Figure 9 shows Hoffman frames and Manley frames).

(a)

(b)

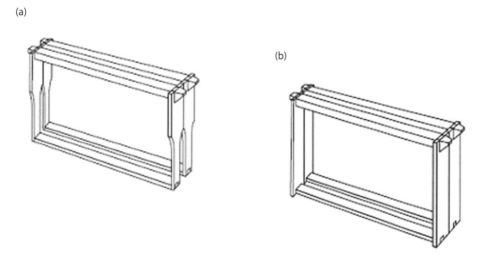

Fig. 9. Keeping frames apart: (a) the sides of the Hoffman Frame are scalloped to minimize contact with each other. This helps you to separate them yet also spaces them correctly; (b) Manley frames are straight down the edges, which facilitates uncapping

Hoffman frames

Hoffman frames are shaped so that they are kept apart at the right distance, but lower down they thin out so that the bees can't glue them together with propolis all the way down. These are the best frames to use for the brood box, and most beekeepers use ten of them in each brood-rearing box, especially when using foundation wax. Try not to use any other frames.

Manley frames

Manley Frames have straight sides, which keep them wider apart all the way down. This encourages the bees to draw out the wax comb further so they can store more honey. These are the frames to use for the honey supers. Because they are wider you would probably use only eight or, at most, nine of them in the box. When you come to extract the honey, the frame's straight sides make it easy for you to slide your uncapping knife along the frame, thus cutting off the wax cappings evenly. Try to use these frames.

Other frames

Many appliance manufacturers provide thin-sided frames that need spacers to keep them apart from other frames. When I started beekeeping using British National-sized frames, small metal add-ons called 'metal ends' were used. These quickly became clogged up with propolis and were dreadful things. Later they were made of plastic, and so they were then known as 'plastic metal ends'!

When holding a frame and looking at a fine queen, for example, you instinctively hold the frame by these devices, which suddenly give way and fall off, causing you to drop the frame and so to lose the queen. In Europe, other plastic slide-on pieces abound, and none of these devices is as good as the Hoffman spaced frame for the brood box and the Manley spaced frame for the honey boxes. My advice is definitely to use these frames if you can, or swap over to them when you can. You will be surprised at just how critical the design of these cheap hive items is in your beekeeping – you will curse nothing as much as a badly designed frame.

One other method of spacing frames is via a castellated ridge at each end of the box along the ridge from where the frames hang. These ridges work but they limit your choices of bee management and frame use in the box and, to me, are annoying. My advice is to avoid them if possible.

Feeders

Frame feeders, (see Figure 10) are plastic frames with sides and an open top. They are used to feed your bees with sugar syrup, when required. To do this you simply remove the outer frame in the brood box and replace it with a frame feeder (see Figure 11). You then fill the feeder with sugar syrup, remembering to place some material in the feeder, such as bits of wood or dried bracken, so that the bees will have a foothold and will not drown in the syrup. There are other feeders available but, in my opinion, the frame feeder is the easiest one to use for the beekeeper with only a few hives.

Fig. 10. A frame feeder out of the hive (note the plastic frames)

Fig. 11. A feeder slotted into the hive on the right

Bucket feeders are cheap and consist of a small plastic bucket with a tight-fitting lid. This lid is punctured with many small holes. The feeder is filled with sugar syrup, the lid is put on and the bucket inverted over the frames. A spare box is required to surround the feeder, and a hive lid is put on this box.

These feeders are very good if you want a slow feed for your bees and they have uses in queen rearing (see Chapter 11). They are also readily available, especially in an emergency, and are very easy to use, but they are definitely not as handy or convenient as a frame feeder.

For large-scale commercial beekeepers, a lid feeder that holds more syrup and that can be accessed without opening the hive is better because, with so many hives, visits to the hives will be less frequent and so the syrup has to last longer.

Foundation wax

Unless you are buying a hive already stocked with bees, your frames should have a wax foundation in them. This is a wax sheet that fits inside the frame and that is impregnated with the hexagonal shape of the honeycomb (see Figure 12). The bees will use this sheet as the basis for building their honeycomb and will 'pull the wax out' – i.e. they will produce wax and add it to the pattern until a honeycomb is formed (see Figure 13).

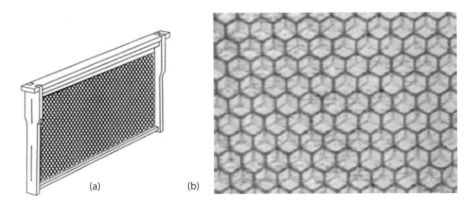

(a)   (b)

Fig. 12. Foundation wax: (a) in the frame; (b) a sheet of wax

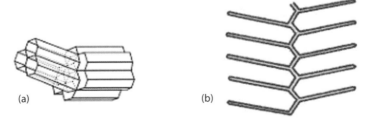

(a)   (b)

Fig. 13. Wax cells: (a) pulled out; (b) sloped upwards to hold honey

Wax sheets can be easily damaged, especially when you want to extract the honey. Wire is usually therefore embedded in the sheet to hold it in the frames and to prevent damage. In the UK you can buy pre-wired sheets to fix into your frames but, in most other countries, the frames will have wires on them and you will have to melt the wax sheets onto them. This is easy and can be accomplished as follows (it sounds complicated but isn't really). Try it:

1. Open up your car bonnet (hood) and attach a red wire to the positive terminal of the battery and a black wire to the negative terminal. (The wires should have crocodile clips at each end for this purpose and, in fact, can be any colour you like.)
2. Attach the other ends to some rubber tubing to stop them touching each other.
3. Place a wooden board wherever it will sit without moving and place your frame on it.
4. Tighten up the wires in the frame so that, if you strum them, they sound like a guitar.
5. Hold up the frame and place a wax foundation sheet into it, ensuring that the top edge goes into the groove in the frame's top bar.
6. Place the frame horizontally onto the wooden board.
7. Attach the black wire to one end of the wire frame and hold it in place with a small tack.
8. Briefly touch the red wire to the other end and gently rub your hand over the wax sheet. The sheet will melt on to the wires and you must then immediately remove the current otherwise you will end up with a load of wax strips.

This all comes with practice. A modification is to have a board with a block fixed to it. This block should be of just the correct height to stop the wires from melting right through the wax and out the other side. I have no doubt you will be able to work out the best way to do this once you've seen everything in action.

You will now have either a load of wax strips or a frame with a wax sheet embedded with wires. Keep going until you have sufficient to fill the boxes. Keep all the wax strips because you can use them as starter strips.

The crown board

Often called the 'inner cover', especially in America, this is just a board that sits on top of the top box under the lid. I don't use them and in fact I can't think what they are for. It was only when I looked at a diagram of a hive that I remembered they existed. I then recalled using them when I started because they came with the hive.

Crown boards often have a round hole in them so that you can invert a bucket feeder of sugar syrup over the hole, but you can do the same directly on top of the frames. I don't think using them makes any difference – they are just another item you have to put somewhere when looking into the hive.

The lid

Lids have a variety of designs. Some are telescopic and fit over the hive completely. Some just sit on top of the hive and rely on strapping to keep them there (these are used mainly by commercial beekeepers). Some fit over the hive at the front and back. Some have integral sugar-syrup feeders, as described above. Most, however, are flat, but gabled lids are available that make a hive look attractive but then, of course, you won't be able to stack the hives on top of each other for moving.

My advice is to use flat, telescopic lids for most flexibility. They don't hinder you too much if you are moving bees and they stay on in winds. If you are definitely not going to stack your hives, then gabled lids look very attractive and, for looks alone, they are a must on WBC hives (see below).

Some commercial beekeepers with large numbers of hives have a fat lid that contains a cavity that can be filled with sugar syrup for feeding purposes. The lid's top has a screw bung and, when removed, a petrol-type nozzle can be put in this and syrup pumped in from a truck-mounted tank. This has the advantage of speed and, because you don't need to remove the lid, you don't upset the bees. The bees can enter the feeder from inside the hive. Robbing is also prevented because any 'foreign' bees will have to pass right through the hive to get to the sugar, and they tend not to do this.

Whatever they are made of, lids must have a tin/zinc cover, otherwise rain will get in. In very hot countries it is helpful to the bees' thermoregulation to paint the lids white.

This is also helpful to the beekeeper. Lids are flat surfaces and thus obey the laws of all flat surfaces – they become covered with 'things'. When out beekeeping you tend to place items on to nearby lids, such as smokers, tools and frames from another hive. I have gone out beekeeping in 50° C (120° F) in Andalucia and I've put honeycombs on scorching hot lids that have melted almost at once. These red-hot lids must also cook the bees and cause them to spend a great deal of time collecting water to cool the hive. When they divert foragers to collect water, these bees are not collecting nectar/honey! In hot places, paint the lids white. You want your bees to collect honey, not water.

CHOOSING THE TYPE OF BEEHIVE

Beehives round the world

There are many types of beehive available, especially on the second-hand market, but my advice is to go for either the Langstroth or the Dadant hive. The reason is that these two are common all over the world and, wherever you are located, you will be able to buy frames, sheets of stamped wax and other items that fit on or into these two designs. The most common is the Langstroth, which may be called other things in other countries but essentially is the same hive. I wouldn't think about buying any hive other than one of these two. Even with these hives, though, you will find there are as many different dimensions to a Langstroth as there are manufacturers, but all the bits will more or less fit together sufficiently well for your purposes.

In the UK, however, the National hive is popular, as is the Smith in Scotland and, if you are located in these countries, you will find many other beekeepers using these. They look the same as a Langstroth, only slightly smaller. All countries have their own indigenous designs, some of which are fine, others terrible. The Spanish Layens hive, for example, is a box designed to make bees overheat, become savage and swarm incessantly, whereas their 'Perfeccion' is in fact a Langstroth by another name – and so it goes on all over the world. Many new beekeepers notice that these hives are just packing boxes on top of each other and don't look anything like the hive of their imagination. This is true, and the reason is that the wonderful-looking hives of storybooks are either inefficient or totally useless for modern beekeeping as well as being cruel to the bees.

One hive that does fit the description and that works well, however, is the WBC – named after its designer, William Broughton Carr, in England. This hive is in fact a series of packing boxes of English National size just like any other hive, but with outer covers that go over the plain boxes and a gabled roof. It is these outer boxes and roof that look nice. This type of hive looks good at the bottom of the garden under the apple trees, and many hobbyists use them.

Going for practicality not appearance

If I wanted just a few hives to indulge my hobby, I would use WBCs and, in fact, I started off with a couple. They are brilliant and the bees in them will produce just as much honey as those in the National hive of the same size. They are, however, unwieldy: you need to remove the outer boxes, which then lie on the ground around you while you are manipulating the bees. These boxes get in the way, so you trip over them usually while holding a frame with the queen on it. They are also very difficult to load up and move because of the plethora of boxes and covers, which fall about and come apart, and you can't stack them due to the gabled roof. So if you just want a few hives at the bottom of the garden and you don't intend to move them to other crops, and beekeeping is just a delightful hobby for you, these are the hives to buy – because they look good. If you think you may be a little more ambitious and may want to take bees to the heather or to other crops to maximize your honey production or to pollinate crops, then don't even think about the WBC. Get Langstroths or Dadants or the most used and sold local equivalent.

I personally would go for a Langstroth. The difference between this hive and a Dadant hive lies in the size of the brood box (i.e. the box in which the queen is confined and where she lays her eggs). The Dadant brood box is larger, and so you usually need only one. The Langstroth box is smaller and so you may need two (more work, more to lift, etc.). Also, using two boxes may be too much for the bees in the winter when the queen is not laying whereas, if you take one box off, it may be too small. Because the Dadant brood box is larger, it may be more efficient for these circumstances. I was once in a remote area of Spain and needed some frames and wax. I was directed to a bar. The bar owner not only sold fine beers but also Langstroth hive equipment and wax sheets. I would have been stuck if I had had any other hive.

There are as many arguments for choosing a particular hive as there are beekeepers. The arguments could go on for ever and all are valid, so my advice is to by a universal type of hive and, really, that is the Langstroth – unless your beekeeping is going to stay at the small hobby level, in which case you can indulge yourself and buy something like a WBC.

BUYING SECOND-HAND HIVES

Many starter beekeepers buy second-hand hives from a local beekeeping association and, in the UK, hives can be purchased at annual association auctions, and this is an excellent way of starting. Not only can you buy equipment at these functions but you can also buy bees. Second-hand equipment is usually very much cheaper than new equipment and you can check whether the woodwork is sound.

The main disadvantage of this approach is that the kit may hold disease, and the main disease that will worry you is American foul brood (AFB). The bacterium that causes this disease has a spore or resting stage if the conditions are not right for its wellbeing. These spores are tough and can stay on equipment for decades. When you put bees in the empty hive, the AFB will resurrect itself and you will be in big trouble. This disease spreads very easily and, from one contaminated hive, it will soon reach your other hives and perhaps those of your neighbours. Eventually the government authorities will come along and burn all your hives and bees. It is that serious.

So be very careful with second-hand kit. If you buy it, run a flame gun all over it, in the cracks and corners and on the under-surfaces. Scorch the woodwork and kill any AFB spores that may exist. Or you can soak the woodwork in potassium hypochlorite, which also kills the AFB. For this, though, you will need a big tank and protective clothing. It is best to scorch everything, while being very careful not to set light to anything. Remember that wax and wood burn very easily.

OBTAINING NEW HIVES OR MAKING YOUR OWN

If you buy new equipment from a beekeeping supplier, you can usually choose between pine and red cedar in the UK but, often, just pine in continental Europe. There are also various grades of wood. I once bought some cheap pine boxes full of knots. After a few months in the sun, these knots became knot holes, and my hives suddenly had entrances all over the place.

Buy the best you can afford or, if you are brave and have a basic woodworking skill, make your own. Free plans for all the hives mentioned above (even the WBC) are available on the website www.beesource.com, and I reckon that, if you want new kit, this is just about the cheapest way of doing it if you are in the UK or USA. I also found that, in Spain, you could purchase beehives so cheaply that it made little sense to make your own.

Many beekeeping supply companies (listed at the end of this book) sell beginner's kits that include everything you need to set up as a beekeeper, plus the bees if required. These kits are well worthwhile in that they are comprehensive and free of disease, but they are expensive.

ACQUIRING OTHER BEEKEEPING EQUIPMENT

Over time you will acquire a whole host of bits of equipment, some useful and some not but, initially, you will need two tools: a hive tool and a smoker.

The hive tool

This is a simple metal bar with two basic designs (see Figure 14). This is a vital piece of kit. You need hive tools to prise apart those areas of the hive that the bees have stuck together with propolis – their all-purpose glue and antibiotic. These tools need to be tough, and those sold at bee-appliance stores are fine for the purpose. You will need dozens of them because you will lose them frequently. This is the tool you put down 'somewhere' in the grass when looking at a queen or some other interesting sight. Then you walk off without it. You will eventually be reduced to using chisels, pen knives, kitchen knives and screwdrivers and, on one occasion, I tried a car key and had to walk home. At this stage you must go to the shop and buy more hive tools.

Fig. 14. Two types of hive tool

The smoker

There are loads of theories as to why smoke calms down bees but it does seem that the smoke in some way affects the bees' sensory mechanisms. It sometimes works the other way round, however – using a great deal of smoke on already-angry bees can make things worse. My Spanish bees (*Apis mellifera iberica*) were usually so savage that, unless blasts of flame were coming out of the smoker, it didn't seem to make any difference. In fact, if anything, they became more enraged. Usually, though, a few puffs of smoke at the hive entrance will keep most bees calm because it induces them to gorge themselves with honey. Then, when removing each box, a few puffs along the top of the frames will keep the bees' heads down. In New Zealand, however, it takes so much to get my Italian bees worked up that I hardly use any smoke at all.

Fig. 15. A smoker.

When you buy a smoker, choose one with a protective grid around it so that, if you pick it up without gloves on, you won't burn yourself (see Figure 15). Also, spend a little more and buy a decent-sized one. Small ones are no good at all because they don't hold much fuel and so have to be constantly re-lit. Make sure, too, that the bellows aren't made of flimsy material. These are the first bits to wear out and should therefore be strong.

I use rolled-up corrugated cardboard as fuel, mainly because it burns slowly, is easy to light with newspaper and it's free (although believe it or not, you can *buy* rolls of it from bee-appliance shops). Old sacking is another good fuel, as is dried grass.

The aim is to get your smoker to produce cool, dense smoke. Prior to inspecting your bees, try to get the smoker going well so that it doesn't go out while you are working on the bees. It is a general rule that most smokers – of whatever make – really work well only when you've just finished inspecting the last hive, and then you have difficulty putting them out before you can go home.

To avoid all this, you can buy liquid smoke that you spray on the frames from a garden spray bottle. Although this seems to work and you don't have the bother of lighting a stubborn smoker, I don't like spraying any liquids in my hives and, when I was an organic honey producer, smoke was the stipulated method. You also have to pay for the liquid concentrate!

The division board

The division board is a board the same size as the boxes with a rim around it. In the rim is a small cut-out. This board is a very useful item that you can easily make yourself in minutes and is used when you want to split a hive into two separate units, both with an entrance. The bees in the lower half of the hive use the normal entrance and the bees above the division board go in and out through the small cut-out in the rim. One example of their use is to start off a two-queen hive to maximize honey production (this is explained in Chapter 6).

CLOTHING

This is a subject very dear to the beginner's heart – and mine! Whether you can tolerate stings or not, it is never pleasant to feel a small gang of bees crawling down your back: on the inside! You know exactly what's going to happen and, by the time you've panicked and torn off your clothing, it's all too late. Bees crawling around on the inside of your veil inches from your eyes and nose are particularly panic-inducing and, again, they usually strike before you can sort the situation out. A sting on the end of, or up, the nose or in the eye is very unpleasant. You can avoid these situations in two ways.

Buying a bee suit

Buy a decent bee suit, not one of those things with separate veils that have drawstrings or that tuck into your top – bees always get in them. I started off with one and nearly gave up because I was stung so much. Buy one with a hood that unzips and that can be thrown back when you've finished. Most of these suits have hoops in the hood that keep the veil away from your face and, if they don't, don't buy one. A good bee suit will cost more, but it's an excellent investment and should last you for years – in comfort.

There are companies that sell excellent lightweight suits for hot countries, but beekeepers with many colonies and commercial beekeepers need a tough suit. Beekeeping with lots of colonies is, effectively, heavy labour, and light suits are torn easily – leading to bees down your back and all the things that follow! I prefer a half suit – i.e. one that covers just the top half of me, like a zip-up jacket with a hood. I prefer it because it is more comfortable than a full suit, but bees do get inside it if sufficiently keen to do so and, if you wouldn't want this to happen, then buy a full suit.

If you are in Spain and you keep the Iberian bee, then wear a thick full suit. Their sting seems to be able to penetrate suit, trousers and underpants in one smooth and flowing movement. Wear your suit with a pair of gum boots with the trousers tucked in, and wear a pair of beekeeping gloves.

Wearing gloves

There are many beekeeping instructional books that tell you not to wear gloves – the reason being that you can't 'feel' what you are doing as well. Gloves can make you clumsy. I know of a beekeeper in New Zealand who won't let his staff use gloves for this very reason. I use gloves and I always have done. To my mind, if anything is going to make me clumsy while inspecting frames of bees, it is constantly being stung. I've tried it and my fingers became so numb that, after a while, I couldn't feel anything and I dropped no end of frames. Repeated stinging also tends to put new beekeepers off.

If you want more 'feel', use washing-up gloves, which avoid the worst of the sting. If you have many colonies, however, these will split very quickly. My advice is to buy a good pair of leather gloves with gauntlets. When you are experienced enough to decide whether these are necessary for you or not, you can then decide what to do with them.

Anticipating stings

The second way to avoid bee stings is to know when the bees are going to sting you or not. This comes with experience and generally works well but, as with all livestock, you never know exactly what they are going to do and they often break the rules of the game.

OBTAINING BEES

Obtaining bees is not difficult and can be accomplished as follows.

Already installed

If you are buying beehives from a local beekeeper, they may come with bees already installed and, in the next chapter we explore what to look out for when inspecting these bees – which is something you will need to do. You wouldn't buy a car without ensuring value for money and it's the same with bees. They could come with a disease, without a queen or with numerous other problems you will inherit.

This is an easy way to buy bees, but a large colony of bees comes complete with guard bees ready to defend the nest and is always more of trial to a new beekeeper than a small nucleus.

Hiving a swarm

This is an interesting way to start but it is unlikely that someone who wants to begin beekeeping would do this without help, even though bees are at their most gentle when swarming. You could let beekeepers or the local association know that, if there is a swarm of bees around, you would like them. This is how I started. My wife obtained a swarm off a beekeeper and transported them to our house in a duvet cover.

If you are a beginner, ask a beekeeper to install the bees for you if you go down this route. Watch and learn (we look at hiving swarms in Chapter 6).

Buying a nucleus of bees

This is the usual method in the UK and continental Europe. A nucleus (or nuc) is a box with only four or five frames in it, and it will contain a frame of brood (or two), a frame of honey (or two) and a frame of comb or even foundation. The smallest nucleus that I have seen had just a frame of brood, a frame of honey and an empty frame. Somewhere in the nucleus (usually on the brood frame) will be a laying queen.

The frames will, of course, be the same size of frame as those in your hives, so you must let the supplier know what size you want. So if, for example, the nuc is a five-frame one, simply remove five frames from your brood box in the hive and carefully put the nuc frames in (see Chapter 5).

The advantage of a nucleus is that it has brood ready to emerge and to contribute to the colony's development, and the queen will have already laid eggs.

Buying a package of bees

This is the most common method in the USA. A package of bees weighs about 1 or 1.5 kg (2 or 3 lb), with approximately 8,000 or 12,000 bees, respectively. The package box has four wooden sides and a screen material in the front and back. It is 22 cm (8.5 in) high, 40 cm (16 in) wide and 14 cm (5.5 in) deep.

An inverted can filled with sugar syrup and placed inside the box provides feed for the bees during transit. Some New Zealand packages are shipped in tubular containers with a gelled feeding source. The package contains a young, laying queen in a small wooden cage with one screened side. The caged queen is well protected during transit and fed through the screen. This contact with the bees improves her acceptance when the package is hived.

The main disadvantage of a package is that it will be around three weeks before any brood emerges ready to contribute to the colony's development.

ACQUIRING GENTLE BEES

The type or race/strain of bee that you acquire is often a matter of chance. If you hive a swarm or obtain hives with bees already in them, then you get what you get and, if the vendor has any information, ask them for this. A swarm is the same. If you buy bees, however, you can look in the beekeeping magazines and often there is a choice.

For gentleness – which is all important in urban situations – the Italian or Cecropian bees are probably the gentlest, while the Spanish or Iberian bee is perhaps the most savage after the Africanized bees of killer-bee fame. (None of the last two types would do well in northern climes anyway.)

The type of bee that is best for your particular micro-climate is a source of endless argument among beekeepers, some claiming that their savage little lot of black bees are the best for the eastern Lincolnshire frosts or, others, that their yellow Italians can gather twice as much honey (probably because they rob other hives) as any other bee in the central Rutland fogs, even if they do need huge amounts of sugar syrup in the winter. As I said before, as a general rule, unless you want to be a commercial beekeeper, go for gentleness (in fact, go for this anyway), and many breeders will produce gentle bees for you to buy as a nucleus. Contrary to much opinion, there is no scientifically proven correlation between savageness and good honey collection.

What you do with this nucleus or package of gentle bees on Day 1 is discussed in the next chapter. Just make sure (unlike me) that you have your beehives and other equipment ready before the bees arrive.

STARTING BEEKEEPING: A SUMMARY

In order to start beekeeping, you will ideally need the following items.

Two complete beehives (at least)
Use the most locally used, modern-style hive (but not the Layens hive in Spain even if it is the most common). If in doubt use a Langstroth or local equivalent. You will need at least one brood box (deep/full) and two supers (shallows, ¾ sized). Use a queen excluder to start beekeeping and use the frames as advised above.

Use Hoffman frames in the brood box and Manley frames in the honey boxes. Avoid frames that require plastic or metal frame spacers (although, unfortunately, these often come with new hives so, despite what I've said, you will probably end up with them). The frames should have standard wax foundation wired into them. You may have to do this. Or, preferably, they should be made of plastic and coated with a light film of beeswax.

A hive tool
In fact, buy several hive tools.

A good-sized smoker
Make sure this has strong bellows and a protective grid around it.

A bee suit
Buy a suit with a zip-up hood/veil.

Good gloves
Purchase gloves with gauntlets – and also a pair of gumboots.

Bees
Use a gentle strain if you can obtain them and take advice from local beekeepers as to the best strain for your area. Be careful whom you believe. My advice would be to use Carniolan, Italian or Cecropian (Greek) bees, especially if you want to keep your bees in an urban area – but more of this in Chapter 5. Many of the local experts whom you seek advice from will say: 'Oh, he (meaning me) doesn't know what he's talking about – he's never lived around these parts – the best bees for around here are . . .', and they'll go on about Lincolnshire frosts and Rutland fogs and you'll end up obtaining a couple of hives full of savage little horrors. I do know what I'm talking about, believe me. I've had them all! More usually, though, you will take pot luck with a swarm or with a hive with bees already in it.

ACQUIRING THE EQUIPMENT

If you want the start of your beekeeping career to go smoothly, make sure you have hives, tools, clothing and this book before you obtain the bees. As noted earlier, I was presented with a swarm of bees in a duvet cover as a surprise birthday present. This wasn't the best way to start! You can obtain this equipment as follows:

- Buy a complete beginner's kit, or individual items from a good bee-supply company. This is the most expensive way. (See the list of suppliers at the end of this book.)

- Obtain second-hand equipment from a local beekeeper or beekeeping association auction. This is cheaper than the previous way but runs the risk of such diseases as AFB. Having said that, if you buy a hive of bees at an auction, it should have had a disease inspection before the sale. Most auctions insist on this and have a visiting inspector. Ask about this. Used, empty hives on their own won't have been inspected and so may contain unnoticed diseases.

- Make your own equipment. This is an economical option, and all plans can be found at www.beedata.com. While this way is possible with the hives, I recommend buying the other tools and clothing new unless items in excellent condition can be had at a bee auction or from another beekeeper.

- Buy bees in a nucleus (or two) from a reputable supplier, obtain a swarm from a beekeeper or buy a package of bees for installation in a prepared hive from a bee breeder/producer. Or you could buy an existing colony in a hive. All these sellers will advertise in the beekeeping magazines or you can ask your local beekeeping association for the swarm. Arrange for the bees to arrive only when you have everything ready.

WHEN TO OBTAIN YOUR BEES

It is easier to buy/obtain your bees in the spring. This is because you will then be able to see how the bees develop in their own year, from being a small colony or nucleus, to growing rapidly, to swarming, to building up their honey stores and, finally, to slowing down for the winter. At the start of spring, your colony will be small and gentle and, as they grow and become more fierce, you too will be growing in experience and will be able to handle it. Also, you will be able to see the queen more easily as she will be small. Buy in early spring.

WHAT NEXT?

Now you have everything prepared and your bees have been ordered for a spring start, you are ready to go on to the next stage of starting with bees.

Chapter 5

Starting with bees

This chapter explains what you do on *day 1* of your beekeeping career – i.e. the lead up to when your bees arrive. You have all the equipment and now need to put your prepared hives in the right place – which must be convenient for you, convenient for your neighbours and suitable for the bees. A general rule is that, the better the site, the better the colony will build up and the more honey you will be able to obtain. Everything you do now is aimed at obtaining a surplus of honey and at maximizing your harvest.

POSITIONING YOUR HIVES

Many commercial beekeepers have to place their hives wherever they can obtain permission from a landowner, but the general principles apply as much to them as to the hobbyist with two hives. It isn't always possible to get it spot on every time, but do your best.

Country areas

If you place your bees placed in a country area miles away from your home, you should try to stick to the following rules. These rules are designed to help you find the ideal location, which may not always be possible. Needless to say, however, the hives are best kept out of sight, sheltered from high winds and away from frost hollows. I have seen bees kept in all sorts of areas over winter periods, and some of these were appalling places. While bees are hardy creatures that can survive most things, if you expect them to thrive in such areas and to provide you with honey, you will be disappointed.

You should also ensure that there are plenty of flowering plants or crops in the area. It is, however, often easier to be more certain of a honey crop in a city than in today's countryside, where thousands of acres of wheat won't amount to much honey, especially as wheat farmers will do their best to eradicate any nectar-bearing weed that dares to pop its head up in the vicinity. Find out what is in the area first, and then try to keep to the following rules:

- Ensure easy access by foot or, preferably, by vehicle.

- Permanent sites must have good nectar sources within 2 km (1 mile).

- Sites must have a water source in the vicinity. This should preferably be in full sun and out of the wind.

- In temperate climates, place hives in the sun. Some dappled shade, however, is useful.

- Sites should have early sources of pollen for brood rearing, such as rock rose, willow or gorse. Books that detail useful plants for nectar and pollen are listed on pages 278-80.

- Sites should be sheltered from the wind.

- Ensure the site is not prone to flooding.

- Make sure the site is not in a winter/spring frost hollow.

- Sites should preferably be out of sight of roads.

- Don't place hives under trees where they can be dripped on during and after rain.

- Keep sites away from HT power lines.
- Keep the area around the hives clear of tall weeds or grass. Cut grass and weeds – don't use spray of any kind.

Minimizing drifting when siting your hives

Drifting is a problem associated with most apiary sites and occurs when bees enter the wrong hive or 'drift' into the wrong hive. This can occur if:

- hives are placed in straight rows;

- there is a prevailing wind; or

- all the hives are identical and facing the same way.

Research has shown that hives at the end of rows are more conspicuous to bees than those within rows, and hives in the front and back rows are more conspicuous than middle-row hives. Bees will, therefore, more readily enter hives in the outer rows at the ends of rows.

The effects of drifting are that some hives can be depleted of foragers, thus affecting their honey-gathering ability, and it can also be a way of spreading disease. With only a couple or so of hives, this is unlikely to be a problem but, as soon as you expand, drifting will become a major consideration.

Drifting can cause large variations in hive yields in an apiary that beekeepers may then ascribe to a failing queen, etc., and the wrong corrective action may then be taken. It is a bigger problem than most beekeepers realize and very few beekeepers control or prevent it, mainly because neat rows of identical hives look tidy and efficient and good to the eye. You won't suffer from this problem, though, because you now know that it really is a big, if hidden, problem and you will no doubt follow the advice below.

Preventing drifting
The following are some ways to prevent drifting:

- Arrange your hives in an irregular manner. Hives situated among trees or shrubs with the entrances facing indifferent directions should not suffer from drifting. The hives are distinctive to the bees, and the shrubs and trees act as landmarks for them.

- Place or grow landmarks in an apiary.

- Arrange your hives in a horse-shoe pattern, or in wavy lines.

- Arrange your hives in pairs with 2–3 m (6½–10 ft) between pairs.

- Paint different-coloured symbols on the hive entrances.

- If your hives are in rows, ensure there is at least 3 m (10 ft) between the rows.

Urban areas

Some may wonder why on earth a beekeeper would keep bees in a city. In fact, some of the best honey comes from city parks and gardens, and some areas are richer in nectar than many areas of the mono-crop countryside zones. There are three important things to think about in urban areas: neighbours, neighbours and neighbours. You might want bees, but your neighbours might not. They like to buy their honey in the safety of a supermarket. They will be scared of bees because many of them think that honey is produced by nice, fluffy bumble bees and so, when they see your fast, horrid little wasp-like things zipping around all over the place, they will not always be pleased or happy about it. Keep them happy by trying to adhere to the hive placements outlined below, and always use known, gentle bees – and give them loads of honey.

The main complaints by neighbours in urban areas are as follows:

- Swarms settling on their property.

- Bees buzzing around angrily and stinging when you are inspecting the hives or taking honey.

- Bees using water sources on their property.

- Yellow staining on washing and cars from bee droppings.

There are two ideal sites for urban bees.

Rooftops

Many beekeepers in urban areas use rooftops for their hives. These sites are ideal as they are the least likely to affect neighbours and the hives, if well placed, can be kept out of sight – out of sight, out of mind.

Enclosed gardens

In urban areas, bee gardens need to be as enclosed as possible, with high walls in front of and behind the hive to encourage the bees to fly high enough so as not to annoy neighbours. Then, if you are using gentle bees, you should get away with being an urban beekeeper.

I have seen, however, just such a beekeeper whose bees had swarmed five times in five days (he had five hives), and all had occupied tree branches, overhangs and other useful bee-type perches in neighbours' property. Very nervous neighbours were doing their best to help the beekeeper collect the swarms by holding ladders and so on, but clearly didn't like the situation. Perhaps not surprisingly, though, because bees are prone not to sting during swarming, none of the neighbours was stung, even though bees were swirling around in all directions. After the worried beekeeper had sorted it all out, his neighbours were much happier about having bees around – and with pots of honey to give to their friends, they even referred to the bees as 'our bees' as they bragged about it all in the pub.

The importance of water sources

All bees need a water source, whether in the countryside or in urban areas, but the location of the water source is more critical in urban areas. All bees kept in urban areas must have a water source on the property or provided by a nearby public water supply, such as a river, pond or lake. If there is no such water supply, they will head for other supplies and, inevitably, they will head for the garden pond or swimming pool of the one neighbour with whom you don't get on and who is implacably opposed to bees in urban areas. This will cause a genuine nuisance, and you will have trouble.

It is very difficult to persuade the bees to change their habits once they have found a source of water, so you need to be on the ball about this before you obtain your bees. Your water supply need be nothing more than a trickle of water, a leak from an outside tap or hose, or a small pond. Bees prefer water with an odour rather than fresh water, and so a little mud and weed won't harm the situation.

Bees from my home apiary in Spain found a small crack in the lid of our septic tank and drew their 'water' supply from this until I managed to seal it up. This occurred even though there was a stream nearby. I did feel a bit guilty about selling the honey for a while after this, and felt it best not to advertise the fact on the jar label.

So, to avoid these problems, provide a clean water supply if one doesn't exist already.

Avoiding complaints

To minimize complaints from neighbours, observe the following rules:

- Don't keep too many hives on the property. Keep two or three at the most.
- Provide a water source.
- Keep gentle bees.
- Maximize your swarm-prevention techniques (explained in Chapter 6).
- Collect any swarms quickly if they do occur.
- Stop bees from robbing (explained in Chapter 8).
- Put the hives in a sunny, sheltered position, out of sight of neighbours.
- Erect a high fence around them to make them fly high after leaving the hive.
- Talk about your bees and their amazing pollination abilities with fruit and crops.
- Give your honey to your neighbours.

Keeping bees in an urban area takes common sense, explanation/education, gentle involvement, if possible, and a huge charm offensive involving honey. You will be surprised to find just how many people take a real interest in bees – if you take the trouble to tell them about bees and as long as they feel safe from them.

The need to prevent drifting is the same in urban areas but, with fewer hives and a lack of space for long rows of hives, drifting will probably be very much reduced. Make sure your entrances face different ways, however.

ARRANGING INSURANCE IN RURAL AND URBAN AREAS

Third-party insurance (at least) is essential if you keep bees in an urban area, and comprehensive insurance is very desirable in a country area. In urban areas, because your hives are on a roof or in your garden, they are not likely to be stolen or vandalized, but they might be the cause of a claim from a neighbour if the neighbour's washing is soiled or if injury occurs. Bees kept in the countryside are not likely to offend anyone, but may be stolen or vandalized in your absence.

In the UK, if you are a member of your local branch of any British national beekeeping associations, you will receive automatic third-party insurance and can increase this at a very reasonable cost. In Spain, basic insurance is provided if you belong to the agricultural union, and it is worth investigating provisions such as these in your own country or state.

As everyone knows, insurance is a complete waste of money until you need it and, if you have it, you will probably never need it. All my brand-new hives (I had just fully re-equipped), full of new, expensive, organically bred queens and bees were wiped out in a forest fire in Spain. The reason the forest fire unexpectedly veered in my direction was that the Big, Black Hand knew I was not yet insured! (I had three days to go.) With no prospect of further income and kids to feed and debts to pay, I had to sell up and take a beekeeping job in New Zealand, where I still reside. As you can see, not being insured was a life-changing event for me and my family. So obtain insurance.

YOUR BEES ARRIVE

Now that your hives are in the correct place, near a convenient water source, appropriately insured and generally out of sight of neighbours, you can install your bees. Just before doing so, however, make sure you have 4 l (8 pt) of sugar syrup (2 l; 4 pt per hive). I make this by mixing 1 kg (2 lb) of sugar with 1 l (2 pt) of water (i.e. thin syrup). Invert sugar is best for the fast development of a colony, and instructions on how to prepare this are given in Chapter 9. Initially, however, use ordinary white granulated sugar and warm water. Stir this well until it is clear.

Placing a hive full of bees

If you have bought hives with bees included, you will probably have taken a look into the hive with an experienced beekeeper and you will know the state of the queen, brood and stores. If not, you should at least ascertain from the seller that they have stores to last them at least a few days.

When the hives arrive you should place them in your prepared positions, generally facing south east in the Northern Hemisphere and north east in the Southern Hemisphere. These facings aren't essential, but early sunlight at the hive's entrance can stimulate bees to an early start. Each hive may arrive with its entrance blocked. Follow the procedure outlined below:

- Place the hive on its stand, which may be a pallet or bricks and so on (I've seen them on rubber tyres – anything to keep the hive floor off the ground), facing in the appropriate direction, if possible.

- Slightly tilt the hive forward.

- Unblock the hive entrance.

- Leave the hive for a couple of days to settle down. This 'couple of days' isn't a fixed figure. If because of work or other commitments you can't look at the bees for another week, look at them then. You will have ascertained from the seller that they have stores and so on, otherwise you wouldn't have bought them. If so, they will be perfectly able to look after themselves.

If, however, you have empty hives with frames of foundation and have purchased nucleus bees, then the following is the simple procedure for installing them:

- Place each nucleus on top of the hive in which it is to be installed, with the entrance facing the same way as the hive entrance.

- Open the nucleus entrance and leave the bees overnight.

- The following evening, place the nucleus to one side, open up the hive brood body and remove four or five (depending on the number of frames in the nucleus) frames from the centre of box and then very carefully (so as not to drop the queen) replace these frames with the frames from the nucleus. It is easy to see a queen in a nuc because there are not many bees, and nucs are very gentle by nature. Ensure that as, you move the frames over, the queen is on one of them.

- With a bar of wood, close up the entrance so that only one bee can get in and out at a time. (Entrance reducers can be purchased but it is easy to use a small bar of wood.)

- Remove one more frame from the edge of the box and replace it with a frame feeder.

- Fill the feeder about three quarters full with 1:1 sugar syrup.

- Close the hive and leave for a week before inspecting it to ensure that the queen is alive and laying.

- Ensure that the hive is tilted slightly forward so that rainwater cannot enter it and accumulate.

If you have purchased a package of bees, then follow this procedure:

- When the packages arrives, place it in a cool, dark room. The ideal temperature is about 18–20° C (65–70° F).

- Give the bees some sugar syrup by brushing or sprinkling sugar syrup (1:1 ratio of sugar to water) over the screen surface.

- Install the bees in the late afternoon so that they will settle down and not drift. Other bees will be less inclined to rob the small colony at this hour.

- Reduce the hive entrance with an entrance reducer or a small bar of wood, as described above.

- Lightly bang the cage's floor so that the clustered bees fall onto it.

- Remove the cage's wooden cover.

- The feeder can will be exposed. Remove this.

- Remove the queen cage and check the queen to make sure she is alive.

- Using a nail, puncture the candy in the queen cage so that the queen can be released more easily by the workers.

- Half the ten frames should be removed, leaving five in the hive. Place the queen cage with the candy end up between two frames. The cage screen should be exposed to the bees.

- Replace the frames that were removed so that there is a total of ten frames.

- Place the package in front of the hive's entrance so that the few remaining bees can crawl into the hive.

- Finally, provide the bees with sugar syrup in the frame feeder.

Or

- Put an empty hive body on top of the new hive.

- Place the syrup can that came with the package inside the hive body, resting on the top bars of the frames.

- In about a week, inspect the colony for eggs and larvae and, while doing this, refill the frame feeder.

- Remove the empty queen cage, ensuring that the queen has got out.

- Look for eggs in the cells.

- If the queen fails, introduce a new queen immediately. If you have no queen available, you can unite the package with another colony or package (see Chapter 8), or you can give the bees a frame of young larvae and let them raise another queen (see Chapter 11).

- Ensure that the hive is tilted slightly forward so that rainwater cannot enter it and accumulate. To do this, place a small piece of wood under the stand's back feet or under the hive's rear if you are not using a stand.

SUMMARY

Ideally you should now have the following:

- Two modern, complete, removable box hives common to your area, or two Langstroth hives.

- Hives situated in an urban or country location.

- Hives consisting of a 'full' brood box and a 'half' super, with a queen excluder in between the boxes. (Other half supers should be made available as the season goes on.)

- Each 'full' brood box containing a frame feeder with sugar syrup, plus nine Hoffman frames with foundation wax, some of which that have been replaced with the frames that came with a nucleus of bees.

- Each 'half' super or honey super having eight Manley frames filled with foundation.

- A gentle strain of bees with a young, laying queen. The queen should be a new queen, mated and laying.

- Other equipment as described above so that, after the week you have given your bees to settle down, you will be able to open your hive ready to inspect your bees, to see what is going on and to really start learning about bees.

Chapter 6

The active season: spring

STARTING IN THE SPRINGTIME

I mentioned earlier that spring is an ideal time to commence beekeeping. It is not the only time, but it is easily the best for a new beekeeper. The reason for this is that you can start with a small nucleus colony on just a few frames and watch it grow through your beekeeping. If you follow the advice in this book, it will grow, and your experience will grow with it. By the autumn, you will have seen colony expansion; undertaken swarm-prevention methods; carried out manipulations to increase honey production; dealt with any colony problems; extracted your honey crop; and perhaps split your hives so that you'll have more next year.

You have a great deal to do in the meantime, however. Your colonies are growing and probably wanting to swarm; varroa will be increasing in your hives; and you will have to assess carefully the amount of room the bees need to deposit their honey. Diseases may rear their ugly heads, and you will have to inspect your colonies at regular intervals to make sure they are not suffering or failing in some way. This is a lot to think about for an experienced beekeeper, let alone a new one, but, if you follow the instructions in this chapter carefully, you and your bees will survive to the summer.

Checking the hives

So, it is springtime, and you have left your newly arrived bees for a week to settle in to their new surroundings. You now want your colonies to expand and, hopefully to produce a surplus of honey that you can extract. You have already helped them by placing them in a good position with plenty of forage available within a mile or so from the hive, and now all you need to do is to ensure they stay disease and problem free and have enough room to expand. In other words, you have to know what is going on in the hive and react to their needs. You will have to do this at least once every month – preferably more often – until the winter. So how do you do this?

First, you should look into the hives to see what is going on. What you are looking for is as follows:

- Is there a queen and is she laying eggs?

- Is there brood of all ages present?

- Are there any signs of diseases/pests? This includes a look at the general cleanliness in the hive, especially the floor.

- Has the colony sufficient food stores (honey and pollen)?

- Has the colony built up in numbers and number of frames covered since you installed them (or since your last visit)?

- If so, have they enough room?

Fairly soon you will also be looking for indications that the colony may swarm and for queen cells in the hive, but we'll deal with those later in this chapter.

This all sounds complicated but it is, in fact, quite logical, and you will become very much quicker at recognizing the telltale signs as you gain experience. Take your time, therefore, and follow these instructions. Let's first look at the bees without opening the hives.

Inspecting the closed hive

As you approach the hives and before you open them, look at the entrances. Much can be learnt about the internal state of a hive by observing the entrance, and Table 1 should give you an idea of what you are looking for.

Observation	Interpretation
Bees fighting at the entrance	Robbing
Pile of dead bees at the entrance	Poison
Dead bees, many still moving	Virus disease
Dead drones at the entrance or drones being removed by workers	Period of dearth; lack of stores
Bees unable to fly or staggering/moribund on the hive or at the entrance	Virus disease (could also be starvation)
Mummified larvae littering entrance	Chalk brood disease (see Chapter 10)
Heavy faeces-spotting on the hive	Dysentery (see Chapter 10)
Dead larvae being thrown out but not carried away	Possible starvation
Pollen being carried into the hive	Usually indicates a healthy colony
Many bees flying at the entrance. No fighting. Bees facing the hive appear to be bobbing up and down	Young adult bees on play/orientation flights; usually late afternoon
Many bees issuing from the hive in a swirling ascending mass	Swarm emerging
A regular column of ants entering the hive. Very few, if any, bees in sight.	Hive or nuc empty. Put your ear to the side of the hive and give it a sharp knock. If silent, the hive is empty. If you hear a roar, then you have a colony in being you need to check out.

Table 1. Observations of the hive's entrance

Some of these observations may still be a bit vague, but all will become clear. This inspection can be carried out every time you pass the hives, even if you do not have the time for a full, open inspection. It takes only a couple of minutes and may alert you to a possible problem, but it should never take the place of a full, open inspection.

Carrying out the full, open inspection

If you are about to inspect a newly installed nuc, there is no need to use smoke before opening the hive. Until a colony has grown and has almost filled the brood box I never use smoke. Small colonies are generally well behaved and calm and, if they aren't, you are going to have a feisty bunch of bees later on. The inspection schedule that follows is for a newly established colony about a week old, but the general principles apply to any colony and, by the time your colony has grown and expanded, your inspections will be following the same pattern.

Lifting the lid

Approach the beehive from the side and, gently (using the hive tool if necessary), lift the lid. Place this on the ground upside down. You do this so that you can place other boxes on top of it later. If it is gabled WBC lid, you have to move it well out of the way so that you don't trip over it as you move around. As I said, I don't use smoke on small nucs because they are usually quiet enough without it but, if you want to see what effect it has, then use a small amount only. Puff it over the top bars quickly and lay the smoker down. You'll see the bees near the top bars quickly disappear and start to gorge honey.

Checking for eggs

Now remove one of the end frames of the box (you could remove the feeder if it is empty). This will give you room to move the other frames about. Gently separate the frames with your hive tool so that you are able to lift out the centre frames without rolling bees against the wax as you do so. The centre frames of a small colony will hold the brood, and it is this you want to look at.

Take out a frame with brood on it and see if there are any eggs in the cells. Hold it up to the light to see the eggs better. There should be one egg at the base of each cell. These are tiny white, stick-like things, and you should have a look at Photograph 1 in the colour photograph section of this book.

If you see more than one egg in a cell and these are laid up from the cell's base, you have the problem of laying workers, and you should go straight to Chapter 8. If this is the case, your colony may well be doomed, and you should ask for advice. If you see no eggs in any of the cells then you either have no queen or a non-laying queen. It is possible you have a virgin but unlikely in these circumstances.

Finding the queen

Now look over the frame for the queen, who will usually (but not always) be on a frame of brood. She will be walking around more slowly than the other bees, and often the first thing you notice is her longer, tanned abdomen. If you see her, have a quick look and then gently lower the frame back into the box. If you have seen eggs and a queen then you know that, barring signs of disease, all is well. If you ordered your bees with a marked queen she will be easier to pick out, but if you can't find her and eggs are visible, it is highly likely the queen will be somewhere around. Eggs are eggs for three days only and so you had a queen three days ago at least and you probably still have one.

If you see eggs but still can't find the queen, make a note of which hive it is, wait another three to four days and have another look. The eggs you saw previously will now be young larvae. If there are plenty of eggs still visible this means your queen is good at keeping a low profile when you are looking for her. Some simply disappear when the hive is opened and can be extremely difficult to find even for the experienced eye, especially in a large colony. In a small nuc, however, she will be much easier to find.

Investigating the brood nest

Look to see if there is sealed brood and unsealed brood in various stages of development. This is normal in a healthy colony, with brood as eggs, young larvae, larvae and larvae in capped brood cells.

Inspecting the brood nest is one of the most effective ways of determining the health of the colony and it can give you a timeline on what has been happening in the colony at various times up to the present. The presence of sealed brood indicates what was happening 9–21 days ago (see Figure 20 later in this chapter). Young, unsealed brood shows what was happening more recently, and eggs and tiny larvae show what is happening up to the present. Young larvae should be pearly white and neatly coiled in their cells, and sealed brood should be covered in neat and clean, slightly convex wax coverings with no holes and no sunken parts.

In a small colony it is easy to see all this, and this is one reason why buying a nuc or package to start with is a good idea. It shows you what to look for early on in your beekeeping career. If you find there are no eggs or young brood and you are unable to find the queen then, after a thorough check to ensure there is no disease, the colony must be united with another colony or a nucleus (see Chapter 8).

Inspecting the stores

Having seen the state of the brood and determined that a queen is present, now look at the stores. The bees must have stores of honey and pollen for survival, or at least a full feeder of sugar syrup. Stores are placed in an arc around the brood area, and checking for the presence of honey and pollen is easy. If they have neither, you must do something about it – i.e. feed them (see Chapter 9).

In European and many other countries bees have evolved with the local plants and, generally, there will be pollen and nectar sources at the right time for them (unless you have placed them in a huge monocrop area). In other countries, especially where honey-bees have been introduced recently, this may not always be the case, especially with early pollen sources essential for brood rearing. In such cases there may be a need for pollen patties (substitute pollen) for the bees to feed on and to give them an early boost.

Lack of pollen can be one of the biggest causes of a colony's failure to build up and thrive. You should be aware of this and, if there is a scarcity of early pollen, ask for advice from local beekeepers. You must then feed the colony (see Chapter 9).

Checking the amount of room

Now look at the amount of room the bees have. There should be enough empty cells for the queen to lay eggs (and remember, she can lay 1,000–2,000 a day) and for the workers to store food. If the nuc is only a week old, there should still be plenty of room or potential room (i.e. frames of foundation for the bees to pull out). This is likely to be the state of affairs in a nuc but, as time goes on, the colony will expand, and you may have to give them more room with the addition of another brood box. If you don't, the bees will feel congested and will swarm. If this happens, you will lose up to about half your workforce, which may well become someone else's workforce.

Methods of preventing, or at least controlling, this phenomenon are given later in this chapter but, I repeat, in a new, young colony indications of swarming are rare indeed.

Looking for signs of disease

You should also look for signs of disease, and this is difficult for a new beekeeper. Again, it is a good idea to start off with a young colony because then you will quickly learn what a healthy colony looks like: what the sealed brood looks like and what healthy eggs and larvae look like (see Photograph 2 in the colour photograph section of this book). Then, anything that looks or smells differently will suggest a problem.

Chapter 10 explains diseases and their symptoms and methods of treatment, and so reading this chapter before each inspection will help to determine if you have any problems. It may also be useful to obtain a copy of *The Beekeepers Field Guide* to take to the apiary with you (see the bibliography at the end of this book). This guide goes through all the signs and symptoms of diseases in one small volume that can be taken into the field. No inspection, however, should be undertaken without looking for signs of something being wrong.

Eradicating pests

You may see wax moths (see Chap 10) in a colony. If you've never seen one before, just about any small, grey moth skittering around on a frame will be a wax moth. There are small and large ones but, either way, kill them whenever you see them.

It is usual to see a few wax moths in a colony and the bees can normally control them, but any indications of wax-moth damage should be investigated because it is often the first sign to a new beekeeper (and many experienced beekeepers) that something is wrong. As noted, however, a healthy colony can control these pests.

Inspecting the floor

Now look at the state of the floor. Gently lift the brood box and, equally gently, place it on the upturned lid – you don't want to dislodge the queen and lose her. The floor will now be visible and, hopefully, you will be using a stainless-steel mesh floor but, if not, the floor should be clean and free of debris. If there is a build-up of debris, give it a scrape clean with your hive tool or swap it for a new floor and clean the old one later.

A very dirty floor could indicate a problem, so look around for any other signs of trouble. If a solid floor has a build-up of water, this means the hive is not tilted forward slightly to allow water to run out of the entrance. Do this now if you need to.

Observing the bees

At this point it may be worthwhile unhurriedly holding up some frames and observing the bees to see what they are doing. Try to make some sense out of the apparent chaos. You could see a bee dancing and telling her mates about a good food source, or you could see a bee with pollen baskets moving towards the pollen storage area. You will undoubtedly see new adults cutting though the wax cappings of their cells and slowly emerging, with all the other bees walking about over their heads.

If you are very lucky and the bees are calm, you could see the queen laying an egg. I've lost several queens in my time while gazing at a queen moving around on a comb – especially a young one. So take a quick look by all means but then gently lower her frame back into the hive. Always remember to replace frames in the same way as you picked them up, unless you have another task in mind, but we come back to that later in this chapter when we discuss building up a colony.

Reassembling the hive

Finally, if you mentally tick off all the above checks positively, reassemble the hive and move on to the next hive, where you should repeat the whole process.

This chapter provides a checklist of all the inspection points, and Chapter 8 a queen/brood-nest troubleshooting guide. Use these guides until you are able to remember each point for yourself. The full hive inspection applies to every hive, whether a nucleus hive or a full colony of bees that is 10 boxes high and bursting at the seams.

After the full inspection

If you have placed your bees in a good area, there should be no need to feed them during the spring, except when starting off a nuc or package as described in Chapter 5. If, after this feed, an otherwise healthy and growing colony fails to gather stores in the spring and early summer, then consideration must be given to moving them to a better area for forage.

If you think there is a problem with the colony, ask a more experienced beekeeper for help. You can easily misread the signs and make the wrong decision based on an incorrect diagnosis, and I think this is one of the most important reasons why you should be in your local beekeeping association. It doesn't matter where you live in the world, there is likely to be one, and the members will (certainly initially) be an essential support group for you. Not only that, with the spread of more exotic diseases among bees and the increasing importance of honey-bee pollination to agriculture, you should be on some recognized register for disease control, insecticide-spray monitoring and so on. Even though beekeepers are often more individual beings than hermits, government or club registration should be compulsory.

So that was your first full inspection of your new, young colonies. You may have sought help and advice from an experienced beekeeper if you noticed anything amiss but, for a young nucleus, problems should be rare. Otherwise, all is well, and you are more conversant with your bees' activities. There is, however, one preventative measure you must take now even if your colonies look healthy: treat them for varroa.

Treating your hives for varroa

Most beekeepers place their bees in areas where a mite – varroa destructor – is endemic. Varroa evolved with the far-eastern honey-bee, *Apis cerana*, and, during this process, the bee learnt to deal with it. In a hive of these far-eastern bees, therefore, varroa lives in a form of mutual hostility with the bees and is tolerated, even though it causes some losses. Probably due to the movement of bees around the world, the varroa mite came into contact with *Apis mellifera*, the western honey-bee, which had evolved no defence mechanism against it and which therefore cannot deal with it. The mite has now managed to invade just about everywhere where bees are kept, even New Zealand – which is as isolated as you can get.

An infestation of varroa mites in your colony will destroy it unless you treat it. The mite doesn't intend this to happen because it will then die out itself. The varroa mite probably assists in vectoring into the bees some or all of the many viruses that are normally endemic in bee colonies but which are kept in check by healthy colonies. By biting into the bees and puncturing the bees' cuticle, the mite may well aid in the ingress of viral particles and bacteria.

Since varroa arrived, we have learnt a great deal about this mite, but there is also much we don't yet know. It may be that many of the so-called syndromes currently affecting the western honey-bee are the result of varroa activity. While Chapter 10 discusses this mite in more detail, suffice it to say here that, if you are in a varroa area, you will have to treat your colonies. There is no avoiding this and, if you don't get it right, the colony will without doubt die out and the wax moth will move in. In the early days of varroa many beekeepers discovered that they were, in fact, wax-moth keepers! This happened to me. Don't let it happen to you.

In the spring when your bee populations are growing fast, so are the numbers of varroa mites, and so you must treat them. This means April/May in the Northern Hemisphere and September/October in the Southern Hemisphere, and then again in the autumn. There are many treatments and many ways of administering them so, because you are starting out, find out what members of your local beekeeping association are doing and follow their example. Once you have treated your hives you can at least be more relaxed about the state of your hives over this period and will have done your best to limit varroa damage.

There is, however, another problem that often arrives quite suddenly in the spring, and that is swarming. Like varroa it is best to recognize that swarming may well occur and to try to avoid this problem. If you fail to do this then you can at least limit the damage.

SWARMING

Have you ever been driving along in the spring and suddenly you heard multiple splats on your windscreen, which became covered with muck? You looked out to see insects heading towards you in their hundreds, and then suddenly all was quiet again. That was probably a swarm of bees.

As your colony grows – and it can very rapidly in the spring – you have to make sure it has enough room. The queen needs room to lay eggs and the workers need room to store honey. If the growing population does not have enough space, the bees will swarm, and this is one of the most perplexing problems in beekeeping. It is especially difficult for commercial beekeepers with perhaps thousands of hives to look after but, even for the hobbyist with just a couple, it can be a daunting task to limit or prevent this phenomenon.

If your bees swarm, there will be a long break in your colony's development because a new queen has to be mated and built up in the egg-laying stakes. There will be fewer bees in your hive to gather honey, and the colony will have to wait for some weeks for new bees to go through the egg to adult-forager-bee process. Your colony may thus not have the time to make a surplus of honey that year and, if it does, it will be very much reduced.

What is swarming?

Swarming is honey-bee reproduction at colony level rather than bee-to-bee sexual reproduction. In this way, honey-bees are able to increase their numbers by increasing their colonies and also to invade new areas. Because this is a natural method of reproduction and dispersal, it is difficult to stop it from occurring. Most swarming occurs from around May to June in the Northern Hemisphere and from September to early December in the Southern Hemisphere.

Preparing to swarm

As a result of certain conditions in the hive, the bees in your colony will raise new queens. The process begins when worker bees make small cell cups on the comb, mostly near to the comb's outer edges and especially along the bottom. These small cups don't necessarily indicate immediate swarming as they may never be used but, once the conditions arise that cause the swarming impulse to manifest itself, the queen will be directed towards these cups and will lay an egg in some or all of them. At this stage, the beekeeper must take note and commence swarm-prevention procedures. The colony will develop these cups into queen cells that are so distinctive they are very easy to recognize (see Figure 16).

Fig. 16. A queen cell hanging from the bottom of a frame (note the 'sculpture' of the cell)

A virgin queen emerges

If left alone, after around 16 days, from one or more of these cells a virgin queen will emerge that will take over the colony, the old queen having departed with the swarm. This new virgin queen will go to the other queen cells, if allowed to by the workers, and will sting through the cell to kill off her potential rivals.

The virgin, however, is now in a precarious position. She has to leave the hive and fly off to a drone congregation area to mate with many drones and then return to the hive. This is a very dangerous period of her life. She could become lost, be eaten, hit bad weather or be sprayed with pesticide. The worker bees may have protected one or more of the remaining queen cells just in case she doesn't return and they need another virgin, and they may have prevented the first virgin queen from harming it. If she mates successfully and returns to the colony without mishap, however, she will be allowed to kill off any rivals, whether they have emerged or not, or the bees themselves may tear down any remaining queen cells.

After-swarms

Occasionally another virgin will emerge that is guarded by the workers until they are sure she is not required, but this system seems sometimes to go wrong. I have seen a swarm with a queen and seven virgins in it. What was going on in the original hive?

This type of occurrence suggests that the second newly mated queen – or even a virgin in a hive – may swarm with half the remaining workers while another virgin mates and takes over, thus depleting the colony even further. This is known as an after-swarm. If a colony sends out several after-swarms, this can make it worthless. I've seen some tiny little swarms that are of no use at all and, if they occur late in the year, they rarely survive.

Prime-swarms

But back to the original plan, in which the old queen in the company of around half the workers departs the hive. This is known as a prime swarm. Older workers are believed to initiate this using both body language and noise signals. The queen is fed less for some time before the flight and her egg-laying rate decreases so that she can fly more easily.

Once the swarm has left the hive, it usually congregates first at some point not far from the original hive. It hangs there for several hours, waiting for the scouts to direct them to the new home. This is the point when most people see a swarm, and it is at this point that it is most easily captured.

Catching a swarm

This is mostly easy – possibly the easiest thing about beekeeping. If you see a swarm leaving the hive or flying past you, follow it until it hangs up. You can then (if it is conveniently sited) shake it into a box, put some sort of lid over the box allowing a small entrance for bees to go in and out, and leave it there, preferably in the shade, until the evening. If the mass of bees stays in the box, this means you have the queen in there and all is well. If the bees gradually leave the box and hang up again, they are clustering around the queen, which you missed. You then have to shake the bees – in one sharp shake, if possible – into the box again hoping that, this time, the queen falls in as well. She usually does. Obviously, if you have an empty nucleus box or something similar, this makes the operation easier, but I have used anything handy – cardboard shoe-boxes, for example. In such situations, you know it is a new swarm and so it will very likely be peaceful.

Sometimes swarms hang in the most awkward places (see Figure 17), making it very difficult to retrieve them and, on these occasions you either have to leave them or use your imagination. I used a ladder to get to a swarm on one occasion. It was hanging off a branch fairly high up in the tree over a small arroyo, or stream. I lifted the box to it and, with my other hand, shook the branch hard. The swarm fell into the box, the ladder fell away and I was left hanging on the branch with one hand, and holding a heavy box of bees in the other. I shouted for my wife to come to help but she arrived centuries too late and I had already hit the shallow water by the time of her arrival. I was lying there, covered with thousands of increasingly irritated bees. Even swarms can go into fight mode if provoked enough and, as usual, I hadn't put any gear on and so the pair of us fled.

A colleague of mine tried to extract a swarm from an electric fence, with comical results. Most beekeepers have 'swarm' stories – a little like fishermen! Suffice to say that you should be careful and treat them gently.

Swarm-collecting equipment

Keep a box handy for catching swarms. You can purchase basic cardboard boxes with ventilation screens for this purpose. The one I use is shown in Figure 18. This doubles as a swarm box for queen rearing and for holding the queen on a comb when I want her out of the way.

Fig. 17. A swarm clustering on a post – difficult to get off. We smoked them up into a box of comb held above them

Fig. 18. A handy swarm box

Another box I use has a removable gauze floor that can be used for any box, super or brood sized. You simply slip the floor on, tip the bees in and place a lid over it (see Figure 19). Then, because they have plenty of ventilation, they can be moved to their final location.

(a)

(b)

(c)

Fig. 19. (a) Gauze floor with aluminium flange; (b) box sitting in the flange of the floor; (c) lid on ready to go (strap if required)

Collecting unknown swarms

If you are asked to come to collect a swarm from someone else's land or house, grasp the opportunity for a free new colony to increase your stocks. You will need a spare hive and wax frames, though, or at least a nucleus box until you can obtain another hive.

Many beekeepers will tell you to avoid unknown swarms because they may have a disease or be a nasty strain, or a thousand other reasons. I say, go to get them. After all, if you were a cow farmer and someone offered you a free herd of cows, would you refuse? Diseases can be treated and nasty strains can be re-queened.

Swarms are programmed to make wax combs and, if you collected them just for this, it would be worth it. In this case, however, try to find out how long the bees have been hanging there. If a swarm has been hanging up for too long and the scouts haven't sorted out a new home or bad weather has prohibited takeoff – or for any other reason – the bees may become irritable, and irritable swarms can explode like atom bombs if you start messing about with them. Perhaps they have been there for so long that they have built comb and have become a colony at this particular site. They will then be normally protective of their nest.

Making a show of swarm collecting

Mostly, however, a swarm will be very gentle and easy to handle. It's great to collect them. You perform a service for others; you obtain free bees; and, if you make sure loads of people are watching (get on your mobile to tell people about it and delay your own arrival for a while – I know a beekeeper who did this), you can look like a hero.

Make sure your audience stays well back because of the 'danger', and advance bravely on the swarm as if going into a war zone. The public don't know that a swarm is the easiest part of beekeeping because they will have seen the film, *Swarm* and, even if they haven't, everyone (except you) knows from birth that bee swarms are deadly! And there you will be, bravely treating them like flies. Don't mess this up, however, because, if you irritate a swarm enough, a few of its members may just start stinging people, and then your reputation will go straight down the drain. Also, by collecting swarms you may save the bees from being classed as pests and destroyed. What a waste of livestock!

Africanized bees

The one big word of caution here is that, if you live in a part of the world (e.g. parts of South America or the southern USA) that has been invaded by Africanized bees, the words above about being deadly may well apply for real, and local laws and regulations may exist to cater for such an event. These could be clearing people from the area if appropriate, calling the authorities and so on. You should know about these laws and regulations and, if you do go near the bees, you should be appropriately clothed.

Researchers and bee breeders are always attempting to improve the honey-bees in their countries and, in 1956, Brazilian researchers imported honey-bees from Africa into Brazil in an effort to improve beekeeping in the New World tropics. The African bees were suited to conditions in Brazil and they began colonizing South America, hybridizing with European honey-bees (hence the name 'Africanized' honey-bees) and displacing the European bees.

Compared with the more docile European bees, Africanized honey-bees are extremely defensive. They attack in large numbers and will sting people and livestock with little provocation. They will even take over European bee colonies by entering them and killing the resident queen.

These bees have since moved northwards at a rate of up to 480 km (300 miles) per year and, today, every country in South and Central America has established populations of Africanized honey-bees. In 1990 they entered the USA and are gradually creeping north. Attempts to flood areas with European drones for mating met with little success: an African queen emerges before a European queen and then, like all queens, she destroys the other queen cells in the colony. A mixed mating, therefore, will always result in an African queen and all that it entails. Beware!

For those in Europe and other parts of the world where Africanized bees are absent, you will have an enjoyable and profitable time collecting swarms. Swarming is a nuisance to you, but there is a flip-side to this – other beekeepers may not be so zealous in their swarm-prevention regime and so, if their bees swarm, they may well become your bees if you can catch them.

What goes on in a swarm?

If no one collects it and a swarm is left alone to hang up, scout bees will constantly go to and fro from suitable sites. They will convey their message about a suitable site to the swarm by dancing on its surface and by recruiting new scouts to view their proposal. It seems a swarm will take up home in the proposed site of those scouts who are able to recruit the most dancers and who dance the most vigorously in favour of their home site.

Once they have decided, the scouts will initiate a mass takeoff, possibly by using a vibrating form of body language and by making a piping sound. The swarm will then head off to its new home, directed all the way by scouts who fly through the swarm in the required direction. If you have seen a swarm moving through the air, it seems to be an aimless mass of insects whirling around in all directions and not really going anywhere. But it is, and you soon realize that it is moving fairly quickly if you try to follow it. It's like an optical illusion: it is easy to follow on foot until it flies over a hedge or a river or other obstacle, and then you can loose it. The scouts dive down to the entrance of the new home and, slowly but surely, the swarm follows and takes up residence.

Taking up residence

Within minutes of taking up residence, the workers build comb, without which the colony cannot function. One of the possible reasons why bees in a swarm are gentle is that, during this process, they are conditioned not to sting. Before leaving their previous home, each of them fills up with honey. Most of this is used to synthesize wax to build the new home, and all the bees are needed for this: no honey, no wax; no wax, no new home. If they go around stinging, they will die and their honey will be wasted.

My point earlier about swarms pulling out wax comb is a serious one. That is their first main aim, and the beekeeper can use this propensity. You always need comb.

Other workers will be out foraging and, within half an hour, the swarm will be a colony. Where previously there was one colony, there are now two – reproduction and dissemination, just like us.

Dealing with the swarm

You, meanwhile, have captured your own, or someone else's, swarm and will have placed it in the shade, ensuring that the container has an entrance. Observe it for a while to make sure the bees are not gradually leaving it and hanging up again. If all is well, you can return home to prepare a hive for it. This requires just one box on a floor with wax foundation on the frames. It's a good idea to give them a good feed of sugar syrup, and so one of the frames could contain some good, clean comb. This will allow the early foragers to store their honey and pollen and may enable the queen to start laying earlier.

Go back to the swarm in the evening when most of the foragers will be back in their temporary home and close the box. Take it to the prepared hive (with the frames taken out), open it and tip all the bees into it. Gently place the frames in the hive with the frame with comb (if you have one) in the centre and the frame feeder with syrup nearby. Fill the rest of the hive with frames, close up and leave them to it.

Another way of putting them into the hive is to prepare a ramp in front of the hive leading to the entrance. For effect, some beekeepers place a white sheet on this. Tip the bees on to the ramp/sheet and you will see the bees march purposefully up the ramp and into the hive. This is fun to watch – in fact it's a wonderful sight – and it is good for the education of others but, for practical beekeeping, it is easier simply to tip them straight into the new hive.

Handling unexpected situations

The above instructions describe ideal situations. To be honest, while these often do occur, things occasionally don't go to plan. The swarm may hang up in impossible situations, you don't have a swarm box handy to put them in, or you have five spare frames only and just two of these have wax and you have no feed. Well all that's OK: bees are hardy creatures. They weren't expecting foundation frames and a feed of sugar syrup anyway. Just do what you can for the moment. Give them the two frames and fill the rest in a couple of days.

Bees can survive without feed for a while, and I've often not given them any at all if good nectar sources were available – which, of course, you have made sure about anyway.

If you can meet the ideal, then do, because it hurries up the process of the swarm becoming a productive hive. If you can't, don't worry: do what you can and give yourself time to sort it all out later.

Putting the swarm back into the original hive

One final way of dealing with a swarm is to tip it back into the hive from which it came – if you know it and if it's one of yours. Many texts advise this. If you definitely *don't* want increase you can do this. The two queens will fight it out and one will live to head the colony.

I did this twice in my early days because I didn't know any better and, on both occasions, the bees swarmed again the next day. If you put them back where they came from, they are likely to swarm again because the original cause of swarming will reoccur. Generally, I try to prevent the swarming process from starting in the first place but, if it occurs and I see it, I take the opportunity of increasing my stocks and giving the swarm some work to do in making comb. I don't advise putting them back in their original hive. Try to stop it in the first place and, if you can't, then use the swarms for increase.

Swarm prevention or swarm control?

Remember, if your bees swarm, half your honey-collecting field force will go and there will be a long gap before the hive is up and running again because the bees will have to wait for the replacement queen to mate and lay eggs. You will then have to wait for these eggs to become bees. So you must do something about swarming, and swarming only happens significantly in the spring.

First, there is swarm prevention and, second, there is swarm control. Swarm prevention is all about managing your colonies so that the swarming impulse doesn't arise in the first place. Swarm control is about letting the bees swarm, but only under your control so that you at least retain the bees. This may occur when you have left it too late to prevent them from swarming or, despite your best attempts at swarm prevention, the bees are still determined to swarm – and it happens. Let's first look at swarm prevention.

Preventing swarming

Very experienced beekeepers advocate many methods for preventing swarming that, to my mind, try to go against what the bees are attempting to do instead of going in their direction. The two main culprits are clipping one of the queen's wings and, in conjunction with this, destroying queen cells. Those who advocate clipping the queen's wings, say this prevents her from flying and so going with a swarm. The theory is that she will rush out with the swarm, fall on to the grass and climb back into the hive. The swarm, in the meantime realizes the queen is not with them and flies back to the hive.

Doing this is neither pleasurable nor profitable and, with the bees back in the hive, the same pressures that lead to swarming in the first place are again in place and the bees are likely to have another go. I saw this in my early beekeeping days. A similar method that at least doesn't mutilate the queen is to place a queen excluder over the entrance so that the queen is prevented from leaving. What that achieves I have no idea.

The swarming process takes a full month out of a colony's productive period, from the moment the queen cups are made to the moment the swarm leaves. The bees will still forage and store nectar and pollen but at a reduced rate compared with a hive that isn't preparing to swarm. All the activities of the bees described above over that month hugely reduce the colony's ability to produce a surplus compared with that of a colony that has been deterred from swarming in the first place. Deterrence is, I believe, therefore, the best overall management plan.

Clipping wings should especially have no part in beekeeping. On a large scale it would be far too time consuming and, on a small scale, it solves nothing. It was prohibited for much of my commercial beekeeping time under EU rules for the production of organic honey. Some will say it gives the beekeeper a better time-frame to inspect their bees and so prevent swarming because the beekeeper destroys the swarm cells before queens emerge. The mathematics of this method's timelines are sound, but that is the only good thing about it.

There are three points here:
1.   In many colonies, by the time you find sealed swarm cells, there is a fair chance your bees have already swarmed and you just haven't noticed.

2. If your bees have swarmed and you destroy the remaining queen cells, you will have destroyed their best chance of raising another queen. Soon you won't have a colony at all.
3. Finding queen cells to destroy is a tricky business. You are likely to miss one, especially in a large colony, and if you miss one your bees will swarm anyway.

Work with your bees, not against them, and consign these primitive old practices to the dustbin where they belong. One notable beekeeper, C.C. Miller of the USA, said early in the twentieth century that 'if a colony disposed to swarm should be blown up with dynamite, it would probably not swarm again, but its usefulness as a honey gathering unit would be somewhat impaired'. Clipping wings, placing queen excluders over the entrance and destroying queen cells have the same effect. There are better ways that work in the direction the bees want to go, so why not use them?

Methods to prevent swarming

Good swarm-prevention methods should reduce swarming with a low degree of colony interference and should be compatible with good colony management for both pleasure and profit. It goes without saying that a very good method is to obtain a strain of bees that has a lower tendency to swarm. This is, of course, not always possible but, if you are in a position to use this method and still keep your beekeeping pleasurable and profitable, don't dismiss it. When considering your swarm-control strategy, try to think in terms of employing the following manipulations in conjunction with each other, not as isolated examples.

Re-queening annually (or at least every two years)

This is one of the best methods for limiting swarming in your colonies, especially if you are a commercial beekeeper and have perhaps thousands of hives. It is difficult under these circumstances to keep such a close eye on matters but, if you re-queen annually, you will at least know that even in your absence the number of colonies swarming in your bee yards will be low. For a beekeeper with only a few colonies it is an easy method to employ.

Research has shown that a queen under a year old with plenty of queen pheromone is much less likely to swarm than a queen in her second year; a two-year-old queen is less likely to swarm than a three-year-old; and so on. The figures are quite remarkable.

Re-queen, therefore, *every* year so that no queen is over 12 months old. Fall or autumn re-queening is perhaps more difficult than spring re-queening, but it has so many advantages over spring re-queening. From my own experience I think the reasons for this are the better weather and the larger numbers of mature drones around. Troublesome spring weather and the chances of fewer drones being available make spring mating less certain. The great majority of professional honey producers re-queen every 12 months. They do this for a reason: less swarming, more eggs/bees.

Reversing hive bodies

In the early spring, reversing hive bodies can be a useful and effective method of swarm prevention. This simply involves swapping the positions of the upper and lower brood boxes (if you have them). Alternatively you can place a second brood box on top of the first. This box should have frames of empty comb, and a frame of capped brood from the existing brood box should be placed in the middle of it. Bees tend to work upwards, and so giving the colony more room for brood and for themselves reduces overcrowding and, in turn, reduces the inclination to swarm.

Start this when you see a number of queen cups or before, if possible. Don't leave it to the stage when queen cells are started. This manipulation is very simple – whole boxes are moved, and this is effective especially if used in conjunction with other methods. After about two weeks, reverse them again if the bees have moved up and keep this up until the end of the swarming season.

Supering up

This involves putting honey supers on to the brood body(s) in time for the honey flow. The first box should be filled with comb, especially if the season is early – bees have difficulty producing wax early on in the year. Putting supers on in time is not only essential for honey storage preparation but it also limits swarming by giving the bees more room in the hive.

Keeping your colonies equal in strength

This can be done in two ways. You can move frames of brood from strong colonies in danger of overcrowding to weaker colonies, or you can swap the positions of weak and strong hives. This latter manipulation can also be quite effective on hives that are near to swarming. In both cases you should ensure that both colonies are free from disease, otherwise you risk the chance of spreading it. You must also make sure the weaker hives aren't weak because of some disease, otherwise you are wasting your time and your bees.

The idea, generally, is again to ensure that strong hives are relieved of overcrowding pressure while, at the same time, helping colonies that are building up slowly. Evening up your hives is, in any case, a good strategy. Hives with even numbers of bees tend to 'do things' at more or less the same time and make apiary management much easier.

Ventilating your hives

Good hive ventilation goes a long way to lessen the swarming impulse if other methods are employed as well. Ensure that your entrances are appropriate for the time of year; that in really hot climates your lids are painted white; and that you use a stainless-steel mesh floor – which can also help in varroa control (see Chapter 10). The use of shade boards over the hive entrance is also a good idea in hot climates.

Controlling swarming

But what if you have missed all the signs and you look in your crowded hive one day during the swarming season and find queen cells? You've left it a little late but you can at least step in here to ensure the inevitable swarm will stay in your apiary in one of your hives and not fly off to some neighbour! Check to see if your colony has already swarmed (a good reason for having marked queens). If it hasn't or if it has and is still very populous, you can carry out the following manipulations.

The artificial swarm (1)

This involves splitting a hive into two colonies. It is easily done:

- Place a brood box on a floor on top of the existing hive, with the entrance facing the opposite way to the hive, or place it nearby in the apiary.

- Take two frames of brood (capped and uncapped) with as many adhering bees as possible and place them in this box.

- Place a frame of honey and pollen either side of them.

- Fill the rest of the box with foundation or comb.

- In between the two brood frames, place a caged queen or a queen cell.

- If necessary, shake in some more bees from a brood frame to make up the numbers.

- Give the new colony some sugar syrup in the frame feeder and place it near to the other occupied frames and close the hive.

- Reduce the entrance to one bee space to discourage robbing, or block a reduced entrance with grass so that robbing won't occur and the bees in the new hive won't rush out and return to the old hive.

- Fill the old hive with comb and close up.

You have now lessened the chances of swarming in the old colony and you have an extra colony that, in this case, is called a 'top'. You can either keep this separate or reunite it with the original to take advantage of a major honey flow. By reuniting the hives you will have done your best to ensure a good harvest, which would have been lowered by swarming. In undertaking this type of manipulation you make sure that the queen is in the original chamber. This is the only disadvantage of this method: you must locate the queen.

The demaree method

This method keeps the hive together so that it can take advantage of a honey flow, but it is time consuming and difficult to do on a large scale. It is, however, an excellent swarm-prevention method for the hobbyist. If you find queen cells in the colony, follow this procedure:

- Destroy *all* queen cells. Don't miss any.

- Place *all* the frames of brood into a new brood chamber.

- Place empty frames of comb in the original brood chamber.

- Find the queen and put her into this empty brood chamber. She will probably be with the brood in the new brood chamber.

- On this new brood chamber, place a queen excluder or a super of honey (which acts as a queen excluder).

- Place the new brood chamber(s) above this.

- After seven to eight days, destroy all queen cells in the upper brood chamber(s).

You can see what is happening here. You are giving the queen a new nest in which there is plenty of room to lay eggs. You are effectively stopping the bees in the upper brood chambers from swarming because they have no queen up there, but you are also allowing for the colony's normalization because you are keeping it all together while preventing the upper part from raising new queens by destroying any queen cells. Overall, the colony retains its bees and so is able to take advantage of any honey flow.

The artificial swarm (2)

The procedure for this is as follows:

- Move the entire hive to a new position.

- Place a new brood box with floor in the old position.

- Put the queen on a frame of brood in the new box.

- Fill the new box with frames of foundation or comb.

- Place the original supers with or without the queen excluder in the new hive.

- Position the old hive anywhere in the apiary.

- Cut out all the queen cells in the old hive.

- One week later, again cut out all the new queen cells in the old hive except one,

or:

- leave them and let the bees choose; or

- cut out all the queen cells and put in a new caged queen; or

- put in a queen cell from elsewhere.

This procedure is effective and easier than it looks but, like all artificial swarming, it splits the colony into two. If you want it to take full advantage of a nectar flow, therefore, you should unite the two halves before the flow starts. The disadvantages of this procedure are evident: you must find the queen, which can be difficult, and if you want to destroy all the queen cells, you mustn't miss any.

Unable to find the queen

If you cannot find the queen and you want to complete an artificial swarm, carry out the following procedure:

- Cut out all the queen cells – *all* of them.

- Split the colony into two, ensuring that each half has eggs and young brood.

- Place one half elsewhere in the apiary.

- Block the entrances of the moved box with grass. The bees will eventually remove it and, by the time they have done this, they will have become accustomed to their new hive and won't fly back to the original one.

- After three days look at each half. The half with eggs will have the queen and the other half will probably have queen cells.

- In the queenless colony, cut out the queen cells, except one. The bees will raise a queen from this. *Or* introduce a queen you have purchased in a queen cage.

The queen removal method

This is another effective but time-consuming method of swarm control where the queen cells are found in a colony. Brother Adam claimed that it was a fail-safe method of stopping swarming in a colony. It is simple and reliable, no extra equipment or boxes are needed, and can be used in conjunction with your annual queen replacement. However, the time between finding and removing the queen and a new queen laying can be as much as three weeks. During this time, the colony may do little work, even during a honey flow.

Carry out the following procedure:

- Find and remove the queen. If you are going to re-queen your hive with a new queen or a queen cell, the old queen must be killed. If you intend to keep her on, place her on a frame of brood and bees into a nucleus box, add some frames of comb and set aside.

- Destroy all queen cells except one. *Or* destroy the queen cells and replace with one of your own. *Or* destroy all queen cells; repeat a week later and, a week after this, introduce a new queen in a cage or reintroduce the original queen.

- Seven days after each step, inspect the colony and remove any new queen cells.

If, after removing the queen at the first step above you see a virgin queen on the comb – and this does happen – she can be left on the comb. The colony with the new virgin will *probably* not swarm.

SUPERSEDURE

One sight some beekeepers see during their inspections is two queens on the frame. Everyone knows there should be one queen only, so what is going on? This situation is probably the result of a natural phenomenon called supersedure.

Supersedure occurs when a colony replaces its queen without swarming. Colonies that re-queen themselves without swarming are rare, however, and it is not yet known why some bees supersede and stay put rather than swarm. Supersedure can therefore lead to increased honey crops with less of an effort in swarm control on the beekeeper's behalf.

There is a wealth of anecdotal evidence to suggest that certain strains of bees are inclined to supersede rather than swarm. Despite the obvious commercial advantage of having supersedure colonies, very little research has been done on the subject. Supersedure queen cells are built from queen cups in the same way as swarm cells. They are therefore very difficult to tell apart. Occasionally the new queen will mate and start laying together with the old queen. The bees will dispose of the old queen later.

Trials in New Zealand claimed that induced supersedure (see Chapter 11 for instructions on how to induce supersedure) was, at best, 75% successful. Trials in the UK showed a 50% success rate. Unless you routinely mark all your queens, you will never know if your bees have supersedured or not.

The supersedure cell

There is no easy way to distinguish a supersedure cell from a swarm cell. There tend, however, to be fewer supersedure cells than swarm cells. Therefore if you find one or two cells only, they could well be supersedure cells. The queen cells' position may also be indicative of supersedure cells: many beekeepers have reported that a few queen cells built along the top edge of the frame or in the centre of the brood frame are more likely to be supersedure cells.

So, if you see two queens during an inspection, this isn't necessarily a problem: you may well have a good colony to rear queens from (see Chapter 11). Earlier in this chapter, the annual (or two-yearly) re-queening of your hives was suggested as a swarm-prevention method. If you do this you must ensure that your queen is accepted, and this can be a problem for some beekeepers. Chapter 8 gives comprehensive guidance that may help you when re-queening.

BUILDING UP THE COLONY

Before we end this chapter on springtime tasks, there are two methods of adjusting a hive that may increase your harvest by helping the bees to get the best out of the main honey flow.

Spreading the brood

The first method helps a colony that is headed by a good queen and that is disease free to build up more rapidly. This is achieved by spreading the brood. It is, however, a labour-intensive method and should be repeated several times. It isn't, therefore, used by commercial beekeepers with many hives but, if you have a few hives only, it is a worthwhile practice.

The procedure is as follows (see Figure 20):

- Move the whole brood area to one side.

- To protect this from cold, place a comb of stores between it and the side wall (this may not be necessary in warm areas).

- Find the comb with the most *sealed* brood (comb 4 in Figure 20 (a)).

- Place it to the right of comb 7 (the last comb of brood in Figure 20 (a)). This induces the queen to move to comb 6 (was comb 7), in which she will lay because this comb is in between two brood combs and is warmer (see Figure 20 (b)).

- Some 7–10 days later, make another such shift (see Figure 20 (c) and (d)).

- Continue until you see a large, even brood pattern.

The main advantage of this method is that you are moving frames within the hive and so there is no danger of disease being introduced from another hive. Also, the brood chamber tends to expand in one direction, making it easier to assess.

While this is a simple and effective way to build up your colony, you should never transfer a frame of brood over an empty frame: chilled and dead brood may be the result. If you take care not to do this, you should see good results.

Using two queens

The second method of helping to increase your harvest is to use two queens in one hive. Experience among large-scale commercial beekeepers has shown that two queen colonies consistently produce better honey yields than single queen colonies. Obviously

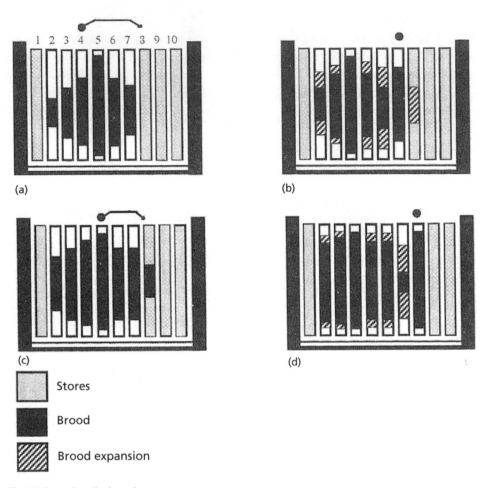

Fig. 20. Spreading the brood

the drawback is that, unless kept apart, the two queens will fight. Special, but simple, procedures must therefore be carried out:

■ Use a strong colony only, preferably treated for nosema (see Chapter 10).

■ Two months before the expected start of the honey flow, divide the colony.

- Place the old queen, young brood (uncapped) and about half the bees in the bottom chamber.

- Above this, place a brood chamber with drawn comb, if available.

- Cover with a division board (see below).

- Place a new queen with capped brood and half the bees in the upper chamber.

- Above this, put an empty brood chamber with drawn comb, if available.

- Carry out brood chamber reversals as swarm-prevention methods in both the upper and lower levels, if required.

- After two weeks, replace the division board with a queen excluder.

- As the flow starts, super up as required.

- About one month before the flow ends, remove the queen excluder to combine both colonies. The old queen is usually killed.

- Winter the colony with the young queen.

This method of increasing your honey harvest means you really need to know your local plants and when they will give nectar so, unless you can predict the flow fairly accurately, it isn't worth doing. One advantage of this method is that it tends to reduce or eliminate swarming because the brood nest is split up and because you use young queens. Also, colonies tend to be equalized during the set-up, which aids apiary management.

SUMMARY

In the spring you manage your hives so that they can take advantage of the honey flow. The following, therefore, are the main tasks for spring:

- **Inspect your colonies to ensure that:**
  - **they have a young queen no older than two years (a marked queen will make this task easier);**

- there are no signs of disease;
- they have sufficient stores of honey and pollen;
- they have sufficient room for the queen to lay eggs and for the foragers to store honey;
- the colony is growing; and
- there are no signs of swarming.

▪ Treat your hives against varroa.

▪ Carry out swarm-prevention measures and, if required, swarm-control measures.

▪ Every time you pass your hives, carry out a quick, external hive inspection.

▪ Utilize methods to increase your honey harvest and to make apiary management easier.

At this time of the year you should carry out these inspections at least every two weeks. Don't hurry them, however, and make sure you are satisfied that you have seen everything you want to see before closing a hive.

Commercial beekeepers with thousands of hives often take at most a couple of minutes over a hive inspection and are able to 'read' immediately the signs of something being amiss. They need to do this because of time and money factors, although I have seen apiaries with hives full of American foul brood that have been missed in the early stages of the disease because of hurried inspections. These bees have to be destroyed and the hives burnt or otherwise treated, which leads to huge extra costs and a very much reduced harvest. So, even for the experts, hurried inspections can be a case of more haste, less speed, causing a large hole in their wallets!

Chapter 7

The active season: summer and autumn

TAKING YOUR BEES TO HARVEST

By now, you have established your apiary in either a rural or urban site, or both. You have inspected your bees every 10 days or so and have made sure that your colonies are growing – they have a young queen and have been treated for varroa. You have carried out swarm-prevention and swarm-control measures where required, and the bees have sufficient room for expansion in the brood nest and enough space to store honey in the supers.

Your management strategy should now be to assist your colonies in building up to their maximum strength before the main flow starts. High bee numbers are important for this flow. A colony of 60,000 bees will collect 50 kg (110 lb) of honey during the season, and two colonies of 30,000 bees will collect a total of 45 kg (100 lb). You will see, that therefore, one colony will collect 5 kg (10 lb) more honey than two smaller ones, even though the total number of bees is the same. Thus six colonies of 10,000 bees will collect only 40 kg (90 lb) of honey in total! Each bee in a large colony will therefore collect more honey than each bee in a smaller colony over its foraging lifetime.

Spring is ending and the worst of the swarming season is over, so what is there to do now? There is a honey flow to attend to and, in many areas, this may well have started. Inspect your colonies: any by this stage that do not occupy to overflowing at least one brood box should be united with another colony (see Chapter 8). Regarding the honey flow, you will probably notice an increase in foraging activity and fresh nectar in the combs.

SUPERING UP

Making sure your bees have enough room to store honey is now a very important issue. If all has gone well, your young colonies will be large and still growing. If you initially purchased colonies of bees rather than nucleus colonies or packages, the same situation should apply. Your aim, therefore, is to ensure you have the maximum number of bees available to take advantage of any honey flow the flora in your area can provide.

You have undertaken most of the manipulations to maximize honey production (i.e. preventing swarming and keeping your colonies healthy) and, if good nectar sources exist, you should now give your bees sufficient room to store all this nectar. To begin with, you should add honey boxes to the hive – a process known as supering up.

Researching honey storage

Research has shown that bees can be induced to store more honey than they require for their own purposes if they have drawn comb available in which to store it. As long as there is a honey flow and sufficient bees, they will keep on storing more and more honey. There are many theories about whether you should place only one box at a time and allow the bees to move into it and, when it is half full, add another box, or about whether you should add the second box under the first or on top of it, or just plonk all your boxes onto the hive in one go.

I haven't seen any research on this but I have always found it easier simply to place each new super on top of the last and, usually, to place at least two supers on at a time. I have generally used drawn comb whenever it was available, and I usually put a comb of honey into a new super from the super below just to 'invite' the bees up. If you need to employ foundation, use it during a good honey flow only, otherwise the bees will not draw it out well.

Placing honey boxes

Many commercial beekeepers, myself included, often move hives to remote areas many hours from their operations base. In such cases, the hives are placed in a position to take advantage of the local honey flow, and several honey boxes are placed on them at once. Then, later on, when time permits another visit to the site, more boxes are placed on the hives if required. This seems to work very well, which suggests that all the theories about how and when to place supers on hives may not be very sound.

It follows, then, that you should put sufficient boxes on to last until your next visit. Putting 'too many' boxes on should do no harm if there is a good flow on, and putting on too few will cause problems for the bees and lessen your honey crop.

There may just be one objection to this policy, however. If there are insufficient bees in the hive to move up into the new supers – especially the top ones – and you have used frames of comb, then the wax moth may enter and damage the comb, sometimes beyond repair. They will do this because there won't be any bees up there looking after things. The moths are unlikely to bother with foundation, however (they prefer used comb), so, if you use comb in the first one or two boxes and then place boxes of foundation, you should be fine.

Whenever you first put the supers on, it should always be before the main honey flow starts. Apart from being a good swarm-prevention measure in the spring, it will stop the bees storing nectar in the brood nest which, in turn, lessens the room for the queen to lay eggs.

Helping your bees to store honey

When conditions are ideal and there is a heavy honey flow on, it is amazing how quickly a healthy colony manages to store huge amounts of honey. When this happens, there are several ways in which you can help your bees to store their honey more efficiently. It is not essential to use supers full of comb when supering up, but it does help the bees if a heavy flow is on. Another way to assist the bees is to have entrances in each of the supers in the form of a drilled hole 1 cm (½ in) across. This saves the bees from having to enter at the bottom of the hives, crawl up through the brood areas, scramble through the queen excluder and move up to the top super to unload their honey. With a hole in the super they can go straight to the storage area, unload and return to the field. Some beekeepers who don't want holes in the woodwork stagger the supers slightly so that the bees can enter the top super immediately upon return.

If you have only a couple or so of colonies, it is easy to experiment with these ideas to gain experience of your bees during this heavy workload time.

Let's assume that your colonies are well and packing in the honey and that you have given your bees more boxes in which to store honey. (Problems that may, and probably will, arise are dealt with in the next chapter.)

HARVESTING HONEY

Honey can be harvested as the season progresses or at the end of the season. This decision is usually based on the existence of the honey flows in the area. For example, if you have an early flow of, say, dandelion and then a later flow of thistle, you may wish to sell the two honeys separately. If you are not bothered, then you can let the honey build up in the hives and extract the lot in one go.

Knowing when to harvest

Honey can be extracted when it has been capped over by the bees on the comb. At this stage, the honey will have been 'matured' by the bees, sealed up and is ready to eat. Often, when you want to remove the honey, not all will have been sealed. I always use a rule of thumb here: if three quarters of the honey is sealed, I am happy to remove it from the hive. This is an important point. If you extract honey that has not been sealed, the water content will inevitably be too high, and the honey will ferment in storage and explode if sealed in a jar or tank. It will also taste foul if this happens. You must remove honey, therefore, only if the majority of it has been sealed over by the bees.

Equipment for honey extraction

Later in this chapter we discuss analysing your honey, and you will see from this the various factors that go into producing a good jar of honey. But before you think of harvesting your honey you must collect some extra equipment. The main piece of kit is the extractor itself, but you will also need an uncapping knife or machine, filters, food-grade containers and somewhere bee-proof to do all this.

This last point is important. I have been in too many situations where extraction was carried out in non-bee-proof areas – even professional extraction plants. If bees can get in, they will, and soon it becomes impossible to work. Thousands will enter and everything you touch will have a bee on it, and your fingers will end up looking like marrows in no time.

Before you remove boxes of honey from your hives, therefore, you will need the following equipment to extract your honey.

Extractor

Types

Extractors can be of the radial or tangential type (the latter so called because the frames sit at a tangent to the direction of the spinner's rotation) and should be made of stainless steel or food-grade plastic. It is important when you spin the frames that the honey from both sides is extracted, and you can do this more easily with a radial extractor because you simply rotate the spinner the opposite way to extract both sides. You don't have to turn the frame over.

With the tangential extractor (see Figure 21), you should spin the frames one way quickly and then remove them, turn them around and then continue spinning. It's usually a good idea then to turn them again and spin again. This extracts the honey from both sides. Larger, more modern machines may have cages that can be turned, and so you needn't keep removing and replacing the frames. Another disadvantage is that this type of extractor places enormous strain on the frames' wax and can destroy the comb. Because of its design, fewer frames can be accommodated. The one advantage is that it is a more efficient extraction process and clears out more honey – but not that much more.

Large commercial companies use all sorts of extraction machines, and a favourite is the box extractor. The frames are uncapped automatically and placed back in the boxes by the machine. The boxes are then loaded sideways into a huge extractor, which turns at high speed to extract some 80 or more frames at a time in their boxes.

All this machinery sounds complicated, but it isn't really. My advice is to go to a bee-supply company or a beekeeper who has an extractor and have a look. Then you will see just how simple it all is.

Fig. 21. Inside a motorized tangential extractor

Obtaining an extractor

You can obtain extractors new from bee-supply shops, or second hand from association auctions or from advertisements in beekeeping magazines. They come with a handle on top for winding the spinner or with small motors. Many tin-plate extractors are offered for sale in the magazines, the reason being that they are no longer regarded as food-grade equipment. You would not, therefore, be able to sell any honey extracted by these machines.

For your first harvest it is a good idea to ask if you can use someone else's extractor, or you could hire one or borrow one belonging to your local beekeeping association. If you decide to buy one, my advice is to buy one with a motor. This is so much easier and it revolutionized my life when I first obtained one.

Some commercial beekeeping companies will extract your honey for you for a fee, but you may not end up with the same honey you put in! Or the same frames!

In some countries there are plants dedicated to extracting honey on a co-operative basis. In such circumstances you will receive back your own honey and your own frames. It is much more fun to do it yourself, however, and so that is what we'll assume you will do.

Uncapping knife

The idea of this implement is to slice off the honey cells' cappings so that the honey can flow out of the cells. This knife could be a simple bread knife with a serrated edge if that's all you can find. You can buy them very cheaply, and the shape of the offset blade renders purpose-made knives easier to use.

Uncapping knives are best used when they are hot so that they go through the wax more easily. You can soak a knife in a bowl of hot water before slicing off the cappings or you can purchase an electrically heated model or even a steam-heated model.

Moving up the scale, there are electric uncapping machines based on a revolving nylon brush that spins very quickly. You put the frame of honeycomb against the brush and this 'rubs' the cappings off. It resembles one of those brushes you find in hotels for cleaning shoes. They are now much cheaper than previously and are coming into the expenditure range of the serious hobbyist. And then there are the professional uncapping machines that cost thousands and that are used by large commercial companies. If this is your first attempt, we'll assume you'll be using some sort of knife and a bowl of hot water.

Honey filters

A honey extractor will extract everything on the comb, including pollen, bits of bee, twigs, pieces of broken frame and so on, and so before you jar up your honey, you should filter it. There is a market for unfiltered honey for those people who regard it as having more health-giving properties than the filtered variety, but most people want a clean-looking product without the bits. A filter can be just about anything, from a muslin bag to a high-performance, high-pressure filter using diatomaceous earth to eradicate the chances of any possible microscopic particles from entering the food chain.

Personally I prefer muslin bags. I started with them and then moved on to an old MOD UK tea strainer, shown in the Figure 22. This still works well. As I moved up to being semi-commercial, however, I used the Strainaway® system, which consists of a couple of buckets on top of each other separated by a filter. The different buckets have different sized filters. By creating a vacuum in the bottom bucket, honey tipped into the top bucket was sucked through the filter and stored in the lower bucket. It was brilliant and easily capable of looking after an operation of 3–400 hives.

Fig 22. MOD UK tea strainer

Other filters are available from bee-supply shops, and these are simply stainless-steel sieves of various sizes through which you pour your honey. They are all very easy to operate.

Honey bucket (or several) with a tap
A honey extractor can hold only so much honey before you need to empty it through a filter to make more room in the extractor. You will therefore require one or more honey buckets for this purpose. These can be made of food-grade plastic or stainless steel, and they must have a tap at the bottom for draining the honey into jars or other containers.

Make a conscious effort to ensure that, before you use these buckets, the taps are shut. Honey is silent when it runs out of containers, and you won't notice it until you tread in it or see it appearing under the door. This warning goes for the extractor as well. I have extracted honey and lost it at the same time because it flowed out of the tap all over the floor – in silence.

And that is it at first. So, armed with your borrowed extractor, bread knife and bowl of hot water, together with your muslin bag and honey buckets with taps firmly shut, you are now ready to take the honey away from your bees. How do you go about this?

Removing honey
Once all your extraction equipment has been collected together and your extraction room is ready (often the kitchen), you can go out to the bees and remove the honey.

The only problem is that there will be hundreds, if not thousands, of bees in the honey supers on the combs and so, first of all, you have to get rid of them. There are various ways of doing this and the main ways are shown below but before you do anything else, check each hive for signs of American foul brood (AFB) and European foul brood (EFB). After you have removed the honey, the empty frames may be placed in other hives, and this will spread the disease.

The various ways of removing bees from the supers are, however, as follows.

Bee escape boards

Many hobbyist beekeepers place a bee escape board between the brood boxes and the supers. The bees go down to the brood box at night through this escape board, and it prevents them passing up again. These boards are simple affairs, with a hole or holes in them. Over these holes, various devices can be fitted that allow the bees a one-way passage downwards.

There is one escape board beloved of the hobbyist: the Porter bee escape, which I found to clog up with drone bees within minutes, so becoming useless. The little wire valves in these things are also propolized by bees and so, again, they become useless and difficult to clean properly. The idea is that you place the board overnight in between the supers and the brood box and return to the hive the next day to remove the now empty supers.

Whichever type of bee valve you use, make sure it has multiple escapes so that, if one becomes clogged up, the bees can use others. Even with a bee escape board, you may experience problems because many bees will remain on the honeycombs overnight, especially when it is warm. The other disadvantage – especially for commercial beekeepers – is that you have to visit the apiary twice: once to place the boards on the hives and then the next day to remove the honey.

Fume Boards

Fume boards are frames the same size as a hive lid covered with tin. In these boards is an absorbent fabric that soaks up a liquid bee repellent. The tin is usually black so that the boards warm up in the sun and thus help the liquid to evaporate more easily. The liquids (which go under various trade names) can be purchased from any bee-supply outfit. By placing the board over the top of the frames in the top box, the bees will move rapidly downwards. It is a good idea, however, to smoke the bees to start them moving before you use the board.

These boards and the liquids must be used as directed. If you overdo it by using too much liquid or by keeping the boards on too long, the bees become thoroughly confused and cling on to the comb, making it even more difficult to dislodge them. If used correctly, the bees will move rapidly down into the next super. After a few minutes you should check that the vast majority of bees have moved down. If so, then remove the super and place the fume board over the next super down so that you gradually move down the hive. In a large apiary, if you employ several fume boards, moving from one to another, you can clear several hives at a time and so complete the task in short time.

It is important that the fumes move downwards into the supers, and so there is now a device that sits on top of the fume board over a hole. This swivels with the wind, and its aim is to direct air into the fume board and thus to blow the fumes downwards. I have found that, if fume boards are used correctly, these are not necessary.

Before using the boards, any holes you have made in the honey super boxes so that it is easier for the bees to fly straight into the supers will need to be blocked up. If you have staggered the supers for the same reason, they will have to be put back together properly so that the bees cannot enter them.

Brushing bees off the frames

Bee brushes
Many hobbyists who have only a few hives use a bee brush to brush the bees off the frames one by one. This is not a bad idea for a few hives, but bee brushes usually become clogged with honey very quickly and I have found that, however gently you brush the bees, they soon become defensive.

The best way to remove the bees is to have a spare empty super available. Pull out each frame, give it a shake to remove most of the bees and then brush the rest off in front of the hive entrance. Place the now bee-less honey frames into the spare super and, once full, cover it up.

Bee brushes can be purchased from any bee-supply company very cheaply and are designed for the purpose. There are those who still advocate the use of goose-wing feathers as a brush. I tried one once: it barely lasted for more than one super of honey (in fact, it didn't even last as long as 10 frames), and it had no better effect than a bee brush, which will last for years. Forget it!

Motorized bee blowers

I must confess I have never used a motorized bee blower, but I have spoken to those who have and who tell me that they are fast and efficient if used correctly. They should be used in conjunction with a stand, on which the supers are placed. This stand is placed on the ground in front of the hive, and the bees are blown downwards out of the super on to the ground in front of their hive, from where the bees can crawl back into the hive. Bee blowers can be purchased from bee-supply shops.

Transporting the supers

Before progressing any further, it is as well to repeat the fact that honey should be removed only from hives that have been checked for diseases, especially AFB.

Once you have removed the bees from the supers, you can load them into your car or onto the truck if you are a commercial beekeeper. This part of the operation can be one of the most unpleasant aspects of beekeeping. For the hobbyist with only a few supers it isn't too bad but, for the commercial operator moving hundreds of very heavy supers onto a truck surrounded by millions of bees that want to get their honey back, usually on a boiling hot day, it can be a very tiring, sticky and slippery affair. Then, at the end of the day, all these boxes have to be moved from the truck into a secure shed prior to extraction.

EXTRACTING THE HONEY

Preparing to extract

You now have your boxes full of honey frames in your extraction facility or, more likely, in your kitchen, and you want to start the final part of the process.

Let's assume your boxes are in your kitchen with your bread knife in a bowl of hot water and your borrowed extractor is sitting there ready and waiting. The boxes should be on newspapers on the floor because, whatever you do, honey will drip. All you need now is to find a spare empty super and place this next to the stack of full ones – the rest is easy.

Extracting

Take the first frame out of the first box and, over a large bowl, run the hot knife cleanly up the comb so that it slices off the wax cappings covering the cells. Turn the frame over and do the same on the other side, and then place the frame in the extractor. Easy, unless the comb is badly formed and you have to wind the knife in and out of its hills and valleys. Once the extractor is full, wind the handle like crazy to turn the machine and the honey will fly out into the base of the extractor. If you have a tangential extractor, you should then turn the frames and spin again until all the honey is extracted. If you are like me you just need to turn on the motor and wait! One problem with a motorized spinner is that, unless you place the frames in the extractor evenly as far as weight is concerned (especially if it is a tangential extractor), you will spend a great deal of your time trying to stop the thing dancing round the kitchen.

Filtering

The honey in the extractor's base will stay there unless the tap is open. Once the level of the honey reaches the level of the spinner, you must pour the honey into the honey buckets through your filter or muslin bag before continuing the process. Don't forget the filtering process, but my opinion is that you shouldn't go overboard with it. A clean-looking product is what you want and, if your stainless-steel filter can remove most of the bits as you pour, you will be pleased with the result.

In Spain my honey sales relied on the fact that I used this simple process. I had information on the label (in Spanish, of course) that my honey was cold filtered, thus maintaining all the product's goodness and value. It worked, and people chose my honey over others just because of this. That was using a cheap, stainless-steel filter hung over the honey bin and, later, the much easier but same principle Strainaway® system.

Pre- and post-harvest work

Occasionally with some crops, such as oil seed rape/canola, the honey crystallizes very swiftly and may even crystallize in the comb unless extracted as soon as it is capped over. If this happens and you end up with some solid combs of crystallized honey, it is probably best to break the combs up and melt them in a large container set in a hot-water bath – a sort of huge bain-marie. This bath should be heated from below and, eventually, the comb and honey will melt. This can then be poured into buckets and recycled or sold.

Another way of sorting out this problem is to place the frames of comb into a warm room for sufficient time for them to loosen up. Most of you, however, won't have this facility. If you are in an area of a crop such as this, you should check your hives frequently and take off the supers of honey individually when they are three quarters full. In other words, you can't do them all at the end of the season.

Another problem you may encounter is that you find brood in the honey supers. This means the queen excluder has failed, probably as a result of damage by your hive tool, and the queen has gone up into the supers. She may still be there or she may have been damaged when you used a fume board or brush to remove the bees prior to taking the supers off. If you see brood in the honey supers, check the hive it came from (if you know).

ANALYSING YOUR EXTRACTED HONEY

Now that you have extracted your honey and poured it into your honey buckets or bins, you should cap it tightly. Honey is hygroscopic and will absorb moisture from the air. The following points should now be noted.

Moisture content

Test the water content of your honey. Honey can ferment naturally due to the presence of wild yeasts and, of course, sugar, and whether it does or not depends on the water content. If your honey ferments, it may explode in the jar just like homemade beer and it will taste foul. Use a calibrated refractometer. This will give you peace of mind.

Moisture %	Liability to ferment
Less than 17.1	Safe regardless of yeast
17.1–18	Safe if yeast count < 1,000/g
18.1–19	Safe if yeast count < 10/g
19.1–20	Safe if yeast count < 1/g
Above 20	Always in danger

Table 2. Moisture content and honey's liability to ferment

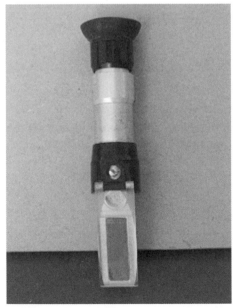

You will see from Table 2 that, if the percentage water content is above 20%, your honey is likely to ferment. The figure is higher for some honeys due to their different characteristics but, for most honey, these figures will apply.

Fig. 23. Honey refractometer

You may ask: 'Where can I get a refractometer?' The answer is from a bee-supply company. They are becoming less expensive. Or you could borrow one (see Figure 23). Or, if you have ensured that you have definitely extracted honey only from frames that were at least three quarters capped (preferably more), you can rely on luck. Most new beekeepers do and, indeed, I did for years and had no problems at all. In fact, even after I eventually bought one in a bid to look more professional, it was only two years later that I found all my readings were wrong because the refractometer wasn't correctly calibrated. So much for professionalism!

Granulation

Another problem that may occur is that your honey soon sets in the containers and so that it is very difficult to get it out of and into jars. There are several things you can do here. First, you can spoon it out of the honey buckets as and when you need it and warm it gently in small quantities. Or you can place your containers in a warm room, if you have one, or even the airing cupboard. It will take a while but, eventually, it will soften and become easier to handle.

Other methods of preventing granulation include freezing the honey, which greatly retards granulation. When you defrost it, however, the honey it returns to its original state. Controlled granulation and creaming are other processes used by commercial packers that prevent honey becoming rock hard, and these are described later in this chapter.

Hydroxy-methyl-furfuraldehyde (HMF)

There is a danger that if you heat your honey too much in order to liquefy it or to make it easier to pack into containers, a breakdown product called hydroxy-methyl-furfuraldehyde (HMF) will increase in quantity in your honey, and there is only a certain amount of this that is legal. HMF is formed by the breakdown of fructose in the presence of an acid, and heat increases the speed of this reaction. The authorities use HMF as an indicator of heat and storage changes in honey, and this can be a real problem for producers in hot developing countries who may have inadequate storage facilities. You won't be able to measure HMF easily, but Table 3 is a rough field test for this. In most countries and the EU, a level of HMF above 40 mg/kg is illegal. It can be seen from the table that honey held at an ambient temperature over 30° C for six months will accumulate more HMF than the same honey flash heated to 70° C for five minutes and then cooled rapidly.

Temperature (°C)	Time
30	100–300 days
40	20–50 days
50	4–10 days
60	1–2.5 days
70	3–5 hours
80	< 2 hours

Table 3. Time for 30 mg/kg of HMF to accumulate (based on three samples).
Source: Kushnir and Subers (1964)

Detecting the level of HMF in honey

The following is a very rough but easy method of ensuring that your stored honey is saleable or at least that it has a low level of HMF. This is accurate to within 95% reliability and it is cheap. The test strips cost only 20p (approximately), although you do have to buy them in packs of 25 minimum:

■ Mix 10 g of honey with 40 ml of *distilled* water at 20° C (i.e. room temperature). Don't warm the liquid.

■ Leave the mixture for 1 hour, keeping it at the same temperature. The glucose oxidase in the mix will give off hydrogen peroxide (H_2O_2).

■ Immerse a hydrogen peroxide strip (Merckoquant 110011 or 110081) into the liquid for 1 second.

■ Wait for 15 seconds and then read off the colour against the colour scale. This scale goes from 0 to 25 mg H_2O_2/per litre. The colour will indicate a number.

■ Multiply the number by 5. The result gives the amount of H_2O_2 in micrograms (μg) as determined by the glucose oxidase from 1 g honey in 1 hour at 20° C. For example, a reading of 2 mg H_2O_2 × 5 shows that 10 µg of H_2O_2/g/hour at 20° C are present.

- If the number is greater than or equal to 10 mg per g per hour, it means that the HMF level will be lower than 40 mg/kg. Reliability = 95%.

- If the result is 0, for example, this means that the honey has been heated too much or has been heated for too long.

This test is not so reliable with certain honeys from thyme or mint because of the higher levels of vitamin C in this honey. The H_2O_2 oxidizes the vitamin and so is reduced. The presence of the enzyme katalase can also upset the results. However, even though this test is not exact, it can give you an idea of an approaching or existing problem, and a bad result may make it worthwhile sending your honey to a laboratory for a full analysis.

You will now appreciate that looking after your honey post-harvest is an important part of being a honey producer, especially if you want to sell the product. Selling honey that requires a chain saw to break into it will not bring you many sales, and nor will honey that blows the lid off its jar in a customer's larder. I have seen both; in fact, I have produced both!

DEALING WITH THE AFTERMATH

Finally, what do you do with the cappings you have left over and all the wet frames?

The cappings

The cappings can be left to drain in a filter or sieve, or be hung up in muslin bags and left to drain. You will be surprised how much honey is left in them. Or you can purchase a cappings cage. This fits into an extractor (of the same make) after removing the frame cages. You then spin out the cappings, leaving lots of fine, white wax particles. This wax is highly valued and should be stored for possible future sale or used to make new foundation (see Chapter 12).

The wet frames

The wet frames can be given back to the bees to clean up but, when doing this, take the precaution of blocking up most of the hive entrances to reduce any robbing (see Chapter 8), or you can take all the boxes full of wet frames and place them near the apiary for a general free-for-all by the bees. Many texts will tell you that this will lead to a huge outbreak of robbing, but I have never found this to be true. The bees will clean the boxes very quickly, and these should then be stored in a safe, dry, light and airy place.

Dealing with wax moths

The big danger of stored comb is from the ravages of the wax moth (see Chapter 10). Wax moths don't like light and so, if you can store the frames in a light place, all may be well, but stacked boxes generally don't let light in except at the top. Many books – and beekeepers who ought to know better – will tell you to sprinkle para-dichlor-benzine (PDB) (moth balls) on top of the pile of boxes. Being heavier than air, the fumes will then sink into the boxes and prevent the wax moths from surviving. Don't go near this. It's carcinogenic and dangerous and could contaminate the wax and future honey crops.

You could, with a little more time, buy some *Bacillus thuringiensis*. Just mix some with water in a garden spray bottle and lightly spray both sides of each frame. This is time consuming, however, except for the hobbyist with a few hives, but these little beasts will kill any wax moth larva that dares to poke its head up and they won't contaminate anything. They will protect your combs all through the winter. Any bee-supply company will sell this under various brand names.

PRODUCING COMB HONEY

There are a few other methods of harvesting honey, one of which requires some skill in ensuring that the bees are encouraged to do what you ask. The first of these is producing comb honey. Comb honey can be produced in two ways.

Using sections

You can place wooden inserts called sections (either round or square) into the frames, each with some foundation in it, thus dividing the area of the frame into a series of smaller frames. You then encourage the bees to pull out the foundation in these. Once pulled out, the bees will fill them with honey and cap them. The round sections are now mainly made of plastic, and the wooden square sections are often purchased as wooden strips that you make up yourself.

People eating comb honey don't want a thick midrib or wires in the honey, and so you should use very thin foundation that can be purchased for this purpose with no wiring. Remember to cut this foundation to fit the sections when it is at room temperature, otherwise it will easily break up. Sections can be used in half and full supers and, to make sure the bees pull out these small frames, the colony must be a very populous one that has started a honey flow, or at least is storing surplus honey, before you put the sections in the hive. If no honey is already being stored, the bees can pull holes in the foundation of the small frames. The trick, therefore, is to replace the super in which the bees are rapidly storing honey with the super of frames with sections.

One beekeeper who regularly produces these sections told me (for I have never used frames like this) that a balancing act is involved here. If you place another super of sections on too soon, you will end up with frames of half-filled sections, but if you leave it too late in supering up and the bees become too crowded, you could end up inducing swarming. For successful comb honey production, however, you do need crowded colonies, so make sure you ventilate the hives well – full, open entrances and perhaps the boxes very slightly staggered. Another point he made is that, once full, the sections must be removed swiftly while the cappings are still white. If you leave them too long the cappings will discolour with millions of little feet crawling over them. Experience tells.

Using non-wired, thin foundation

Another way of making comb honey is to use full frames of non-wired, thin foundation and, when you harvest the honey (again with dispatch to prevent discolouring from the bees' feet), you cut the comb with a comb cutter (see Figure 24) and place each delicious slice into a plastic container made for the purpose (see Figure 25). These comb cutters are cheap devices – just like large cookie cutters – and I have had much success with this way of producing comb honey. Basically, hive management is easier and the process itself is easier.

Fig. 24. A comb cutter

(a)

(b)

Fig. 25. (a) Cut comb in a container; (b) a round section

Mixing comb with honey

Many beekeepers use up odd chunks of honeycomb or empty comb by placing the chunks in a jar and then filling this with honey. This is a useful method of using up odd bits of comb. I found, however, that the honey would often set faster than usual, making the whole thing look very unattractive and so unsaleable. Ultimately I either produced liquid honey or cut comb honey. I stored the comb in a freezer until it was ready for sale. It kept well, and it also kept away the wax moth and other predators. Freezing also prevented any wax-moth eggs from hatching.

GRANULATED AND CREAMED HONEY

Granulated honey is liquid honey seeded with a fine-grained, starter honey. About 5–10% of the honey should be made up of this seed honey or starter. The seed honey's small glucose crystals are spread throughout the honey by a stirrer and held at an optimum temperature for crystal growth. If the seed honey is heated slightly in a warm room so that it spreads easily, it will mix better.

Stir the honey at 20°C (68°F) – not more – until it is thoroughly mixed, and then store it in a cold room at around 14° C (57°F). This will achieve the finely granulated honey that is popular with the public. This method is named after its discoverer and is known as the Dyce process.

This honey may set hard, and so creamed honey is also produced. This is honey that will not set hard. It is produced by a process that involves turning finely granulated honey in a stirrer that incorporates air into the mix and reduces the size of the glucose crystals.

Most beginner beekeepers, however, prefer to start off by producing plain, well filtered liquid honey. I have included the information above about comb, granulated and creamed honeys to give you a taster of what is to come in your beekeeping career.

INSPECTING THE HIVE POST-HARVEST

After the bees have settled down, inspect all the hives to ensure the queen is present (you may have damaged or lost her during the harvest), that there are no diseases and that there are adequate stores. (Remember you have just taken away most of them.)

That is your year up to the harvest. It wasn't difficult, was it? It should, however, have been interesting and, if you've got this far, you've done pretty well. Below is a general timeline for your activities throughout the active beekeeping season, just to remind you of your tasks.

MARKETING HONEY

This book doesn't pretend to be a marketing manual, and methods of marketing vary widely in different countries and very much according to your circumstances. I would say, however, to be bold and imaginative. Tell people of the benefits of local honey.

When selling honey in Spain, I packaged it in small hexagonal jars and placed these in small, open, wooden crates. With an attractive label telling the customer that it was cold-filtered honey straight from the hive and showing a local scene, and going further to name the honey after the local village, I outsold all the competition. I was selling 250 g (8 fl oz) jars of honey for more than the competition was selling 1 kg (2 lb) pots! My honey was especially attractive to the local hippy community (one even asked me if I had any marijuana honey; I didn't even know if the plant gave nectar – I still don't!). It was also attractive to the Moors in Gibraltar for use in their coffee and tea, and the pots were small enough for tourists to take home in a hand luggage as souvenirs.

Go boutique if you are a small producer and you can make money but, before you sell anything, make sure you know the labelling rules and all the other compliance-related laws. These often change, especially in the EU.

This chapter has assumed you have had few, if any problems, with your colonies – and, if that's the case, this would be a fine achievement, but what if something does go wrong? In the next chapter we have a look at some of the problems you may encounter and what to do about them.

THE YEAR SO FAR: A SUMMARY (Northern/Southern hemispheres)

- January/March–June/July: Assemble all the required equipment and hives. Prepare an apiary site in either an urban or rural location. Decide on your source of bees.

- April/May–September/October: Receive your package/nucleus of bees and install them. After installation, carry out a full hive inspection. Remember what was discussed in Chapter 6.

■ **May/June–November/December:** You may be starting out at this point if you are being given a swarm. If so, install it and carry on. Carry out swarm-prevention and, if required, swarm-control activities. Continue with hive inspections.

■ **July/August–December/January:** Super up as and when required. Keep up the checks. Prepare your harvest equipment. Harvest as required if separate honeys are needed, or especially for any fast granulating crops.

■ **August/September–January/February:** Harvest and post-harvest activities. Store the empty boxes taking precautions against the dangers of wax moths.

Chapter 8

Dealing with problems

Problems can arise in a colony of bees at any time of the year, and it is for this reason that you should carry out regular inspections of your hives. Over the season, your records will show you which hives are doing well and which aren't, and this can give you an advantage if you want to breed your own queens later on. Obviously, you will breed only from queens who have demonstrated desirable traits, and this will show up in your notes. But, in a more immediate timeframe, you may find problems during one of your regular inspections or you may just be experiencing problems generally with some or all of your hives.

This chapter should help you to counter any problems you may come across in your inspections, and it offers advice on strategies and methods that can assist you and your bees to increase your output of surplus honey.

LAYING WORKERS

Causes and symptoms
This is a problem for beekeepers who are unable to check their colonies at regular intervals, or whose intervals between inspections are too long. The signs are easy to recognize. When carrying out your inspection, you see several eggs in one or more cells, and these eggs are not right at the bottom of the cell where they should be. What has happened is that the queen has died or is unable to lay eggs – possibly as a result of damage when manipulated by the beekeeper. For some reason, the workers have been unable to raise another queen from a young larva, and so the colony has become hopelessly queenless.

When this problem occurs, the pheromonal imbalance in the colony – especially the lack of queen pheromone and open-brood pheromone – causes the ovaries of some of the workers to enlarge and so they start to lay eggs. Not being able to mate, the workers can lay only drone eggs, and this they do in worker cells. The resulting drones are small and useless, and the colony is doomed. Small, isolated drone cells made out of worker cells are, therefore, another sign that there are problems in the colony (see Photograph 3 in the colour photograph section of this book). Quite a few workers may be at this game, and they compete with each other, resulting in many eggs laid in single cells. A worker's abdomen is not as long as that of the queen, and so she can lay the egg only part way down the cell (see Photograph 4 in the colour photograph section of this book). Other workers may remove many of these eggs because they don't recognize them as queen eggs. The brood pattern, therefore, is always very spotty and uneven, with empty cells scattered among the small, domed drone cells.

The easily visible symptoms of laying workers, therefore, include the following:

- Spotty and uneven brood.
- Small drone brood only present.
- The number of eggs per cell.
- Egg position.
- Drone brood in worker cells.

Removing laying workers is difficult because they look the same as other workers and because there will probably be quite a few of them. Introducing a new queen to a hive with laying workers is, however, often a waste of money: the colony considers itself queen-right and will not accept the new queen.

There are, fortunately, two methods that may work, and these are described below. It is, however, often best to disband a colony in this state.

Solving laying-worker problems

First method

This is the treatment most likely to work and to cause the fewest problems:

- Move the entire colony 200 m (220 yd) and take out all the frames.

- Shake the frames onto the ground and brush all the bees off them.

- Set aside any frames with drone brood or eggs to deal with later.

- Return the bee-less hive to its original position and place a frame of young brood, a queen cell or a caged queen in it. Feed if necessary.

- Close the hive and leave it alone for a week.

- Clean all the eggs and drone cells out of the set-aside brood frames and return them to the hive.

The theory here is that the non-laying, normal worker bees will know the area and will fly back to the hive, whereas the laying workers may never have left the hive and so won't know the way home. I have carried out this method and it works, although I'm sure that, in some cases, a few laying workers managed to return to the hive.

Second method

A second method is to add a frame of open brood each week until the bees start queen cells. The presence of open brood may induce the bees to raise a queen of their own. Once they have started queen cells you can regard the colony as being 'normal' again, and you can either allow the queen cell(s) to remain or destroy them and introduce your own cell or a caged queen. I have tried this method twice and it failed both times, but other beekeepers have told me that it has consistently worked for them.

Bad ways to deal with laying workers

Some texts advise a couple of other methods for dealing with laying workers – re-queening with a push-in cage and uniting the colony with a queen-right colony. I have included these methods here only in the hope of preventing you from carrying them out.

First method

I especially don't advise re-queening with a push-in cage. This cage is large in area with legs at each corner. These legs can be pushed into the wax comb, thus stabilizing the cage and confining the queen to that area of comb. The cage also prevents the workers from getting to the queen and killing her. The queen lays eggs in the cells in the cage, and the bees that emerge from those cells regard her as the queen. When the cage is eventually removed, the colony should accept her.

I don't like this method for two main reasons. First, it takes a long time: the queen has to lay eggs and then you have to wait three weeks for the first new adult bees to emerge. By this time the original colony outside the cage will be in a very poor state and will probably be infested with wax moth because of the insufficient number of bees to look after the household. Secondly, if the bees don't accept the new queen on release, you've wasted both time and money. Don't bother with this method.

Second method

The second method I advise against is to unite the laying-worker colony with a good, queen-right colony. It could work, and I have done it once successfully and once unsuccessfully, but the danger is that the laying workers may just kill your queen – and then what? You have given them a larger colony to wreck. Murphy's law states categorically that, in cases like this, you will end up with another queenless colony.

COPING WITH AGGRESSIVE COLONIES

One problem you will come across in your beekeeping career will be that of very aggressive colonies. These make beekeeping unpleasant, and even the hardiest of beekeepers doesn't like being continuously pasted by their bees. Compared with, say, Italian or Cecropian bees, my Iberian bees were, generally, extremely aggressive. I did, however, have one colony of gentle Iberians, and I kept the queen in it for as long as possible to breed from her. She wasn't my queen to start with (I picked her up in a swarm), but she had a faded red dot painted on her back and so I called her Rose.

Unfortunately only a couple of her offspring had nice natures, and after three years, I found Rose dead on the hive floor.

A variety of factors may influence how aggressive a colony becomes. As a general rule, established colonies are more aggressive than small nuclei, and so any test of aggression should be made when a nuc grows into a colony. The degree of aggression also depends on the beekeeper's perception – I inspected a colony of so-called aggressive Italians in New Zealand and thought they were flies!

The factors that may influence a colony's aggressive tendencies and possible remedies are listed in Table 4.

Cause	Remedy
Queen genetics/race genetics	Re-queen from a gentle race of bees
Hive being robbed by wasps/bees	Find and destroy the wasps nest (see the section on robbing later in this chapter)
Hive being disturbed by large animals	Resite hive or fence off hives
Hives badly sited – under power lines, near a busy road, under dripping trees, etc.	Resite hives
Bad weather (affects some colonies)	Work in good weather. Obvious!
No honey flow	Check for sufficient stores
Beekeeper works an aggressive colony, which then disturbs other colonies	Always work the aggressive colony last
Colony found to be queenless	Re-queen if no laying workers/disease
Bees affected by spray poisoning	See the section on spray damage later in this chapter
Too much use of smoke. This can make some colonies aggressive	Use only the minimum of smoke

Table 4. The causes of, and remedies for, aggressiveness

The following points about aggressiveness, however, should also be noted:

■ There is no direct correlation between aggressiveness and honey collection.

■ Bad handling and the crushing of bees by the beekeeper will make colonies aggressive. When I worked in a team of beekeepers in New Zealand, none of us would work near to one team member who was rough with the hives. Despite the heat, he would wear full protection and an undershirt, whereas the rest of us – from cooler countries and unused to heat – wore as little as possible and thus got pasted by his bees. I sent him on a charm course.

■ In some areas of the world, the most common cause of aggressive bees is animal attention and predation, especially by bears and skunks.

Inspecting a colony of aggressive bees

It's all very well having a table showing you what to do about aggressive bees but, if you are in the position of having to inspect one, how do you go about it? It's a daunting prospect at times, so why not make it easy? Carry out the following moves, which should be planned with military precision:

■ In the early evening of a good flying day, seal up the aggressive hive's entrance. Do this quickly, using a sponge strip prepared for length and thickness in advance.

■ Move the hive 10–15 m (11–16 yds) to the side and open it.

■ Place a hive body, lid and floor on the original site. Place in this one or more combs of honey and pollen and an empty comb to collect the returning foragers.

■ Leave for an hour or two or, preferably, overnight for things to settle down.

■ Inspect the colony (most of the stinging foragers will be in the dummy hive on the original site).

■ During your inspection, kill the queen and, the next day, introduce a gentle, caged queen or a queen cell from a gentle colony.

■ Because the bad lot in the dummy hive are now queenless, re-queen these with a known, gentle queen or a queen cell from a gentle colony.

You could, however, bungle the issue and irritate the bees even more than usual while carrying out the above manipulations so that they become totally out of hand. The best advice I can give is to cover everything up quickly and go home. Retry the next day with a better operations plan.

DEALING WITH ROBBER BEES

If robber bees sound like something out of the Middle Ages, then this is probably because robber bees operate on the same lines as the original robber barons of old. Robbing occurs when bees from one or more colonies attempt to enter and rob the stores of other hives. This is a serious problem in that, if it gets out of hand, some hives may lose all their stores and many of their foragers in the fighting, thus hugely debilitating that colony. Small nucleus hives that get in the way can easily be wiped out. Some bees are more inclined to rob than others, but Italians are usually the first in.

Most robbing outbreaks are the result of feeding the bees, and honey or syrup exposed in the apiary – especially during a period of dearth – can start it off. Within minutes, a scout finding the honey tells her mates, and the problem grows from there. Feeding small nucleus colonies can also cause problems. These are small and, due to their small numbers, are unable to defend themselves against large-scale attack.

Colonies that are low in numbers because of disease are especially problematical. They are often robbed out by bees from larger colonies, who then spread the disease all over the apiary and beyond. American foul brood (AFB) can be spread this way and, if left unchecked, can wipe out an entire apiary.

Robbing is easy to detect during an external hive inspection and, if you notice the following signs, you have an outbreak on your hands:

- Greatly increased activity at the hive's entrance.
- Bees fighting at the colony's entrance.

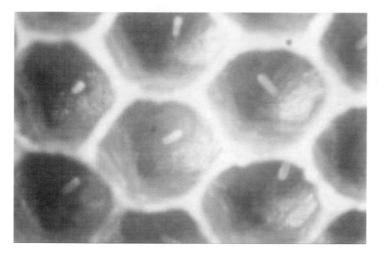

1. One egg at the base of each cell

2. Healthy sealed brood

3. Small, isolated drone cells – a sign of laying workers

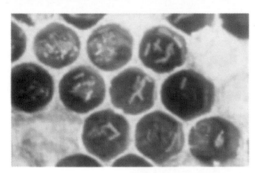

4. Multiple eggs per cell, laid part way down the cells

5. Queen introduction and travel cages, with two virgin cells at the front

6. Placing a new queen into a hive in a frame wrapped in newspaper

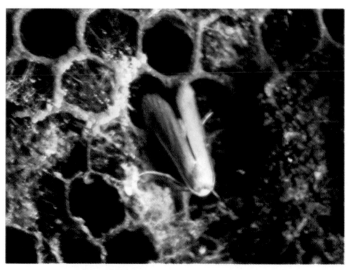

7. A lesser wax moth

8. Wax moth damage

9. Spotted brood pattern
(pepperpot)

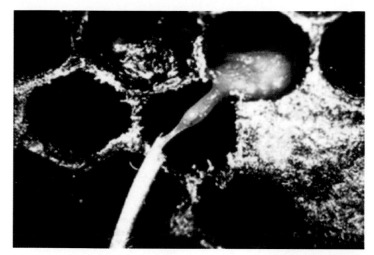

10. AFB: the telltale rope of a dead larva

11. *Varroa destructor*

12. Varroa on larvae

13. Varroa mite on an adult bee

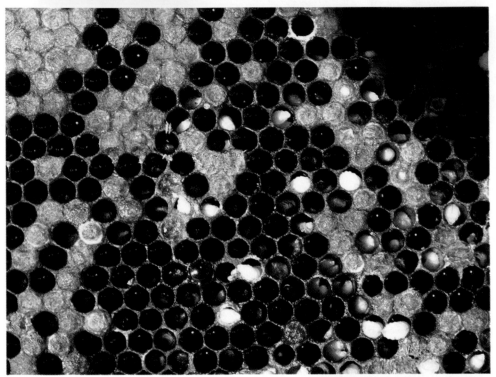

14. Typical view of suspected parasitic mite syndrome

15. *Tropilaelaps clarae*

16 The typical deformed wings of a *Tropilaelaps clarae* or *Varroa destructor* infestation

17. Adult small hive beetle

18. Small hive beetle larva

19. Small hive beetles on comb

20. Moving bees on a large scale at night. No entrance block and no covers

21. Jobbing beekeepers in New Zealand

22. Dragging out the bee truck

- Much debris at the hive's entrance, especially wax particles as a result of the bees ripping the comb apart to steal the honey.

- Many bees entering and leaving every small crack in the hive.

- The whole apiary alive with bees flying in all directions, combined with the above points.

Treating robbing

Once robbing starts it is very difficult to stop, but the following actions should help if one of your hives is being robbed:

- Block up all cracks in the hive(s) with grass, mud or whatever else comes to hand.

- Reduce the hive's entrance to one bee space.

- If available, lean a glass screen or board across the hive's entrance. This will confuse the robbers and, in conjunction with the other controls, can help greatly. If nothing comes to hand, place straw or grass across the entrance. Again, this will confuse the robbers.

- Alternatively, swap the hive being robbed with the robber hive. This is a little drastic and, if several hives are involved, it might not solve the problem unless done in the evening just before everything settles down.

- If the situation is very serious, consider moving the robber colony or the robbed colony to another apiary at least 2 km (1 mile) away.

- If the apiary has a water supply, spray the bees with a hose. They will then go home.

Preventing robbing

The following precautions will help to prevent robbing in the first case:

- Don't spill honey in the apiary during times of dearth.

- Ensure that small colonies and nucleus colonies have entrances reduced to the minimum, especially if feeding them. If they haven't got small entrances, when feeding stuff grass into the entrances to reduce them to one bee way. After splitting colonies, reduce the entrances to the splits to one bee way until the colonies have grown in numbers.

■ Make sure all your hives have crack-free boxes and joins.

Treat robbing seriously. It disrupts and destroys colonies and is highly instrumental in spreading disease.

UNITING COLONIES

There will probably come a time when you will have to unite one colony with another. There is a variety of reasons for this. For example, a colony may have lost its queen and have dwindled because you did not have a replacement queen. To utilize the remaining bees, you could unite these with a healthy colony. Or you may have carried out the artificial swarm procedure to prevent swarming but don't need the extra colony. Some weeks later, you could unite the two parts. This may help your honey flow – remember, one big colony is better than two smaller ones.

Before uniting colonies, however, it is essential that you know the reason why you are doing this. For example, if a colony is queenless or weak, you should know why. It would be pointless uniting this hive with another if it had a disease: you would be giving the disease to the healthy hive. So, before uniting colonies, check for disease. Also, if you have a good queen you want to keep in the healthy, large colony, make sure that, when you unite this colony with a weaker colony, the latter hasn't got a queen in it you didn't find. Murphy's Law states that, on an occasion such as this, the two queens will fight and the better one will lose.

The problem with uniting colonies is that you are trying to combine two units of bees that will immediately fight each other when you put them together and, in the process, you will lose lots of bees and possibly one or both of the queens. You have to convince the bees they are not enemies so that they unite peacefully. You can do this in two main ways.

Method 1

Give the bees time to get used to each other. This can be accomplished quite easily:

- Open the larger queen-right hive.

- Place a sheet of newspaper over the open box, over the bees, and make some slits in the paper with your hive tool.

- Lift the smaller, queenless hive off its floor and place it on the box covered by the newspaper.

- Leave alone for a couple of days before checking that the colony has united.

On the very many occasions I have done this, I have found it works 100% of the time. It's a bit slow and cumbersome, but it does work.

Method 2

The second way to get the bees used to each other is to confuse them. This can be accomplished by changing their odour. The fastest way I have done this is to give a very swift squirt of non-toxic room-odour spray to each box.

Open the larger queen-right hive and quickly spray the bees in the top of the box. Then, just before placing the box with the queenless bees on top, quickly spray the bottom of this box so that the bees all smell the same. By the time the spray wears off, the bees will be accustomed to each other.

Other than room spray, I have also used sugar-syrup spray and flour. They all work but I don't really like spraying chemicals or powders into hives, and sugar-syrup spraying can cause an outbreak of robbing. My preferred method is to employ the slower, more awkward newspaper.

PREVENTING SPRAY DAMAGE

Spray damage is a huge problem born mainly of ignorance on the part of farmers and orchard contractors. The simple fact of the matter is that insecticides kill bees, and anyone spraying insecticides near an apiary without warning the beekeeper can be prosecuted. Herbicides can also kill bees – even those with labels on them saying 'safe for bees'. Many herbicides contain agents called surfactants that make the liquid stick to the plants' foliage. This also sticks to adult bees, which then return to the hive and pass it on to the young larvae in the brood chamber. The larvae may then die. So, although a herbicide may be safe for adult bees, it will eventually reduce or even kill the colony.

Most farmers are aware of the problem and will warn beekeepers they know of that they are going to spray. Beekeepers, however, also have a responsibility either to be in their local association's spray scheme (which will send them spray notices) or to make themselves known to local farmers so that they are aware of the existence of bees near to their land.

Protecting your bees

So, if you receive a warning of spraying nearby, what should you do? There are two main strategies. First, if you have other apiaries, you can move the bees to another area. Before you do, however, make sure there are no spray warnings for that area about which you may not have been notified. Secondly, you can close the hives so that the bees can't fly.

The first expedient is obvious. You load up and move (see the section on moving hives later in this chapter) prior to the spraying and move back afterwards. The second is a little more complicated. Bees shut in a hive unable to fly may panic, overheat, suffer stress or undergo meltdown. In other words, you may kill your bees by trying to protect them just as easily as the insecticide may. The answer is to ensure that, at all times, your bees have food stores, room to move, ventilation and water. If you can ensure this, you can shut your bees up.

Follow the advice below so that your bees survive the chemical warfare so prevalent in modern-day agriculture and horticulture:

- Place a frame feeder full of sugar syrup in the hive.

- Remove the lids from your hives and place soaked sponges on the hives' top bars.

- Place a shallow, empty box on top of each hive.

- Staple a gauze cover onto this box.

- Place a tin lid on this new gauze lid. Raise this above the gauze lid by using slats of wood. This keeps the rain out.

- The night before the spraying, stuff the hives' entrance with gauze or place a mesh across the entrances, (i.e. something that will allow air in but won't allow the bees out).

Your bees are now prepared. If it is hot, you must keep the sponges wet by pouring water on them, as required. As soon as the all-clear is given, remove the entrance meshes to allow the bees to fly.

Alternative method
With this method you can leave your hives as they are: you simply cover an entire hive with a black tent made of sacking or hessian. Make sure the edge of the tent around the hive is secured snugly to the ground. The bees will tend not to leave the hive, and those few that do will not be able to get back in. The only thing you have to remember is to keep the sacking wet. This way the bees won't overheat. In research trials this method was used with no entrance blocks, and it significantly reduced bee mortality. I've tried it and it works well.

If your bees do suffer from spray poisoning, first make sure you have made the correct diagnosis: the symptoms of spray poisoning look very much like some diseases. If you are sure it is spray damage, then all you can do is hope that the queen hasn't been harmed and that the colony will build up again. Obviously, you mustn't unite a poisoned colony with a strong one.

MOVING HIVES

Problems

For various reasons, you may have to move your hives to another apiary (for example, to avoid spray damage, to pollinate a certain crop or just because you are moving). Moving bees isn't difficult, but there are two major problems.

If you move your bees within their radius of foraging, then, once you have moved the hive, the foragers will all fly back to the original position. This means you should move your bees at least 2–3 km (1–2 miles away). Even if you move them 18 m (20 yds) they will fly back to their original position and cluster there. If you move them just a metre, however, they will usually suss things out and go to the right place. There are ways around all this, as I explain below.

The second problem is that, if you move your bees during the day, you will lose most of your foragers because they will be out. You can, however, block them in the night before with equipment similar to that used for spray protection (mesh entrance block and gauze lid), and then move the hives the next day. The bees will panic and suffer stress but, if you have provided them with room, water, food and ventilation, they should survive.

I carried 20 colonies from Toulouse in France down to near the southern tip of Spain in an enclosed van. By ensuring that each hive had an empty box on top and a gauze lid, and by squirting water from a hand-held spray into the top of each hive every hour, the bees survived the three-day journey and were perfectly well at the end of it, if a little angry when released.

You could, however, move your bees on an open truck at night or in bad weather. They will all be in the hives because it is night or raining, and you can load them with no precautions other than to ensure they are well strapped down and won't move. We moved all our bees like this in New Zealand with no cover and with no entrance blocks. It was essential to arrive at the destination by dawn, though, and when on one occasion this didn't happen, many bees were lost.

Precautions

Before moving your bees you must ensure the hive boxes won't come apart. This includes the floor and the lid, unless the lids are telescopic. Use straps, staples between the boxes or clips of some kind. Metal straps are, in my opinion, the best method.

On the journey through Spain, I crashed the van, and the staples holding the hives together flew apart and so did the hives. I was unable to continue that day simply because of the number of bees on the windscreen blocking my view. I didn't dare open the window or they would all have gone. I waited until nightfall when the bees dutifully went back to their boxes. I then managed to reassemble the hives and nail them up.

The basic rules for moving bees are, then, as follows:

- Always strap the hives up tight.
- Ensure the hives won't shift and are strapped down well.
- Move your bees more than 2–3 km (1–2 miles) away so that you have no problems with your bees returning.
- Move your bees up to a metre away and your bees will have no problems in returning.
- At night, load up, strap down and go.
- In bad weather, load up, strap down and go.
- During the day, shut the hives the night before when all the bees are in, and allow plenty of room, ventilation and water.
- For short moves of up to an hour, block the hives up at dawn before the bees are out and then go.

The short move

But what if you need to move your bees only 18 m (20 yds) or so? This can be done but it is a little laborious. You could take 18 days to do this by moving a metre a day, or you could move the hive and place a dummy hive with comb on the original site to collect the foragers. Then, at the end of the day, you put the dummy hive onto the moved hive. That evening, block the entrance with grass and, by the time the bees manage to chew their way out, they will have gathered that something is different and may then take new orientation flights. You may need to repeat this procedure until the foragers learn where they are meant to be. I've done this with not too many problems but, as I said, it is laborious.

DEALING WITH QUEEN PROBLEMS

Seeing problems on your inspections

If on an inspection you see no eggs and no young larvae, but you do see a marked queen, you have a problem. Unless you can replace this queen quickly, your colony will soon dwindle as older workers die and are not replaced by younger bees. Sooner or later the queen will disappear, and you will end up with a laying-worker situation. It is evident in this example that the queen has stopped laying and something needs to be done. Problems with the queen can strike at any time. Sometimes a queen will simply stop laying due, perhaps, to some genetic fault, or because she has been damaged during one of your inspections. This happens much more frequently than beekeepers think. The brood pattern of a healthy colony is an ellipse of sealed brood cells neatly waxed over with slightly raised wax cappings (see Photograph 2 in the colour photograph section of this book). Around this mass of sealed cells should be open cells with pearly white larvae in them and, as you look towards the edge of this area, the larvae become younger until, finally, you simply see eggs. The outer edges of this 'arc' of brood are often the stores area for honey although, in healthy colonies that are building up swiftly in the spring, the brood frames are usually just slabs of brood.

The above may not be exactly what you see but that is the general idea. Any areas of capped brood with too many uncapped, empty cells that give a spotty or pepper-pot appearance mean trouble. It could be that inbreeding is causing the queen to lay too many non-viable eggs and the workers are removing them, or it could be the result of diseases, such as AFB or European foul brood (EFB) (see Chapter 10). The worst sight of all is a brood pattern with, mostly, empty cells and isolated drone cells made out of worker-sized cells (see Photograph 3 in the colour photograph section of this book).

Table 5 is a troubleshooting guide that should help you to identify queen problems and to determine the causes of the problems and ways of treating them. Note, however, that many queen problems are also caused by the following:

■ Queens are damaged or killed during manipulations.

■ Queens are introduced while the old queen is still present.

■ A queen is introduced when laying workers are present.

■ The beekeeper's inability to find queens, thus making the wrong assumptions.

Problem	Cause	Treatment
No brood present	No queen/failed queen	Re-queen or unite the colony. Make sure it is not a natural time for a break in egg laying, (e.g. winter)
Sealed brood only; no eggs	Colony swarmed	Check in 3 weeks for eggs/young brood
Drone brood only; 1 egg per cell	Drone-laying queen (queen failure)	Re-queen/unite the colony
Drone brood only, often in worker cells; eggs not at base of cell	Laying workers	See the treatment outlined earlier in this chapter
Mix of drone brood in worker cells; normal capped brood; several eggs in some worker cells	Laying workers	See the treatment outlined earlier in this chapter
No brood; small queen, excitable on the comb	Virgin queen, delayed mating/not yet mated. Newly arrived postal queen	Check for eggs in 1 week

Supersedure cell(s) formed after queen introduction	Common; cause unknown	Remove cell(s); can be cut out and put in a queenless nuc
	Badly mated queen	Check brood pattern; if bad, allow supersedure
	Cells were present before introduction	Destroy cells
Queen in introduction cell dies	Not fed by workers or cage balled	Laying workers may be present
Introduced queen killed after release	Old queen present	Remove old queen prior to introduction
	Unnoticed virgin present	Leave her to mate or kill her and re-queen (see later in this chapter)
	Laying workers present	See earlier in this chapter
Spotty brood pattern	Queen failing	Re-queen (see later in this chapter)
	Inbreeding depression	Re-queen (see later in this chapter)
	Disease, especially AFB, EFB and PMS (parasitic mite syndrome)	(see chapter 10)
	Very heavy flow; cells filled before queen can lay	Give comb for queen, super for honey
	Pesticide poisoning and insufficient nurse bees. Dead larvae being removed	Add more bees or unite if serious
Small but good brood pattern	Newly mated queen	Inspect again in 2/3 weeks

	Slow laying queen	Re-queen or accept the situation (see later in this chapter)
	Not enough bees to look after brood	Allow colony to build up or, if serious, add more bees or unite
	Not enough room for queen to lay	Provide comb/clear brood nest
Poor brood pattern (larvae of different ages grouped together)	Inbreeding, leading to removal of diploid drones and re-laying by the queen	Re-queen if serious (see later in this chapter)
Swarm cells present	Colony preparing to swarm	Carry out artificial swarm procedure
Two queens present	Supersedure queen and daughter	Leave alone if no fighting. Old queen will disappear. Or split hive
	Swarm(s) waiting to go	Virgin(s) will probably leave with the swarm

Table 5. Queen/brood-nest troubleshooting guide

Introducing a new queen

There are many situations that may require you to re-queen a colony, and this is usually a very straightforward task – as long as you can get hold of a queen. Comparatively little research has, however, been carried out on the act of re-queening, despite its importance in beekeeping. The research that has been done suggests, firstly, that the receiving bees need time to adjust to the new queen and that, during this period, she should be protected from those bees that are finding it difficult to adjust. Secondly, there should be a balance between adult bees, brood and the queen. So if your bees are, say, very aggressive and you want to put in a queen from a known gentle colony or race, to increase your chances of a successful introduction, you should make sure the new queen is similar to the old queen (i.e. well mated and laying well). In an illuminating experiment, two American bee scientists swapped similar queens back and forth between colonies 292 times without loss.

In the main it is difficult to achieve this like-for-like, especially if you receive a queen through the post. So let's take a look at some methods of queen introduction that should increase your chances of success. Remember, though, that nothing is certain with bees, but there are some rules of thumb that, if obeyed, can improve the odds:

- The most important rule is that the receiving colony *must* be queenless. This sounds obvious but it is often ignored by those who can't find the queen. Such people hope for the best, leaving the queens to fight it out. You can, however, be sure that the old, feeble, arthritic and half-blind queen will defeat the new, strong and virile young thing you introduce. So, after you have de-queened the colony or nuc, check that a virgin hasn't just emerged that is patiently waiting for mum to swarm. It's surprising how often there is more than one queen in a hive. A swarm that appeared on our land one year had one mated queen and five virgins in it. All these were in the hive together.

- The second important rule to remember is that smaller colonies or nucs accept new queens more readily than large colonies. It is best, then, to introduce a new queen to a small nuc made up for the purpose.

Finally, if a colony loses its queen during the late autumn or winter, it is usually best to unite it with another colony to take it through the winter rather than introduce a new queen.

Re-queening annually
The annual replacement of the old queen with a new young queen or queen cell is the main reason for re-queening. Annual re-queening gives you the best chance of producing more bees and so more honey, and it is also the best way of reducing swarming. You can either buy a queen or queen cell from a breeder or produce one yourself (see Chapter 11). Buying a mated queen is more expensive than buying a queen cell but less risky. The queen in the cell has to emerge, leave the hive and enter a world full of predators,

such as birds, mate, return safely to the hive and then start laying. Something could go wrong at any time during this period.

Annual re-queening also allows you to retain the strain of bees you are happy with. It also keeps all the colonies on an even footing, thus making apiary management much easier.

Autumn or spring?

You can re-queen in the autumn or spring, and there are distinct advantages to both periods. In the autumn, the hives are generally strong and, usually (but not everywhere), the weather is stable and so better for mating. There are also likely to be more drones around (in cold, wet springs, drones are fewer in number, immature and may not fly due to bad weather).

In the spring, on the other hand, you obtain a new queen that will be young and better able to take advantage of the honey flow. By re-queening in the spring you also lessen the chance of swarming.

Some commercial beekeepers with thousands of hives swear by autumn queens, but most hobbyists re-queen – if they are going to at all – in the spring when colonies are smaller and more easily managed. My advice is to re-queen in the spring if you are a new beekeeper or a hobbyist but to re-queen in the autumn if you are a commercial beekeeper relying on the honey crop for your income.

Buying a new queen

If you buy a new queen, she will arrive in a cage made of plastic or wood (see Photograph 5 in the colour photograph section of this book) with two or three attendant bees, and there will be an exit hole in the cage blocked by candy (see Chapter 9 for a candy recipe). There will be a plastic cover over the outer part of the hole. This is to prevent the caged bees from chewing their way through the candy and escaping. It may be you are unable to put the queen into the colony for a day or two, and in this time the bees can chew through a great deal of candy! So, before you put the queen in the colony, you *must* remove the plastic cover so that the bees can chew their way out. By the time they have done this, the queen will normally have been accepted by the colony – as long as it is queenless.

If you are unable to put the queen in straightaway, she can be kept in the cage but she must be protected from fly spray or other insecticides and from drying out in the heat. Two or three times a day, therefore, drop some water onto the cage. I don't think there is any need to remove the attendant bees from the cage before putting it into the hive.

The bees in the hive need time to accept the new queen, and this is where the cage and the candy come in. The bees will immediately sense a new set of pheromonal signals and odours from this new queen and would probably kill her if you just put her in the hive. Young bees are also more receptive to a new queen than older bees. The re-queening method shown below recognizes this fact: its aim is to make the whole business easy and painless.

Opening cages is always a problem because, if the queen escapes, you will lose her. If you really must open the cage for some reason (for example, to remove a dead attendant), open it near a closed window. If the queen then escapes she will fly to the window and you will be able to catch her again. (Remember, queen bees won't sting even though they have a sting.)

The most successful ways of introducing a new queen into a hive are described below.

How to re-queen

Method 1
Collect together the same number of spare boxes, floors and lids as the number of hives you want to re-queen – what you are going to do is make some mini-hives or nucleus hives. Using a piece of wood, make the entrances to these small hives just one or two bee spaces wide. Place the nucleus hives on the lids of the hives you are going to re-queen, but facing in the opposite direction. Block the entrances with grass.

In the hives you want to re-queen, first make a split by removing from them two frames of emerging brood, one frame of stores and a frame of empty comb. The emerging brood should cover only about half of the frame. Don't brush off any bees because you are going to need them and, as these are brood frames, they are likely to be young nurse bees. These frames must be placed in your new nucleus hive.

Place the brood frames together, and put the stores on one side and the comb on the other. You can fill the rest of the box with foundation. Many beekeepers have nucleus boxes that hold only four or five frames. Use one of these if you have one. If you haven't, don't worry – just use an ordinary box with a floor and lid.

Shake the bees off two or three other frames into the new nucleus you are making. These will be more nurse bees. Replace the frames in the hive.

As you place each brood frame into the nuc, you must check that the old queen isn't on it and that there are no queen cells. This is important – the whole thing will fail if you do not ensure this.

When all is ready, push the queen cage onto one of the brood frames in the nuc. This should be in a position three quarters the way up the frame, and the cage's escape hole should be facing slightly upwards so that any dead attendants won't block it. Don't push the cage onto the brood comb along its flat surface because the bees outside need to communicate with the queen. Shove it into the brood frame at an angle. In other words, the cage should be between the two brood frames at an angle so that the bees can reach most of the sides and with the escape facing slightly upwards.

Three days later, check for eggs and ensure that the bees have unblocked the entrance. If all is OK and eggs are being laid, leave for another three weeks until brood is being capped over and all is well.

Now go into the main hive and kill the old queen. Then unite the two boxes using the newspaper method described earlier in this chapter, placing the nuc on top. If you are employing a smaller four-frame nucleus box for the new queen, you will first have to place all the frames into a normal-sized brood box and then fill the rest with comb before uniting.

This method is easy and it works very well. It allows the main hive to continue as normal, with their queen until you are sure the new queen is viable, and it hardly disturbs the colony's life at all. The bees that are accustomed to going in and out of the nuc in the opposite direction will soon learn to adapt, and all will carry on as normal with a new, low-swarming, heavy-laying, young queen. Easy!

Method 2

This method also works well and is for those who want a quick-fix, low-tech application. The theory is the same as the first method but, in this case, you install the queen straight into the main hive without using a nuc:

- Remove and kill the queen of the colony to be re-queened. Destroy any and all queen cells.

- Leave the colony queenless until the next day.

- Remove a frame of capped and emerging brood from the colony.

- Press into this frame the queen cage.

- Wrap the entire frame in newspaper, stapling the newspaper ends along the top bar (see Photograph 6 in the colour photograph section of this book).

- Make a few slits in the paper with your hive tool.

- Lower the entire frame into the colony.

- Check for queen release in three days.

- Check for eggs a week later.

INTRODUCING A NEW QUEEN: A SUMMARY
Even easier!

If you keep it simple and try to understand what the bees are doing, you should have no trouble with queen introduction. You must, however, remember the following points:

- **The colony accepting a new queen must be queenless.**

- **All queen cells must be destroyed, including those made after the colony has been made queenless.**

- **Queens are more readily accepted by small colonies and nuclei.**

- **In large colonies, queens are more readily accepted early or late in the active season or during a heavy honey flow.**

- **The bees may build queen cells or supersedure cells even after apparently accepting the new queen. These cells must be destroyed, and you must check that the new queen is still around.**

Basically, there is no method that offers a 100% guarantee of queen acceptance, but the methods outlined above are well tried and tested and invariably work. Remember, with the above methods you can substitute a queen cell, either purchased by you or made by your bees. Or you can even purchase small, plastic queen cells into which you can put a virgin queen. A thin film of wax is placed over the exit hole, and the cell is placed on a frame of brood hanging downwards. I have never tried this but have heard from others that it works.

There will be other occasions when you will need to re-queen a colony (for example, when you find a failed or dead queen or a colony in which the queen has disappeared). You can employ these two methods just as easily for these circumstances.

Many beekeepers are very nice people who don't like to kill a queen. I'm afraid I'm a bit like that so, if she is a one-year-old, you can place her in a nuc and grow the nuc into a colony, but you need to take combs from your other colonies to make up the nucs, and that may not be in your management/harvest plans. Also, this will effectively double your stock-holding which you may not want (or have sufficient boxes/frames/lids, etc.), and half your stock will be new queens and half one-year-olds. This may make things difficult for you, so it really is best to kill the old queen. As one commercial beekeeper told me: 'A queen is just a production unit. Nothing more.'

Chapter 9

Overwintering your bees: autumn to spring

PREPARING FOR WINTER

Now that you have completed the harvest and your colonies have settled down again, you should start thinking about two things – storing your honeycomb and preparing your hives for winter. For most beekeepers, the management of their bees is really centred around honey flows, and the early autumn may be a time when you wish to move your bees to the heather (in the UK), for example, or to a late crop if you are in Spain. Before you do this, remember that the colony must be inspected to make sure it has:

- no diseases (see Chapter 10);

- sufficient bees for the purpose (it's no good taking a depleted stock); and

- a laying queen.

Apart from storing honeycomb and preparing for winter, the only other task after the harvest is to go right through your apiary and inspect every hive. Winter is approaching, and your colonies must go into winter as strong as possible. If there is any uniting to do to boost certain weak colonies, do it now before wintering the hives down.

Moving your hives for the winter

If colonies need to be moved to winter sites, this is the time to do it. For many beekeepers – especially commercial operators – honey-collecting and winter sites may be a long distance apart. As we saw in Chapter 8, moving hives is stressful to the bees and so, after moving them, another inspection is warranted.

Your winter sites should be as sunny as possible – i.e. south or north facing, depending on where you are. They should not be prone to flooding, should be protected from the prevailing wind and not be in frost hollows. The sunnier the site the better because, the more the bees can fly and 'un-cluster' themselves, the better their chances of survival.

Surviving the winter

Essentially, you prepare your colonies to survive the winter on two brood boxes. The queen will soon cease laying and, during very cold weather, the colony will go into a cluster formation to maintain brood temperature. Little if any foraging will be done, not only because of the cold but also because, even on sunny days, there will be no nectar sources. So, even if the bees fly to void themselves, they will collect no food.

In order that your colony will survive the winter, therefore, you should ensure the following:

- It has a laying queen.

- There are sufficient reserves of bees. I suggest 15 frames of bees for cold winters and at least 6 for mild ones. The more the better.

- It has no diseases (see Chapter 10).

- It was treated in the autumn for varroa as part of your treatment plan.

- There are sufficient stores to take it through the winter. If not, feed the colony (see below). Remember, stores include pollen.

- The queen excluder has been removed (it can be stored in the lid).

- There are two brood boxes for the bees. Some authorities believe that winter losses are reduced if three boxes are available for the winter. I have had no problems with two.

Now examine the state of the woodwork and hive, and carry out the following tasks:

- Clean the floors. If necessary, scrape them or replace them with new ones.

- Check that the lids are sound. The tin should not be rusty or holed. Make sure the lids fit well and won't blow off in wind. If necessary, strap them on.

- Check that the boxes' woodwork is sound. It should have no holes or splits in it: these will let in the rain and wasps. Swap any damaged boxes for sound ones.

- Because the bees tend to cluster in the empty brood area, ensure these frames are surrounded by frames of stores (both pollen and honey). These should be in the bottom brood box. As the bees tend to move upwards during the winter, the upper brood box should also have frames of stores, especially honey around the brood frames. Any brood frames that still have brood can be placed up there.

The bees will begin to cluster as the temperature falls below 18°C (64°F). As the temperature goes lower, more bees will cluster until, at around 13–14°C (55–57°F), all the bees will be clustered. They cluster to ensure that the brood-nest temperature remains at 34–35°C (93–95°F). If the temperature goes lower, they will tighten the cluster; if it rises, the cluster will loosen. If the temperature drops dramatically, the bees will cluster very tightly and will sometimes remain like this and not move. In this way they can become divorced from their stores and will starve. It is a pitiful sight to open up in the spring to find a cluster of dead bees just below the stores of honey.

Additional tasks for overwintering your bees

Any frames of comb you want to replace can be put at the sides of the boxes. In this way they will at least be protected from wax moth. They can be removed, melted down and replaced on your first spring inspection.

Top ventilation of the hive is beneficial for the bees, but not too much. One or two corners of the lid propped up by a matchstick should be sufficient. This will enable a throughflow of air and will prevent the build-up of condensation and moisture. Remember that the bees are not trying to keep the hive warm – only the cluster itself

– and so a throughflow of cold air won't harm them. The lid, however, should be secure at all times so that it won't blow off in the wind.

Install an entrance block or mouse excluder. Mice entering the hive for warmth during the winter can be a real problem. If wasps are a problem, use a tunnel entrance. These can be purchased from bee-supply shops or, better still, can be made at home. Essentially, this is a tube fixed to the floor board that runs from the entrance into the hive. Wasps don't like entering these and will leave the colony alone.

Organizing winter stores

It is very important that your colonies have enough stores to last them through the winter. The amount required will depend on what your winters are like. Below are the storage requirements for the Northern Hemisphere. These requirements are the same for the Southern Hemisphere – you simply need to amend the words accordingly:

- Northern climates (cold): average winter temperature <7°C (45°F). There should be a minimum of 40 kg (90 lb) in three brood boxes. As a rule of thumb, the following amounts are required: 10 kg (20 lb) in the bottom box, 15 kg (33 lb) in the middle box and the rest in the top box.

- Temperate climates (e.g. the UK/NZ): average winter temperature −4 to +10°C (25 to 50°F); 15–30 kg (33–66 lb).

- Southern climates: average winter temperature 10–20°C (50–70°F); 8–15 kg (17–33 lb).

So what does all this look like in terms of frames of honey or cans of syrup? When working out the amount of stores your bees should have to enable them to survive the winter, use the following approximate weights of honey in the comb (the figures have been rounded up):

- Each Langstroth frame should contain approximately 3 kg (6.5 lb) of honey.

- Each shallow Langstroth frame should contain approximately 2 kg (4.5 lb) of honey.

- Each British Standard (BS) frame should contain approximately 2.5 kg (5.5 lb) of honey.

- Each shallow BS frame should contain approximately 1.5 kg (3.5 lb) of honey.

- Each deep Modified Dadant frame should contain approximately 4 kg (9 lb) of honey.

Note: each full ¾ Langstroth frame covered with bees has approximately 2,300 bees; each full Langstroth frame covered with bees has approximately 3,500 bees.

The above figures will vary, however. For example, a rare super that contains perfect combs correctly bee spaced and totally sealed will have a greater weight of honey than poorly built combs.

Calculating the sugar syrup stores

If the stores are short, you will need to feed your bees with sugar syrup (preferably invert – see below):

- Each 5 l (1 gal) of heavy syrup will increase the colony's stores by 3 kg (7 lb).

- In 5 kg (10 lb) of honey there is 4 kg (9 lb) of sugar.

- So, if the colony is 5 kg (10 lb) of stores short, feed 4 kg (9 lb) of sugar syrup.

It follows that, for other shortages, you should multiply the amount of shortage by 0.8. You should then have the correct amount of sugar syrup to feed.

Preparing for the winter: a summary

Always ensure (and I repeat this) that the honey reserves are properly organized. In cold areas, many authorities recommend a three-box wintering unit with reserves in all three boxes, but that none of the boxes should be honey bound. In mild areas where inspections can be carried out, there should always be at least four combs of honey and pollen. These combs may be part filled.

Similarly, the colony must have sufficient pollen reserves – something many hobby beekeepers ignore or fail to understand. Again, this pollen must be available in or next to the cluster. Pollen patties (see below) provided near to the cluster four to five weeks before the availability of natural pollen should stimulate brood rearing. A lack of pollen will cause the colony to dwindle in late winter and early spring.

Remember also the following:

- Bees don't die of cold. They starve.

- Bees don't try to heat the hive. They maintain the cluster temperature.

- The autumn sugar-syrup feed can be used to administer fumagillin (see Nosema, Chapter 10) in those countries that permit its use.

Many texts suggest that, around Christmas (or in mid-winter in the Southern Hemisphere), you should place some sugar candy on the hive's top frames or over the feed hole if you use an inner cover. If you follow the advice given above, there should be no need to do this – I don't recommend messing around inside the hives until the spring unless this is for some experimental purpose, such as to see if the drones are still around in midwinter or some other such investigation. By all means unblock the entrance if it is covered with snow and, of course, do something about floods or hives being blown over, but otherwise leave it all alone – until the spring!

MAKING FEED MIXES

We have discussed how much and when to feed your bees, but how exactly do you make these feeds? Below are recipes for sugar syrup, invert sugar syrup, queen candy and pollen substitute. Candy is used for such purposes as blocking a queen-cage exit so that the bees have to chew it away, thus giving them time to become accustomed to the queen, and it can also be used as a quick, emergency feed left on top of the bars if no syrup is available at the time.

Invert sugar

When bees collect nectar, they invert the sugars in the nectar by the addition of enzymes. This enables the bees to pack more of the resulting sugars into the cells than would otherwise be the case because inverting a disaccharide (sucrose) into its two component sugars, glucose and fructose, effectively doubles the concentration of sugar molecules. Using invert sugar means that the bees can skip this stage, and it gives your colonies a huge boost. It is particularly effective as a spring feed and as a feed for nucs and small colonies. For those interested in the science of this, the chemical reaction is as follows:

$$C_{12}H_{22}O_{11} \text{ (sucrose)} + H_2O \text{ (water)} = C_6H_{12}O_6 \text{ (glucose)} + C_6H_{12}O_6 \text{ (fructose)}$$

This reaction is enabled by the presence of an enzyme that is not shown in the formula.

Many texts advise inverting sugar syrup by acid hydrolysis – i.e. employing acids of various types. My advice is *don't*. Acid hydrolysis is dangerous because you need to heat the sugar to near boiling point and also because the acids themselves are dangerous. Unless you know how to halt the reaction at the right time, it will carry on breaking down the sugars into dangerous products, including raising the hydroxy-methyl-furfuraldehyde (HMF) levels enormously, and so you will end up poisoning your bees. I know of many beekeepers who have done this and who didn't realize why their colonies were dwindling. They ascribed all sorts of other reasons for the deaths when, in fact, they were the result of the feeding regime. Remember, feeding your bees is meant to help them, not kill them. I recall one beekeeper complaining that hot sugar had wrecked his honey pump!

Recipes

The recipe below for invert sugar syrup uses active baker's yeast. It is designed for large commercial quantities but if the hobbyist beekeeper wants to use invert sugar syrup it is easy to reduce the quantities as long as the proportions are kept. This method is safe and won't poison your bees or injure you.

Sugar syrup

For a thick sugar syrup for autumn feeding: 1 kg (2 lb) sugar to 500 ml (1 pt) water.

For a thin sugar syrup for spring stimulation or pollination feeding: 1 kg sugar (2 lb) to 1 l (2 pt) water.

Invert sugar syrup

This is especially recommended for the spring build-up. It is designed for large quantities:

1,000 l (220 gal) sugar syrup at 30–40°C (85–105°F)
250 gm (8 oz) dried *active* baker's yeast
1 l (2 pt) warm water

- Mix the yeast with a cup of sugar syrup and the 1 l (2 pt) warm water (around 35–40°C; 95–105°F).

- When it starts to rise, pour the mix into the 1,000 l (220 gal) vat of sugar syrup and stir well.

- Increase the temperature of the sugar syrup to 65°C (150°F), ensuring that it remains for at least 2 hours between 45 and 55°C (110 and 130°F).

- Once the temperature reaches 65°C (150°F), turn off the heat and allow to cool.

Queen candy

For this recipe you can use bulk-purchased sugar syrup or your own homemade syrup. It makes sufficient candy for around 350 queen cages. The sugar syrup made is from 2 cups of white sugar to 1 cup of water:

2 kg (4 lb) icing sugar
¼ teaspoon tartaric acid
2 teaspoons glycerine

Or, more expensively, honey and icing sugar mixed to a stiff paste. This is more difficult to maintain as a firm mixture.

Pollen substitute

When used at the right time, pollen substitutes can be a vital supplement for colonies. Start feeding them about 4 to 5 weeks before brood rearing commences, and keep feeding until natural pollen is plentiful:

1 part sodium caseinate (a readily available dairy derivative)
2 parts dried *non-active* yeast.
Sugar syrup to make a stiff paste (ensure that the sugar syrup is not fermenting, otherwise the patties will blow up)

Combine in a cake mixer or a commercial baker's mixer if large quantities are being made. Fill small paper bags with the mix and, when you give them to the bees, open the upper side of the pattie bag.

Note: avoid the use of soya protein in bee feed. I once read some research that said it has a deleterious effect on the queen's ovarioles. The trouble is, I can't find that research again.

STORING SUGAR SYRUP

Sugar syrup will ferment very readily if wild yeast enters it or if the baker's yeast is not killed off following inversion. To kill sugar-tolerant yeasts in syrup, either use the syrup immediately or, if you need to store it, make sure you kill off the yeasts using the temperatures and times shown in Table 6.

Temperature (°C)	Time (minutes)
51.7	470.0
54.4	170.0
57.2	60.0
60.0	22.0
62.8	7.5
65.6	2.8
68.3	1.0

Table 6. Temperatures and timings to kill yeasts in sugar syrup

THE SPRING START

Unlike last spring when you started off with nucleus hives or package bees or even a swarm, you now have overwintered colonies to look after. Spring is when the whole shooting match starts again. The queen begins to lay (she has probably been laying since around mid-December), but now her egg-laying rate increases. The colonies build up and swarming pressures arise and are dealt with. You increase the number of colonies if you didn't do this in the autumn, and so the year gradually repeats itself. Except that no two years are ever the same. The bees follow the seasonal variations in temperature, rainfall and flower availability and, generally, ignore your requests for order. Yet again, therefore, you must go with the flow and try to organize things to your own advantage and to the advantage of your bees. So, when do you start and what do you do?

The spring management of overwintered colonies

As the daytime temperatures increase, the winter cluster will break up. During a warm sunny day in February/March (September in the south) when the bees are flying strongly, lift off the lid and have a look into the hive. Look at the brood to ensure that the queen is healthy and laying eggs and that there is brood of all ages in the brood nest. The bees will most likely have moved up into the top box, and it is useful at this stage to reverse the boxes. If there are no eggs, the queen has failed. If she is still alive she should be killed and the hive united with a healthy stock.

Check there is no disease (the likely one would be nosema (see Chapter 10), which can strike at this time). If there are no signs of nosema but the colony fails to develop normally, then suspect this. Inspect the stores of both honey and pollen. If necessary, give a frame feeder of syrup. Beware of robbing and, if this occurs, try to put a stop to it immediately.

Providing your bees with pollen

The need for pollen in the early spring is something many beekeepers don't seem to understand. In fact, the whole subject of pollen is often only vaguely thought about by many beekeepers, but it shouldn't be. Many are satisfied if their bees have plenty of honey or syrup, but plenty of pollen is vital for healthy brood development and, without it, a colony may fail to build up and may dwindle. Many beekeepers ascribe this to nosema and so miss the fact that the real culprit is a pollen shortage.

If there is insufficient early pollen then a pollen substitute should be given (a recipe for this is given above). Feed your bees according to the instructions given above. In Europe there are usually early pollen sources, such as willow or rock roses, but this may not always be the case, so keep an eye on the situation. Pollen is vital for a colony's build-up. Don't forget this.

Anticipating swarming

Once you are sure the colony is healthy and fit and developing nicely, just make sure the woodwork is sound, that the hive is not damp and that the floor is clean – and you will be all set again for the swarming season.

At this time of the year your bees are probably preparing to swarm, so you should carry out all the swarm-prevention measures outlined in Chapter 6. But swarms will also be emerging from other beekeepers' hives. The scouts from these potential swarms will be looking for new homes and, if you want to increase your hive numbers without any real effort, now is the time to set up bait hives. I always set up some of these and so usually benefit from some new blood in my apiaries.

Setting up swarm traps and swarm baiting
A swarm trap can be made as follows:

- Make up a bait box from an old hive body (a full-depth Langstroth size is recommended), although it is best to use a hive body you currently employ in your apiary. Ensure this is free from disease.

- Fit it with a floor without an entrance and make a lid.

- Put in two old combs that are free of disease and another two of foundation.

- Close the box and drill a hole ½ in (10 mm) in diameter near the bottom of the box's front.

- Place the bait hive 3 ft (1 m) above the ground, away from direct sunlight and in a place that is sheltered from high winds.

- If a swarm enters, when the bees have ceased flying, transfer them to the appropriate hive and return the bait hive to its original position.

- After a couple of days, treat the swarm for varroa.

This method is very inexpensive – you simply use old kit and just sit and wait. However, if the box is left too long, wax moth may become a problem and, if the weather is hot, the foundation may buckle (unless a plastic foundation is used).

A variation on this method is to use foundation only and a pheromone lure (nasonov pheromone – see below). This is, however, more expensive than the previous method. Commercial swarm lures are also available.

When setting swarm traps and baiting swarms, remember the following:

- Propolis and other remnant hive odours are powerful attractants to scout bees (this is the most likely scenario in nature).

- Swarms generally prefer hives containing propolis to those that do not.

- Swarms prefer hives containing old comb to hives with remnant odours but no old comb.

■ If you use a nasonov pheromone lure, swarms are attracted solely on the basis of this lure. Old comb and remnant hive odours are not important.

Research has shown that odours from substances not of bee origin are neither attractive nor repellent to swarms. The same research demonstrated that odours from bee diseases were similarly neither attractive nor repellent. Beekeepers who employ other attractant substances are, therefore, basing their swarm-attracting, methods more on luck than judgement.

Nasonov pheromone

Nasonov pheromone is named after the nasonov gland on the bee. This pheromone is used by bees as a signal to other bees that says 'we are here – this is where the nest is. Come on in'. Often, after an inspection or when you have just hived a swarm, you will see bees standing at the entrance with their rear ends facing you, fanning their wings. If you look closer you will see a small white patch near the bee's rear-end between seventh tergite, or segment. This is the gland from where the pheromone originates, and the bees are wafting it into the air as a signal to the others. It is also employed to orientate returning forager bees back to the colony.

This pheromone includes a number of different terpenoids, including geraniol, nerolic acid, citral and geranic acid. Bees use these to find the entrance to their colony or hive, and they may also release them onto flowers so that the other bees know which flowers have nectar. The amount of time they expose their gland seems to depend on reward expectations, the bees having acquired this information on previous foraging visits to the food source. In other words, if they expect a great deal of nectar, they will expose their glands for longer, even though on the current foraging trip the nectar reward is lower.

A synthetically produced nasonov pheromone can be used to attract a honey-bee swarm to an unoccupied hive or to a swarm-catching box. Synthetically produced nasonov consists of citral and geraniol in a ratio of 2:1. There has been much research in the USA on employing other honey-bee pheromones, such as the queen mandibular pheromone, to attract swarms more effectively and for making swarm lures.

THE BEEKEEPING YEAR: A SUMMARY

That is the beekeeping year. If you follow a routine of hive inspections, taking action as and when necessary, and if you catch any swarms you are notified of and put up baits for others, you will enjoy the beekeeping year ahead.

This final section takes you through the beekeeping year and highlights the main tasks on a month-by-month basis. This regime depends on the climate in your area, and so should be adjusted accordingly.

January/August
- Make sure all your equipment is in order and is clean. Patch up clothing and renew items, if necessary.
- Check you have enough frames and foundation for the year ahead – or at least to start off with.
- Order new queens if you are going to re-queen your colonies in the spring.

February/September
- Your first hive inspection, if the weather permits.
- Check for stores and feed if necessary. Don't forget the pollen.

March/October
- Maintain your inspection and feeding schedule.
- Remove mouse guards.
- Prepare your re-queening equipment (nucs, etc.).
- Raise new queens if you are using your own queens. (Starting this too early may result in a failure to mate adequately.)
- Check your stored comb for wax moth and spray if necessary.

April–May/November–December

- Start re-queening your hives if spring is your re-queening season. Check for queen cups and cells and signs of swarming. The swarming season varies a great deal so don't be taken by surprise.
- Super up hives if necessary. Certainly put at least one super on and keep a close eye on the situation.
- Commence swarm-prevention manipulations, such as reversing hive bodies.
- Carry out your inspections at regular intervals of around a week to ten days.

June–July/January–February

- Keep up with the honey supers.
- Extract spring honey, if required
- Maintain vigilance for signs of swarming.
- Keep up with swarm-prevention or swarm-control measures.

August/March

- Extract the main harvest.
- Commence queen rearing for autumn queens, if that is when you re-queen.
- Split hives for re-queening.
- Move hives to winter sites, if necessary.
- Start preparing your hives for the winter.

September–October/ April–May

- Winter down the hives after a thorough inspection.
- Prepare the hives according to the advice given in this chapter.
- Store surplus frames and comb after treating them for wax moth.

November–December/May–June

- Use the winter for wax rendering, for making new boxes and frames, etc.
- Repair old, damaged equipment
- Keep an eye on the hives to make sure there is no animal, flood or snow damage.

January/July

- Go on holiday to get away from it all.

That, then, is the year in brief, and should be adjusted according to your circumstances. It all sounds complicated but, in fact, there is nothing difficult in any of it and, if you follow the advice in this book and follow the bees, you will sail through the year with great enjoyment and a huge amount of satisfaction.

Chapter 10

Controlling diseases and pests

MANAGING DISEASES AND PESTS

Diseases and pests are a huge subject, and volumes have been written on them. They are complex and sometimes difficult to understand, yet it is important that all beekeepers are aware of the diseases and pests that can afflict a colony.

All livestock suffers from a range of problems, and bees are no exception. The only difference with beekeepers is that, by and large, they can't call in the vet. It is up to them to do something about their colonies, and the best way to go about this is to develop what is known as an integrated pest management (IPM) system. This is the management of pests employing a combination of methods that include economic, ecological and toxological factors while emphasizing biological (as opposed to chemical) controls and economic thresholds. The basic components of an IPM programme are:

■ prevention and awareness (by regular inspections and thorough knowledge);

■ observation and monitoring; and

■ intervention (where necessary).

Your apicultural extension officer or local association will be able to advise you on this, and you should seek that advice.

This chapter is designed to give you an overview of the common diseases and pests that affect colonies of bees, to provide you with advice on preventing disease striking in the first place and to suggest treatments and solutions when this does happen.

Disease diagnosis and treatment are really up to you. While advice can be sought from other beekeepers and local extension officers, they won't be around when you are out inspecting your bees, and, as noted above, it's no good calling the vet!

Because of its importance, I advise you to obtain a specialist book on the subject or to use *The Beekeeper's Field Guide*, which offers advice on diseases for beekeepers in the field (see the 'Further Reading' section at the end of the book). There are some diseases you must report to the authorities in most countries and states, and you should know the rules about this. Failure to report could lead to legal action. There are no 'worst' diseases because most, if left untreated, will kill your bees, but there are some that require more immediate attention than others, such as American Foul Brood (AFB).

The first many beekeepers know they have a problem is when they open up their hives for an inspection to find them all crawling with wax-moth larvae, which look up and say: 'Where were you, mate? We've taken over in here now.' Sadly this happens all too often to beekeepers who don't check their hives properly.

Let's start our look at diseases and pests with wax moths which, although not a disease, often invade a colony because a disease or other problem has wasted it and made it unable to defend itself.

WAX MOTH

Wax moths perform a vital service to bees in the wild. They destroy diseased hives and so help to prevent the spread of disease. Colonies with genetically weak components in their queens or drones may also fail and be destroyed by wax moths, again helping the bees to eradicate their less viable elements. Unfortunately, the moth is essentially after food for its larvae and won't distinguish between wax combs in colonies and wax combs you have stored for the winter. Where there is wax comb, there will be wax moths, and these can be effectively protected only by healthy colonies that can control the pest. It is not uncommon to see one or two moths in the more remote corners of a healthy hive, but any signs of wax-moth damage mean there is a problem in the colony.

Identifying wax moth

Identification is easy as, apart from the death's head hawkmoth that is seen only rarely in colonies in hot countries, the wax moth is likely to be the only moth around. They are silvery-grey/brown, dull and ordinary and come in two sizes.

First, the greater wax moth (*Galleria mellonella*) (1.3–1.9 cm or ½–¾ in long) is usually found in most beehives, and the bees normally repair any damage it causes as soon as it appears. It is for this reason that most beekeepers are unaware of it until the bees lose their ability to defend themselves and the moth larvae take over.

The problems this moth causes in warm countries are more acute because such conditions favour continuous reproduction. If you live in a warm climate, keep supering up to the minimum required; otherwise, I found that the wax moth will take over in the top unused super where there are few bees to stop them. The female lays her eggs in small crevasses in the hive, and these hatch out into white grubs with a brown end. The lesser wax moth (*Achroia grisella*) is smaller (see Photograph 7 in the colour photograph section of this book) and more silvery in appearance, and its larvae are correspondingly smaller than those of the greater wax moth.

Damage

The grubs move through the comb, eating honey, pollen and beeswax. The tunnels they make through the comb are silk lined and full of frass. These tunnels are easily seen and are just the beginning (see Photograph 8 in the colour photograph section of this book). When they have grown (up to about 3 cm (1¼ in) for the greater wax moth) the grubs will hollow out a shallow, boat-shaped depression in the woodwork, spin a cocoon and pupate. They do this in large numbers and, if you are unfortunate enough to see this, you will know you have left things very late. The smaller moth larvae usually pupate singly. By this stage, the comb will have been reduced to almost nothing and will be held together by moth silk rather than by anything else. This is a horrible sight.

When surprised, both moths remain still, hoping not to be seen. As soon as you try to kill them, however, they will start to move rapidly.

Protecting against wax moth

The only protection against wax moth is to keep your colonies strong and healthy. If a colony is failing, consider uniting it with another one (after checking it has no disease). Protecting stored comb is difficult. Wax moths won't usually infest clean comb that has no pollen or other debris in it, and they never (in my experience) attack foundation. They seem to need used comb that has ingredients other than wax in it – they will attack, for example, comb with honey in it, or comb containing pollen, brood, old brood remains, cocoons and so on.

Stored comb

If you are storing comb, spray them with *Bacillus thuringiensis*. This bacterium can be purchased from bee-supply stores and, when mixed with water and poured into a hand garden-sprayer, can be sprayed easily on to the combs' face. The bacterium will protect the comb without fail and won't contaminate anything except the wax moth larvae. This treatment usually lasts throughout the winter. It is quite a task if you have thousands of combs to treat but, for the small producer, it is very cost effective.

Freezing comb kills all stages of the pest. When you store comb over the winter in a shed, keep the boxes in a cool, well-ventilated place with a spacer between them to let in light: wax moths shy away from light.

In cold climates you can store your supers on top of your hives with a mat or escape board between them. This will allow limited bee access but will keep the supers cold.

Whatever you read elsewhere, don't use PDB (para-dichlor-benzine) crystals. They work, but have been shown to be carcinogenic. Remember, beeswax is a chemical sponge that will soak up just about anything. It's best not to fumigate combs for the same reason. It will also contaminate the honey if you try to use these crystals on honeycomb.

Stored pollen and propolis

Stored pollen and propolis that has been harvested (see Chapter 12) will also be attacked by wax moth, and for this reason should be sealed tightly in storage. Pollen traps placed on your hives should be emptied at least twice weekly. I well remember selling what I thought was a barrel of propolis to a buyer who later found he had bought a barrel of maggots.

Remember that, if you do find moth damage in your hives, look for the reason why the moths have managed to cause this damage. It could be because of disease.

BROOD DISEASES

Diseases affect either the brood or the adult bees. Here we look first at those that affect the brood. Diseases are sometimes difficult to recognize, especially in their early stages, so, if you think there may be something amiss, ask for advice. The worst thing you can do is nothing, and other beekeepers will be willing to help simply because they don't want infected hives in their areas. Most areas also have bee-disease inspectors of some kind, and it is much better to meet them earlier rather than later.

American Foul Brood (AFB)

AFB is probably the most serious of the brood diseases. It is highly infectious bacterial disease and can be spread by drifting bees, by robbing and by the beekeeper moving from an infected hive to others during inspections. Colonies that have AFB must be destroyed. By this I mean that the bees must be killed and brood frames burnt. Woodwork other than the frames may be saved, depending on state or national laws, but must usually be thoroughly sterilized. In many countries outbreaks of AFB must be reported to the appropriate authority, and it is these who deal with the problem. In other words, the outbreak is taken out of the beekeeper's hands.

Damage

AFB is caused by the spore-forming bacterium *Paenibacillus larvae* (formerly classified as *Bacillus larvae*). Larvae up to three days old become infected by ingesting spores present in their food. Young larvae less than 24 hours old are, however, most susceptible, and infected larvae usually die after their cells are sealed.

The big problem with AFB is that, when the vegetative form of the bacterium eventually dies, it produces millions of spores. This means that each dead larva may contain as many as 100 million spores. It is these spores that can be spread so easily, especially by the beekeeper and by the bees which drift into or rob other hives.

Identifying AFB

Identifying the early stages of AFB is difficult but possible and, because this disease could destroy all your colonies, it is worth looking out for it every time you inspect your colonies. Look for the following.

In the early stages, the combs may or may not have the pepper-pot appearance typical of the disease. 'Pepper pot' describes exactly what you may see – a brood comb with sealed brood but with many gaps in the sealed brood that resemble the holes in a pepper pot (see Photograph 9 in the colour photograph section of this book).

The cell cappings may be dark brown and sunken. At this stage, you can tease out the brown remains of the larvae. These will be like a thread about 2 cm (1 in) long. A matchstick pushed through the capping and slowly pulled it out should extract the telltale 'rope' of a dead larva (see Photograph 10 in the colour photograph section of this book.

Sometimes the cappings are perforated and, instead of being pearly or creamy white, the larvae are discoloured.

Later, the larvae dry out and become difficult to remove as a result of the pupal tongue that projects from some of the now scale-like larvae to the centre of the cell.

Colonies infected with AFB really do smell foul. Get to know the nice smell of a healthy colony. Then, when you smell something different, suspect AFB.

Treating AFB

Treating AFB is difficult and, in some countries, beekeepers are not permitted to treat it themselves. Know the rules and, if in doubt, ask. Treatments for AFB include, however, the following:

Burning

Burning the hives and bees is one way of ensuring an end to the matter, but this is not as easy as it may appear. You have to wait until all the bees are in the hive in the evening when you shut the entrance, open the lid and pour petrol into it. This kills the bees almost immediately and the hive can then be burnt. You must be careful. I know of an apiary inspector who poured in the petrol and then dropped in a match. He almost blew himself and the beekeeper up.

The UK and New Zealand have a markedly reduced the incidence of AFB because of their policies of burning.

Burning the frames and bees and then sterilizing the scraped hive parts with sodium hypochlorite is also effective. The hive parts should be cleaned before they are soaked in a solution of sodium hypochlorite for at least 20 minutes. Use gloves and overalls if you employ this method.

Irradiation

Irradiating the hive parts and combs is effective but is not practical for most beekeepers. It is also expensive.

Using the bacteriostat oxytetracycline

The bacteriostat oxytetracycline (which goes under several tradenames, such as Terramycin), can be an effective treatment and prophylactic. Its use, however, is fraught with the danger of the bacteria becoming resistant, and so it should never be employed without expert advice. Many states and countries have banned its use except by the authorities, and some have banned it altogether. Again, know your local rules.

My advice is not to use it at all — it's just another chemical that will contaminate your honey, wax and bees. If you want an alternative to this chemical, read 'Eradicating AFB without the use of drugs' (see the 'Further Reading' section at the end of the book).

To sum up the main points about AFB:

■ This is probably the most infectious honey-bee brood disease.

- Its name bears no relationship to its geographical spread.

- The early stages are not easily identified, so ask for advice if you think something is amiss.

- The larvae die *after* the cell has been capped.

- It appears that AFB is becoming resistant to oxytetracycline, and the inexperienced use of oxytetracycline may contaminate the honey.

- If you leave AFB unchecked, it will destroy the colony and spread to others.

- If you have handled a colony with AFB, sterilize your hive tool, wash your bee suit and burn your gloves.

- Try not to blow yourself up when using petrol to destroy an infected hive.

European Foul Brood (EFB)

Like AFB, EFB is a bacterial disease. The causal agent of EFB is the bacterium, *Melissococcus pluton*, which infests the guts of bee larvae. Although considered less damaging to a colony than AFB, it should never be underestimated and should be attended to if and when detected. The bacterium does not form spores, although it can overwinter on comb. Because it doesn't form spores it's not as infectious as AFB and, if it is caught in its early stages, the colony can usually be saved.

EFB is often considered a 'stress' disease – a disease that is dangerous only if the colony is already under stress for other reasons such as frequent moves, other disease problems, pesticide poisoning and so on. If the colony is given the chance to build up, however, it can usually survive.

Identifying EFB

The following are the signs of an EFB infestation:

- The larvae die of starvation because of the action of the bacteria in the gut, and they change to an off-white colour – not the pearly white of healthy larvae.

- The larvae adopt unnatural positions in the cells and are not coiled neatly.

- The larvae appear to 'melt down' and to lose definition.

- The bees do not usually cap infected cells, but larvae that are capped *may* die of the disease and, in this case, the cappings are sunken and often perforated (pepper pot).

- The later stages of the disease produce a foul smell – often worse than AFB. In both diseases this smell depends on which secondary bacteria infest the larval remains after death.

Treating EFB

Treatment may not be necessary in an otherwise healthy colony, although you may have to report an infestation to the statutory authorities in your area. The bacteriostat oxytetracycline will prevent and cure the problem and many texts advocate this, but its use is not really recommended unless a bee-inspection officer advises it and then only under their direct guidance. Personally, I wouldn't employ it at all. Its overuse can cause resistance and, without doubt, it can contaminate the honey.

Try to remove the cause of stress, and boost the colony's efforts to build up, perhaps with a frame of brood and bees, if possible. If the disease is not too far gone, then all should be well. There is no need for chemicals.

Remember that, because this disease is caused by the starvation of the larvae, it can be hidden in, for example, queen-rearing colonies where high levels of feeding are undertaken. If this is the case, the larvae are able to overcome the parasitic nature of the bacteria.

The name EFB bears no relationship to its geographical spread, and very few areas of the world have escaped it. At the time of writing, New Zealand has no EFB. It is important you know the rules in your area concerning the reporting and treatment of EFB.

Sacbrood

Sacbrood is a viral disease (*Morator aetatulae*) that does not usually cause severe losses. It mainly occurs early in the brood-rearing season when the ratio of brood to bees is high. Most beekeepers don't notice it mainly because it affects a small percentage of larvae only. Adult bees detect and remove infected larvae very quickly and so, if the beekeeper does notice the problem, this is usually because it has progressed to a stage where the workers can no longer control it. Therefore, by the time the beekeeper observes the symptoms, the disease may be too severe for the adult worker population to handle.

Both worker and drone larvae are affected. Pupae may be killed occasionally, but adult bees are immune to it. Dead brood is often scattered among healthy brood. Nurse bees are suspected of transmitting the disease by carrying the virus from cell to cell. It is also believed that robber bees spread the disease by taking contaminated honey from one colony to another. The spread of this disease is another reason why drifting and robbing should be prevented.

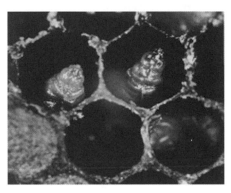

Fig. 26. Sacbrood larvae: typical position

Identifying sacbrood
The following are the signs of a sacbrood infestation:

- If the cells have been capped, the cappings may be perforated (if so, also check for AFB/EFB).

- If the cells are open, identification is easier. The larva's head, the first part of the body to change colour, becomes dark brown to black. If lifted from the cell, the abdomen is bloated, resembling a watery sack.

- Death usually occurs after the cell is sealed and the larva has spun its cocoon.

■ The larvae die in an upright position in the cell, and this is very noticeable (see Figure 26).

■ The larva eventually dries to a scale resembling a Chinese slipper or gondola. This does not adhere tightly to the cell wall and so, unlike AFB scales, the workers can remove them. By doing this, however, they tend to spread the virus throughout the hive.

■ After a few weeks the larval remains are no longer infective.

Treating of sacbrood

Strong colonies and regular re-queening seem to be the best means of combating this disease – no antibiotic is effective at preventing or controlling it. Colonies suffering from this virus usually recover spontaneously when the honey flow starts because, at this time, there are fewer adults in the hive to pass on the disease.

Chalkbrood

Chalkbrood is a disease caused by the fungus, *Ascosphaera apis*, and it affects unsealed and sealed brood. It can be triggered by a change in brood-nest temperature. When there are insufficient nurse bees to cope with extreme weather conditions (e.g. for cold clustering and heat fanning), the brood may be left unattended. The first larvae affected are usually those around the edges of the brood, where the brood temperature may be higher or lower.

Stress of any kind can result in chalkbrood: high or low temperatures, wet or dry conditions, an increase in CO_2, poor nutrition, a failing queen, poor hive management and moving hives. In other words, all sorts of environmental factors have been linked to the disease at one time or another, which means the trigger is not completely understood.

Identifying chalkbrood

Chalkbrood is fairly easy to recognize, especially in its later stages, because the hive's floor and front will be littered with small hexagonal blocks of chalk-like material. Initially, the larvae are covered by a fluffy white fungal (mycelial) growth, which looks like white mould on bread. The larvae are, at first, swollen inside their cells, but, later on, dry out to become hard, white or grey/black, chalk-like mummies.

The fungus can affect larvae in unsealed (as in sacbrood) or sealed cells. The cell caps are either light or dark, and are sunken with many with perforations like AFB, EFB and sacbrood. Indeed, chalkbrood symptoms may be mistaken for other brood diseases (such as AFB, EFB and sacbrood), and even, for white pollen. If you become at all confused – and most of us do – ask for advice from your local bee-inspection officer or from other beekeepers.

In a hygienic colony, if the bees detect dead larvae under the cell caps, they chew holes in cappings and remove the mummies within ten days. The mummies are dropped onto the hive floor and, later, outside the entrance, where they can usually be seen on the alighting board.

Treating and preventing chalkbrood

There is no chemical cure or treatment for chalkbrood although, in recent years, many patent liquids have been marketed as cure-alls. Management practices that reduce the stress on the hives and, thus, that reduce the number of chalkbrood spores, are probably the best way to prevent and manage the disease. Maintaining strong, healthy colonies is also important in the management of chalkbrood.

Other management practices are as follows:

- Provide good ventilation in your hives. Research has shown a possible link between chalkbrood and CO_2 levels in hives.

- Add young adult bees to your hives.

- Do not force your bees to spend the winter in a hive that is over supered. This will lead to chilling.

- Avoid opening your hives in cold weather.

- Try not to stress your colonies (for example, by moving them too much).

- Feed your colonies with sugar syrup, fresh, uncontaminated pollen or supplements.

- Maintain strong hives by regular re-queening.

Some hives are more susceptible to chalkbrood than others. Most of this variation is due to differences in the bees' ability to uncap and remove diseased brood. By selecting queens with hygienic traits, outbreaks of this and other diseases can be reduced.

OTHER BROOD PROBLEMS

There are two other, principal brood ailments: chilled brood and bald brood. Neither is very serious, and the first can be prevented by good hive management.

Chilled brood
Chilled brood is caused by chilling. Brood of all ages die because of a depletion in the number of bees looking after them. This could be caused by pesticide poisoning, insufficient bees in a hive that has been split after carrying out an artificial swarm or any other reason. Always be careful, therefore, when splitting hives or making up nucs that the brood have enough bees to look after them.

Bald brood
Bald Brood is so called because it occurs when the cell cappings are removed while the larvae are still inside. This is not a disease but is the result of greater wax-moth larvae chewing through brood cappings in a straight line. It is also the result of a genetic trait in some strains of bee, where small patches of brood are left uncapped.

If the problem is due to wax moth, the bees remove the silk tunnels and leave the larvae bare – for some reason they fail to re-cap the cells. The cappings are not always completely removed, and so there may be a slightly raised ridge at the edge.

If the problem is due to the genetic trait, you will see small patches of bald brood rather than straight lines.

Treating for bald brood

There is no treatment for bald brood other than to re-queen if it seems to be a genetic trait, or to build up the colony by uniting it or adding brood if the problem is wax moth larvae. Remember, a large, healthy colony can deal with wax moth predation.

Brood disease problems: a summary

Because of the similarity especially of the early symptoms of the brood diseases so far described, the points below should help you to distinguish them:

- AFB: The larvae are ropey and discoloured (dark brown) in unsealed cells or, in cells with perforated, sunken discoloured cappings. The larvae dry to hard scales that are difficult to remove.

- EFB: The larvae are in an unnatural position in and around the cell walls. They may be white through to a discoloured, yellow to dark brown. The larvae are watery, granular or, occasionally, ropey.

- Sacbrood: The larvae are discoloured, brown through to black. Chinese slipper or gondola-shaped larvae are found in capped cells or under perforated caps. These can easily be removed.

- Chalkbrood: The larvae are white and mouldy. Hard larvae (mummies) are white or grey/black and are found in the cells on the floor or on the alighting board at the front of the hive.

- Chilled brood: Larvae of all ages die at the same time. The problem is usually confined to the periphery of the brood area.

- Bald brood: The larvae remain healthy and pearly white. They usually pupate normally.

ADULT BEE DISEASES

Nosema

Nosema apis is a unicellular parasite of the class of *Microsporidia* that is now considered to be a fungus. *N. apis* has a resistant spore that can withstand temperature extremes and dehydration. It is a very widespread disease of honey-bees and, when the spores are eaten by adult bees, they germinate and invade the gut wall. Here they multiply and produce more spores that are passed out in the waste.

Nosema is common in spring and autumn, and many beekeepers treat the condition with an antibiotic substance called fumagillin (the tradename of which is Fumadil B), added to an autumn feed of sugar syrup. Fumadil B (prepared from *Aspergillis fumigatus*, the causative agent of *stone brood!*) inhibits the spores reproducing in the ventriculus, but it does not kill them.

Identifying nosema

There are no specific external symptoms of nosema, but the colony's failure to build up in the spring could be an indication of the disease. Many beekeepers believe that, if their bees have dysentery, this is a sign of nosema. This is not so. Nosema can be spread rapidly by dysentery via nosema spores in the faeces the cleaning bees will eat, but dysentery is not in itself an indicator. Some texts will tell you that bees crawling around the hive's entrance may also be a sign of nosema. Again, this is not so. It is more likely to be a symptom of a viral disease or even of pesticide poisoning.

If you believe one of your colonies has nosema, you can do two things to check this. First, you could obtain the advice of the bee-disease officer in your region, who would probably ask for a certain number of bees to be sent to the laboratory for analysis, Second, you could grind up some bees and look at them under a microscope yourself. You don't need much power to see the very evident rod-shaped spores.

Alternatively, you could carry out a field test on a few of your bees (preferably around 30) from each suspect hive. To carry out this test, follow the procedures outlined below:

■ Grab your bee. Don't use gloves – you will probably be stung but you will get hold of the bee better.

■ Remove the bee's head. Pull it off gently – slowly but surely. Remember, you are doing this for the benefit of your bees generally. This severs the mid-gut from the head. The bee may continue to struggle even when headless, and this can alarm some people.

■ Grasp the very last segment of the bee's abdomen with a pair of good tweezers and, gently holding the thorax with your other hand, slowly but firmly pull the sting and last segment away from the bee.

■ The rectum and mid-gut will follow. Keep pulling slowly and firmly. Don't pull too suddenly or too hard – otherwise something will break and you'll have to start again. The bee may still be struggling.

■ After the mid-gut has emerged, hold it over a piece of white paper. The mid-gut can now be seen easily.

■ Study the mid-gut. If it is tan coloured and wrinkly, it is healthy. If it is smooth and white, it probably has nosema.

Nosema ceranae

Unfortunately, Spanish researchers have identified another type of nosema – *Nosema ceranae* – that is widespread in the Spanish honey-bee, *Apis mellifera*. *N. ceranae* evolved with the far-eastern honey-bee, *Apis cerana*, but these findings indicate that this parasite had now moved out of Asia to Europe. The disease has been reported in France, Germany and Switzerland. More worryingly still were the massive colony losses in Spain during the winter of 2005–6, some of which have been linked to nosema. Nosema may also have caused the huge colony losses in Spain in 2004–5, from which my own bees suffered, or these losses may have been due to varroa or some other pathogen and the nosema simply multiplied in the remains of the dead bees.

Nosema is usually less of a problem in warm climates and so, in common with other beekeepers in the region, I had done little to prevent it. At the time of writing, Spanish and other researchers are still evaluating the problem. The world is becoming smaller by the day, and what were once exotic diseases are spreading very rapidly to western honey-bees.

Treating Nosema apis

Good colony management, as well as chemicals, can keep nosema at bay:

- Make sure the colony goes into the winter with a young and prolific queen and with many young bees (another reason for autumn re-queening).

- Ensure that the colony going into winter has adequate stores of honey and pollen (see Chapter 9).

- Feed fumagillin as sold under the tradename Fumadil B. If fed in sugar syrup to overwintering colonies, this can markedly reduce the incidence of nosema the following spring. Follow the manufacturer's instructions carefully because under or overuse can negate the effects. If feeding this medicated syrup, do not then feed your bees with non-medicated syrup because this will dilute the beneficial effects of the chemical. Use fumagillin only where permitted.

Nosema is very widespread, so don't underestimate its effects on your colonies. It is thought to be the cause of early queen supersedure and, as there are so few visible indications of the disease, it is regarded by many as a sort of silent killer.

Dysentery

Dysentery is not a disease but a symptom of something being wrong. It is caused by excess water accumulation in the rectum and it can spread nosema (but remember, it isn't a sign of nosema). It can be recognized easily: there will be greatly increased faecal spotting on and around the hive's entrance. A bad case of dysentery can cover the entire front of the hive.

Treating dysentery

As dysentery is not a disease, look for the problem. This could be contamination of the food supply or unsuitable winter stores. Ensure that any food given before and during the winter is not contaminated.

The prevention of dysentery, like so many other problems, is basically down to good beekeeping practice.

Virus paralysis disease

Two different viruses – chronic bee paralysis virus (CBPV) and acute bee paralysis virus (ABPV) – have been isolated from paralytic bees. In Europe and North America, ABPV has been shown to kill adult bees and bee larvae in colonies infested with the mite, *Varroa destructor* (see below). This mite damages bee tissues and, in so doing, probably acts as a vector, releasing viral particles into the haemolymph. The biology of bee viral diseases, their relationship with mites and their effects on bees are the subject of many investigations in university departments and government bee laboratories around the world, especially in the light of new developments in such bee problems such as parasitic mite syndrome and colony collapse disorder (see below).

Identifying virus paralysis disease

Virus paralysis disease can be identified as follows:

- The bees will be crawling around the hive's alighting board or entrance in a semi-moribund or moribund state, often in large numbers. These bees will not react if you prod them.

- These bees are usually unable to fly.

- They often appear blacker in colour than other bees and shiny as they become hairless.

- A close examination will often show that these bees have extended abdomens.

- The bees are often refused entry to the hive. This situation looks remarkably like pesticide poisoning when bees are refused entry and die outside the hive in large numbers. Don't confuse the two. This situation can also be symptomatic of starvation, so this is yet another confusing signal.

Acarine (tracheal mite)

When assessing its effects on bees, the mite, *Acarapis woodii*, has caused much controversy. This mite inhabits the prothoracic trachea of the honey-bee – the thoracic opening nearest to the bee's head on the thorax. These openings are really air inlets that allow air to enter the bee's blood stream. The mites enter this opening a few days after the bee emerges when the hairs surrounding the opening are still soft.

Bees seem to vary in their susceptibility to this mite. In the USA, for example, it is a major problem whereas, in Europe, it is a minor player and causes little damage. This might not always have been the case, however. In the early years of the twentieth century, the so-called Isle of Wight disease had a huge effect on British and European beekeeping. During studies of this disease, the mite was discovered and immediately blamed for every colony death. The mite may have been the culprit, or it may have been part of the problem of vectoring viruses into the bees. Or the mite may have been there all the time undiscovered when along came a new virus for it inadvertently to vector into the bees. Suffice to say, every colony death at the time – whether caused by starvation or something else – was blamed on this new mite. Diagnostic features and symptoms were described and, of course, new remedies were sought.

The symptoms (which are still described in some texts today) include crawling at the hive's entrance, crossed wings (K wing) and other wing troubles. These seem to me, however, to be more likely to be associated with a viral disease. Treatments (which are still touted) include 'Frow mixture' which was devised by a Lincolnshire beekeeper and which consisted of nitrobenzine, saffrol and motor-car petrol. It seemed to work – or at least it was used when the problem was passing, and Frow was rightly honoured for his efforts. The thought of putting something like Frow mixture in a hive today would, rightly, fill anyone with horror, yet some texts still advocate its use. Don't use it.

Identifying acarine
There are no certain field methods for determining an infestation. Dissecting the bee and a microscopic examination of the trachea is the only way. There are no visible symptoms.

Treating acarine
Certain evaporative treatments, such as those using menthol or formic acid and which are used for varroa control, can be employed for the treatment of this mite, but it is best

to obtain expert advice. You may have made a misdiagnosis and, in Europe in any case, treatment is generally unnecessary.

Varroa destructor

In many texts this may be called *Varroa jacobsonii*, but it has become evident that, hiding under this name, are two are different beasts. The name now given to the specific mite that affects us all is, very aptly, *V. destructor* (see Photograph 11 in the colour photograph section of this book). It is *V. destructor* that has caused so much trouble for many of the world's beekeepers since it jumped from its natural host, the far-eastern honey-bee, *Apis cerana*, to the western honey-bee *Apis mellifera* – a bee that didn't know what to do about it.

The topic of varroa and its effects on honey-bees is vast and one that we are only just beginning to understand. For example, its relationship with other 'syndromes', such as parasitic mite syndrome and colony collapse disorder, is the subject of furious research. Because this mite has had such an impact on the economy of beekeeping, therefore, I think it is important that we have a look at it in some detail.

When the mite first arrives in a country, by and large it takes all beekeepers by surprise. Most were hoping that it simply wouldn't appear but, when it does, many beekeepers suddenly become wax-moth keepers. I did in Spain. I had moved from the UK where there was no varroa at the time to a country where there was, and I should have known better. I was then new to the game and I hope that, if such a thing happens again, I will be better prepared. You must be.

Life-cycle

The mites reproduce on a 10-day cycle. The female enters a honey-bee brood cell and, as soon as the cell is capped, she lays eggs on the bee larva. These eggs hatch into several females and usually one male (see Photograph 12 in the colour photograph section of this book). The young mites hatch in about the same time as it takes the young bees to develop. When the young bee emerges from the cell after pupation, the varroa mites also leave and disperse to other bees and larvae. The varroa mite prefers drone cells to inhabit and breed in because the cycle and timing of drone development suit it better, but it will also infest worker cells.

When on adult bees (see Photograph 13 in the colour photograph section of this book), the mite sucks the bees' blood by piercing their cuticles. It is then that the bees are thought to be more prone to infections from existing bee pathogens. With the exception of some resistance in the Russian Primorskiy bee, *Apis mellifera* is defenseless against these parasites and, unless the beekeeper intervenes with treatment, the colony will have died out by the autumn.

Identifying Varroa destructor

On adult bees the mites look like small, crab-shaped, red/brown blobs 1.5 mm wide and 1.1 mm long. They can be missed because they tend to blend in with the colour of the bee, so look carefully. Mites can be seen, however, more easily by uncapping drone brood and lifting them out.

Assessing colony infestation

The natural daily mite fall can be employed to assess varroa infestation (see below). In severely infested colonies, there will be a rapid reduction in the number of adult bees, and some or many of the adults will have deformed, ragged wings and deformed abdomens. In severely infested colonies, foul brood-type symptoms may be also seen, and this may lead to a diagnosis of parasitic mite syndrome, which is described later in this chapter.

The following methods should help to determine varroa infestations in your hives. It is also worth checking to see if the mites have become resistant to the usual chemical treatments. Such resistance has occurred in many countries as a result of abusing the chemicals, and it has taken many beekeepers by surprise (an easy way to check this is also shown below).

Drone brood inspection

Test 100 cells. If there are, say, 5% with varroa, you have a low infestation. If there are, say, 25% with varroa you have a high infestation.

Natural mite-fall inspection

This method involves counting the mites that fall off the bees naturally during the normal course of the day. You can do this by inserting what is known as a 'sticky board' onto the hive's floor. These can be purchased from most bee-supply shops. The fallen mites adhere to this board. After 24 hours, count the mites on the board. Depending on whether you are in the Northern or Southern Hemisphere, if your count is 6 mites in May/November; 10 mites in June/December; 16 mites in July/January; and 33 mites in August/February (or below) your colony is running along fine, but keep a close eye on it. If the count is in excess of these figures, the colony will collapse before the end of the season.

Sampling the whole hive for varroa numbers

Normally, only about 15% of the mites will be on the adult bees in a hive in full production. A correction factor is therefore needed to account for the rest:

- Using a clean, sticky board as above, place Apistan or Bayvarol in the hive to kill the mites (see 'Treating Varroa destructor' below).

- After 24 hours count the mites. Assume an 85% kill rate.

- Divide number of mites counted by 0.85.

- If the hive is in full production, multiply the result by 6.

- If the hive is not in full production but has brood, multiply it by 3.

- If no brood is present, then no correction factor is required.

This method should give you an idea of the total number of mites in a hive. A rule of thumb for working out the approximate total number of mites in a colony is, however, as follows:

- November–February (May–August): multiply the daily mite fall on the sticky board by 400.

- March–April (September–October) and September–October (March–April): Multiply the daily mite fall by 100.
- May–August (November–February): Multiply the daily mite fall by 30.

Ether-roll field test to determine varroa numbers
This is an easy test you can carry out in the field:

- Collect about 300–500 bees in a jar.

- Spray ether into the jar for 1–2 seconds (use a can of Quick Start ether).

- Rotate the bees for about 10 seconds.

- Put the bees on a piece of white paper. Do this immediately after the 10 seconds.

- Spread the bees around to dislodge all the mites.

- Count the mites. In this example, let the number of mites seen be 5.

- Divide the number of bees in the hive (see Chapter 9 for an estimation) by the number in the sample (e.g. 25,000 bees in the hive ÷ 500 in the sample = 50).

- Multiply 50 by 5 (the number of mites seen) = 250.

- Multiply 250 by 6 if the hive is in full production = 1,500. *Or* by 2 if not in full production but contains brood = 500. *Or* by 0 if no brood is present = 250.

Note: Fine sugar or soapy water can also be used instead of ether.

Field test for mite resistance to chemicals
Again, this test can be carried out in the field:

- Cut out a 9 mm × 25 mm (⅓ in ×1 in) piece of Apistan strip (see below). Staple this to a 125 mm × 75 mm (5 in ×3 in) piece of card.

- Place the card in a 500 ml (1 pt) glass jar.

- Prepare a light, metal-mesh cover for the jar.

- Shake the bees from 1 or 2 combs into an upturned hive roof.

- Scoop up about a quarter of these (about 150) and place them in the jar with a sugar cube.

■ Cover the jar with the mesh lid and store upturned in the dark at room temperature.

■ After 24 hours, place the upturned jar over some white paper and hit it to dislodge the dead mites. Count the initial mite kill.

■ Replace the lid and put the jar of bees in a freezer until they are dead (1–4 hours).

■ Take the jar out of the freezer and hit it again to dislodge any dead mites that were not killed before. Count these.

% kill by the chemical strip = Initial kill ÷ (initial + final kill) x 100.

The number killed by the chemical strip = the initial kill. Add this number to the number killed by freezing the bees (the final kill). Divide the initial kill by the sum of the initial kill and the final kill and multiply the result by 100. This will give you the percentage killed by the chemical strip. If this is less than 50%, the mites are probably resistant to chemicals.

Treating and protecting against varroa destructor

Timing
The timing of the treatment is important. *Treat* your bees in the spring when large amounts of brood provide the ideal conditions for varroa infestation. If you don't, your colony could collapse in the late summer. Use an authorized miticide, such as Apistan or Bayvarol (see below).

To *protect* your colony against a varroa invasion, treat it in the early autumn, after the harvest. For this, use an organic product, such as oxalic or formic acid. This will slow down the mites' resistance to miticides and the formic acid will penetrate the wax to kill the mites capped in the cells.

You should usually assume you have varroa in your hives even if you can't see them. Contact your local beekeeping association to find out what everyone else is doing and when. Concerted action against these mites assists everyone and helps to guard against a re-invasion of your colonies. Treatment also reduces an infestation to a level that can be tolerated by your bees.

Many treatments are available, including ones suitable for organic honey production (although, in my opinion, these are more difficult to use). When I produced organic honey in Spain, for example, legislation restricted the chemicals and methods I could employ in the fight against varroa but, even though this involved more work, I found it extremely satisfying.

Treating varroa is a very complex and fast-changing area. There are several prevention and control strategies, and you should always keep up to date with the latest innovations and talk to your local adviser. The following are some of the treatments commonly available.

Chemical controls (miticides)

Bayvarol, Apistan, Apivar, Check Mite and Apitol (see Figure 27) are proprietary treatments produced and designed to kill varroa. These comprise synthetic chemicals. They are usually reliable and effective when the mites are not chemically resistant. They are also quick and easy to use.

Fig. 27. A chemical treatment for varroa (Bayvarol strips) and an organic treatment (Apilife Var)

'Organic' controls

Thymol, formic acid, lactic acid, oxalic acid and other essential oils are 'soft' chemicals that are reliable to varying degrees but, for good effect, they must be employed at the right time and in the right circumstances. Some, however, are very temperature dependent. I found, for example, that those based on thymol could cause the bees to abandon the hive and abscond if employed when the temperature was too hot. This is particularly the case with homemade thymol treatments. Commercial treatments are, however, available based on some of these substances – such as Apilife Var (various oils and thymol; see Figure 27), Apicure (formic acid) and Apiguard (thymol).

The biggest problem with essential oils compared with such chemical treatments as fluvalinate (used in Apistan) is the small difference between the amount of the substance that will kill the mites and the amount that will kill the bees. Fluvalinate, for example, is 800–1000 times more toxic to varroa than to bees, whereas the best essential oils are only two to four times more toxic. This doesn't apply to all oils, however. Thymol is not toxic to bees, for example. Unless you know what you are doing, therefore, it is not wise to make your own treatments using various oils because you may well be assisting the varroa mites in finishing off your colony. Further, oils may well contaminate the wax and the honey in the hive and may well be dangerous to humans. Be careful, therefore, using these treatments.

Devices for the efficient use of oxalic and lactic acids are also commercially available. One of these is simply a heated spoon that contains crystals of oxalic acid. The spoon is plugged into a car battery, inserted into the hive's entrance and turned on. The crystals then vaporize in the hive. This process takes about two minutes.

Biotechnical controls (manipulations)

If carried out correctly and at the right time, *drone-brood trapping* can dramatically reduce the number of varroa and will not affect the colony as much as worker-brood trapping (see below). This method is based on the fact that, as mentioned earlier, varroa mites are more attracted to drone brood than worker brood.

The frames of drone brood (in which the varroa mites prefer to live when starting their reproductive cycle) are removed from the hive and destroyed. This method may hence affect the number of drones in the area and thus queen mating. Personally I have never liked methods that alter the natural dynamics of the hive and the apiary.

Nevertheless, this method can be carried out as follows:

- Place a drone frame in the colony. These can be purchased from bee-supply shops or you can put drone foundation wax-sheets into the frames yourself.

- The workers will now clean the cells in these frames and the queen will recognize that they are drone cells from their size. She will therefore lay unfertilized drone eggs in the cells.

- In about 10 days the drone cells are sealed with the mites inside them.

- You should now remove the sealed drone-brood frame and put it in a freezer to kill the drone brood and mites. Alternatively, you could open the drone brood cells with an uncapping fork (available from bee-supplies shops) and lift out the larvae.

Researchers say that, if there is no worker brood in the colony, this method can remove over 90% of the mites with a single treatment. If there is worker brood in the colony, they will compete with the drone brood in 'trapping' the mites, and so the efficiency rate will be lower.

There is now even a device that will kill the mites in the cells without having to remove the frames. The Saartan 'mite zapper' was developed in the USA and comprises heated wires embedded in a drone brood frame. When the cells are sealed, an electrical current is passed through the frame and thus the mites and drone larvae are killed. The house bees will then clean out the cells.

If done correctly, *worker-brood trapping* is very effective in reducing varroa numbers but it affects the colony because you are removing your future foragers. I don't recommend it. *Hive splitting/drone trapping* is also very effective and is popular in Vietnam but, again, it will affect the apiary's overall ability to maximize the honey harvest.

Mesh-bottomed floors were discussed earlier in the book. While not effective on their own, they help to reduce varroa numbers, and mesh floors are better for colonies anyway.

Varroa mites often fall off the bees onto the floor. They then clamber back onto a passing bee and recommence their damage. If there is a mesh floor, they will fall out of the hive and be lost. A floor devised by a Belgian apiarist employs this principle of losing varroa mites. It consists of a series of long, smooth tubes with gaps between them. The varroa mites are unable to cling onto the tubes and thus fall out of the hive. This is a simple and apparently effective method but is very expensive to purchase.

Heat treatment works but is time consuming and is only 50–80% effective, according to US research. It is currently popular in Russia. The theory is that adult female mites are more sensitive to temperatures above normal brood-nest temperature (34° C; 93° F) than are the bee larvae and pupae themselves. If you heat the bees in a colony up to 44° C, (111° F) for 4 hours, the varroa mites on the brood will therefore die but the larvae will, in the main, survive. There will still be a great many mites on the adult bees, though. With its limited kill rate (compared with other methods) and the undoubted stress it puts on the bees, I would not recommend this method.

Finally, *co-ordination with your neighbours* helps to reduce re-invasion from untreated stocks and can play a vital part in any varroa treatment programme. Many beekeepers, however, fail to recognize this. If they did, this would make life a great deal easier –and cheaper – for everyone.

Biological controls

Breeding programmes mainly involve the selection of genetic traits that are hostile to the varroa mite's reproduction cycle or worker-bee traits that actively remove or hinder the mites. The 'suppression of mite reproduction' (SMR) has been extensively studied in the USA, and the selection of traits in the honey-bee population that effectively limit the mite's reproductive ability seems to be bearing fruit. These programmes are not easily carried out, but all beekeepers should keep up to date with varroa treatments and methods of control.

Research is showing that the *pathogenic fungus, Matarhizium anisopliae*, may also be effective in the biological control of varroa – at least, as effective as fluvalinate.

Parasitic mite syndrome (PMS)

I have included this syndrome because of its association with varroa. 'Parasitic mite syndrome' (PMS) is the name given to a range of abnormal brood symptoms associated with the presence of varroa in both brood and adult bees. The symptoms, which were first noticed by beekeepers and the US Department of Agriculture Bee Research Laboratory in the mid-1990s, were found in association with infections of both varroa and acarine (the tracheal mite) (see above).

It is suggested that PMS could be caused by the varroa mite vectoring the acute bee paralysis virus (ABPV), and possibly other viruses, into the honey-bee larvae. However, in one piece of research, US scientists analysed samples of adult bees from colonies with PMS and found that in the majority of cases, neither ABV, Kashmir bee virus (KBV) nor any of nine other bee viruses were in evidence. Therefore, while these viruses may be one of the causes of the syndrome, other factors cannot be ruled out.

PMS affects both brood and adult bees and is usually associated with colony collapse, especially in the autumn. The symptoms can appear at any time of the year, although they are more prevalent in mid-summer and autumn. These symptoms are, however, often difficult to interpret and can be very easily confused with the symptoms of AFB, EFB, sacbrood and various viral diseases (see Photograph 14 in the colour photograph section of this book). Because commercially available, easy-to-use tests for AFB and EFB can now be purchased, the first thing to do is to test for AFB/EFB and other problems. One way of differentiating the symptoms of PMS from AFB is the lack of a foul smell. Similarly, if the larvae have dried to scales, these can be removed easily, and they will not rope if a stick is pushed into the cell and slowly extracted.

Identifying PMS

Once other problems have been eliminated, look for all or some of the following symptoms (the notes in brackets indicate symptoms similar to other diseases and problems):

- The presence of varroa in the colony (PMS is always associated with varroa).

- A reduction in the colony's population (most diseases).

- Larvae of all ages are affected.

- Larvae stretched out in the cells with their heads raised (sacbrood).

- Crawling, moribund bees leaving the hive (viral diseases/poisoning/starvation).

- The possible supersedure of the queen (nosema).

- The presence of varroa on the pupae.

- The cappings perforated or the cells left uncapped by the bees (AFB).

Tropilaelaps clarae

This mite is similar to varroa in its effect on a colony, but it can be distinguished easily from varroa by its elongated shape, as opposed to the crab shape of varroa (see Photograph 15 in the colour photograph section of this book; compare this with the varroa mite shown in Photograph 11). *Tropilaelaps clarae* is not yet a pest in most countries outside its natural, far-eastern range but, like varroa it could spread, and beekeepers are asked to keep an eye out for this new danger.

Identifying Tropilaelaps clarae

As noted above, *Tropilaelaps clarae* is smaller than varroa, and it is elongated, not crab shaped. If the infestation is high, there will be an irregular, punctured brood pattern and malformed brood. The adult bees may have deformed wings (see Photograph 16 in the colour photograph section of this book).

Similar diagnostic tests to varroa can be used to determine a *T. clarae* infestation, particularly an inspection of the capped brood.

Treating of Tropilaelaps clarae

Treatment is similar to that used in varroa control. *Tropilaelaps clarae* has, however, one major weakness in that it cannot exist outside the cell for long. Brood-less periods will therefore clean the hive of mites.

Remember the following points about *T. clarae*:

- It can cause colony collapse faster than varroa.

- It can mate outside cells as well as inside cells (unlike varroa).

- It cannot live outside cells for very long, and this is a major weakness. This means that, during brood-less periods such as cold winters, the mite cannot survive in a colony and will be cleared out.

All beekeepers – even in areas without *T. clarae* – should keep an eye out for it.

OTHER PESTS AND DISORDERS

Small hive beetle
The arrival of this pest in the USA and Australia has been a major blow to beekeeping in these countries. The small hive beetle can eat the brood, destroy the comb and quickly end a colony's life. Its home is Africa where it is regarded as a minor pest of honey-bees, but its presence outside this area is, like so many pests and diseases that have spread throughout the world, a disaster. Beekeepers in beetle-free areas of the world should look out for this pest and report any findings immediately.

Identifying small hive beetle
The one easy thing about this beetle is that an infestation is easy to recognize:

The adult beetle is about one third the size of a bee and can be seen readily, as can their larvae. The beetles are initially reddish brown but mature to black. The adults have two distinctive, club-shaped antennae (see Photographs 17 and 18 in the colour photograph section of this book).

- When a hive is opened, adult beetles can be seen running across the combs to hide from the light (see Photograph 19 in the colour photograph section of this book).

■   If the infestation is heavy, adults may be seen on hive floors and under lids.

■   Small, pearly white eggs, smaller than bee eggs, can be found in irregular masses in crevices or brood combs.

■   If you leave pieces of corrugated cardboard in the hive, the beetles will be attracted to them for shelter and so readily found if their presence is suspected.

■   The smell of fermented honey (caused by the larvae excreting in the honeycomb) is distinctive.

■   The larvae are similar in size to wax moth larvae. After 10–14 days they are 10–11 mm (⅜ in) long. They have three pairs of small proto-legs near to their heads and spines on their backs.

■   The larvae do not produce webbing or frass in the combs.

■   Infested combs have a slimy appearance.

Points to note about the small hive beetle

A few points to remember about this devastating pest include the fact that both adults and larvae will eat bee eggs, brood, honey and pollen, thus very quickly destroying the entire colony. Before this happens, however, when heavily infested, a colony will often abscond. Heavy infestations can reach tens of thousands of larvae, causing partial comb meltdown and fermented, spoiled comb that is repellent to the bees.

Some other interesting points about these clever little beasts include the fact that beetles have been found in bee swarms! Imagine capturing a swarm only to bring death and destruction to your own and your neighbourhood beekeeping. Another point is that, the day after an apiary inspection, there appears to be a huge influx of beetles. It seems that the inspection releases hive odours thus attracting beetles that can detect these odours up to 15 km (10 miles) away! Opening a hive also provokes the existing beetles in the colony to lay eggs, and stored comb in a honey-extraction room is especially at risk of infestation. It seems that whatever you do makes the situation worse!

Treating of the small hive beetle

Beetle traps may be effective, and some are now on the market in the USA. Some of these, however, are merely corrugated cardboard strips. The beetles hide in the corrugations and the strip can then be removed.

Fluorescent-light, larvae-attracting traps can also be used, as can soil drenches in front of the hive – the larvae use sandy soil to pupate in, preferably near to a beehive. Chemical strips may also be placed in the hive, and good hygiene is important, especially in the extracting room.

Colony collapse disorder (CCD)

This is a new and little understood phenomenon in which the worker bees from a colony suddenly disappear. Since 2004, in certain parts of Europe, there has been a dramatic rise in the number of disappearances of honey-bee colonies, and these disappearances are for no apparent reason. The colonies were left with no adult bees, but brood and stores were often present.

Bees very rarely, if ever, abandon brood and stores and, if they do, robbing from other hives usually ensues. Again, after abandonment, the wax moth settles in and destroys the comb. On the occasion of these mysterious disappearances, however, neither robbing nor wax moths were evident. I encountered this problem in Spain in 2004 when I found many of my colonies suddenly empty. One week I had healthy colonies but, a week or so later, they were eerily empty of adults. There was still food on the table but no bees. The brood were dead because of chilling, but there was no robbing and there were no wax moths which, in Spain, are very fast workers because the climate favours their lifestyle. Other beekeepers put it down to bad beekeeping on my part, while (I found out later on) suffering the same problem themselves. They admitted that they, too, had problems only when these disappearances became known as an official 'disorder' and therefore was not their fault!

After a while, however, I began to think it was me, and I vowed somehow to change my way of beekeeping. Being then an organic beekeeper, I employed many different management strategies compared with my neighbours, and so I began to believe that these strategies were at fault. I didn't have to worry for long, though, because a forest fire devastated many of my hives and, in search of a new income I moved to New Zealand. About a year later I read about CCD in Spain and realized that I was possibly one of its first victims – or at least one of the first to admit to it.

Causes

The cause or causes of the syndrome are not yet well understood, but many have been proposed, including environmental change-related stresses, malnutrition, Israel acute paralysis virus, mites, pesticides (such as neonicotinoids or imidacloprid) and genetically modified (GM) crops with pest-control characteristics, such as transgenic maize. The newly discovered variant of nosema (*Nosema ceranae*) has also been postulated as a cause of the problem.

Somewhat tongue in cheek (although it is what I believe), I wrote the following in the editorial for the February 2008 edition of *Apis UK*, the online beekeeping magazine:

> The problem of Colony Collapse Disorder (CCD) seems to be the 'new varroa' talk of the day in the bee and public press. I can well remember the days not so long ago when varroa was the only thing that beekeepers talked about – and perhaps it still should be. I have been in the beekeeping world a comparatively short time (around 18 years) and my main interests in it have been both the production side of things and the scientific side of beekeeping research. I happily trawl through an awful lot of research articles for *Apis UK* for example and I have watched over those few years as new and exotically named syndromes have appeared on the scene – Varroasis; Parasytic Mite Syndrome; Virus diseases of various kinds; a new variant of Nosema and now CCD, and as I read various bits and pieces and listen to people talking on the subject, except for the new variant of nosema, it usually all comes back to varroa. I could be spot off here but that's what it all looks like to me.

> There is also I believe the very underestimated effects of stress on bees to think about. Many beekeepers place enormous stress on their colonies. I did. Moving them from winter quarters to pollination where they could obtain no nectar (kiwifruit) and feeding them copious amounts of sugar and then moving them hurriedly from Gold fruit orchards to Green fruit and then equally hurriedly

to dump sites to congregate for the big moves to manuka areas many hours away. Then splitting them for increase and finally back to often inadequate and damp winter sites (because of any lack of alternatives). Then the process starts all over again. The stress in the colony must be enormous and our moves were minor compared to the multiple shifts I have read about in America. Ally all this to the arrival of a new and devastating mite that assists in the vectoring of existing harmful viruses into stressed and debilitated colonies and I think most humans would give up the ghost. The effect on bees must be catastrophic and so it would seem. They are disappearing. So would I. Let's hope that science can help sort it all out because I'm sure that in this particular case, evolution needs a hand.

YET OTHER PESTS

Bee eaters and other birds

There are many other pests that can make the beekeeper's life difficult, and these include the bee eater, which I have knowledge of from Spain. These delightful-looking birds (they are a little like kingfishers, to whom they are related) can have an amazing effect on the habits of bees. During the day, my bees would fly at low level in a zig-zag motion to try to protect themselves. The number of bees killed this way was not, however, too significant, and I firmly believe the problem is overstated.

The destruction of bee-eater nests in earlier years, for example, backfired. This spread the birds' range, forcing them to colonize new areas that previously had no problems. Bee eaters can, however, have an effect on queen-rearing operations because they tend to prey on larger bees. This could be a major problem when you are trying to mate your queens.

Other birds, such as herons, may attack a beehive's woodwork in their efforts to get at the bees, especially in the winter when there is little else around, but, again, however great their effect on the individual beekeeper and apiary, their overall effect on beekeeping as a whole, and on bee-kind generally, is small and limited in scope. In fact, it is insignificant.

Other animals

Similarly, I have watched toads sit at the hive's entrance and take bees. I have also seen a preying mantis lay her egg sack in the shelter of one of the hive's handles, presumable so that her offspring could build up on my bees! It was all fascinating stuff.

Perhaps one problem that may be more serious is wasp predation. The best way to deal with wasps is, perhaps, to place bottle wasp-traps near each hive – bottles with sweet liquid or beer in them. The wasps can then enter but can't get out. Other than that, you can follow the wasps back to their nest and destroy it. I have done this on many occasions. I don't like doing it because I believe that even wasps have their purpose – they act as the vultures or carrion crows of the insect world – but, now and again, needs must.

There could also be a problem with oriental hornets, such as the mandarin hornet, if ever these spread to other shores. This beast can decimate a colony in no time simply by sitting there and decapitating the guard bees and then going for the brood. However fascinating this might be, it would obviously go against your management strategy. The eastern honey-bee has sorted this problem out. It balls the hornet with a group of bees, and then raises the temperature in the ball to a degree more than the hornet can stand. The bees can survive this temperature but the hornet dies. The western honey-bee, *Apis mellifera*, doesn't know this trick, so watch out for the hornet.

Bears are a problem in both Spain and the USA and, I imagine, in areas of eastern Europe and Russia. The USA and Spain have designed strategies to deal with the bears, and the Spanish even encourage them by placing primitive hives in old, stone bee enclosures with broken walls for the bears to ravage. The bees are then replaced with more from modern hives located in bear-safe areas. Any commercial hives damaged by bears are assessed quickly by independent, non-governmental experts and compensation is paid – again quickly. Even the beekeepers are happy with this regime, and so they do not try to kill the bears, which are very few in numbers.

In the USA, where bears are not an endangered species, different strategies are being developed as the authorities realize that increasing urbanization and the destruction of natural habitats mean that both farmers and wildlife need somehow to be accommodated. Skunk predation in the USA can also lead to very defensive bees and colony destruction. Finally, in some countries, ants are a major pest.

All this seems to boil down to the usual dilemma of people, their agriculture and wild life. While none of these problems should be dismissed, solutions should be sought that enable beekeepers to maintain healthy apiaries and, hopefully wildlife to keep up their numbers. This is, however, an ongoing development well beyond the scope of this book.

SUMMARY

This chapter has attempted to cover the subject of diseases and pests as comprehensively as an introduction to beekeeping allows. This is a huge area, however, and each disease could have a volume of its own. To the beginning beekeeper, the whole thing may be difficult to grasp.

To summarize, therefore:

- Remember that the diagnosis of diseases can be difficult. Some, such as chalkbrood, are more readily identifiable than others, such as EFB, the visual symptoms of which are often confused with other diseases and problems.

- In many cases (e.g. foulbrood), it is easier to identify a diseased colony if you know what a healthy one looks like.

- If you have doubts about a field diagnosis, seek advice from someone competent or contact the statutory authority. It is inadvisable to do nothing in the hope it will go away. *This is especially important in cases of AFB and EFB which, in some countries/states, are not notifiable diseases.*

As noted above, the main thing is to know what a healthy colony looks and smells like. Similarly, know what healthy brood looks like, and know what eggs correctly laid at the base of each cell look like. Know how many bees you should expect to see in a colony, and know what sort of activity you should see at the hive's entrance on a sunny day. If you know these things then, if you notice anything different or smell anything different, either follow the diagnostic advice given in this book or, better still, ask for advice from a bee-disease officer or an experienced beekeeper. By doing this you will learn how to deal with these problems and you will know which ones to report to the authorities.

My final piece of advice is that, if your bees have a disease, don't try to hide it. AFB in your hives, for example, can be embarrassing – it suggests to others that you are not a competent beekeeper, and so many people hide the fact and try to deal with it on their own. The reality may be, however, that it is your neighbour who is not a competent beekeeper – the disease had to come from somewhere! I remember a beekeeper in Lincolnshire whose bees contracted AFB. He immediately rang not only the bee-disease officer but also the rest of the beekeepers in his association and said: 'If you've never seen AFB, here's your chance. Get round here quickly before they are destroyed.' I went round, saw my first AFB and learnt from it. That's the way to do things.

Chapter 11

Rearing Queens and breeding bees

This chapter has been written as an introduction for those who want to move on to producing their own queens and perhaps breeding their own bees. There are many very good books on the subject, and if you are keen on rearing queens for yourself or for sale to others, or if you simply want to explore the world of bee breeding, it would be wise to study these texts. This is just a taster to get you started.

First, all queen-rearing methods are centred on one basic fact of bee biology: nurse bees can turn one-day-old female (worker) larvae into queens by enlarging the young grubs' cells and feeding them on a steady diet of hormone-rich royal jelly. Every technique in queen rearing is thus based on introducing tiny, one-day-old larvae that resemble a small comma to a group of queenless – and thus highly motivated – nurse bees.

WHY REAR YOUR OWN QUEENS?

You already know that you should replace your queens at least every two years, and you know the great advantages of doing this in terms of reducing swarming and increasing honey production. You can, of course, buy your queens from a reputable supplier but, to save money and to increase your enjoyment of beekeeping, you can also produce your own, and this is not at all difficult. In fact, if you leave your bees alone, they will do it for you: they will produce queen cells full of viable virgin queens that you can use to replace your old queens with.

This isn't, perhaps, the best way of going about this, however. It is uncontrolled, and you won't know until it happens just how many queen cells you are going to have available. Also, the cells may come from hives that have characteristics you don't want to propagate, such as a tendency to swarm excessively, foul temperedness or aggressiveness. Sure, you can use queen cells like this in an emergency, but most beekeepers will agree that controlled, planned and simple queen rearing is a far better bet.

Queen rearing means what it says. It does not necessarily mean queen 'breeding' – i.e. the selection of certain traits and breeding for these over several generations until the 'perfect' queen is produced. This is indeed carried out by some beekeepers and research labs in an effort to sort out the varroa problem or for the selection of hygienic bees that will be resistant to American foul brood (AFB) and, indeed, the last part of this chapter explores selective breeding. In the first part of this chapter, however, we just look at ways to produce your queens, preferably from colonies that are good tempered and strong (so that a small amount of 'breeding' comes into it) and in a simple and controlled fashion.

I have, therefore, included three methods here that are simple and easy, but there are many other methods. If you want more information, you should read a specialist book on the subject, and these are listed in the 'Further reading' section at the end of this book.

CHOOSING THE TIME OF YEAR TO RE-QUEEN

Before you begin to rear your own queens you should decide at what time of year you want to re-queen your hives. Autumn or spring are the two choices, and the relative advantages of each season were discussed in Chapters 6 and 7. One thing you must understand at all times, however, is that queen rearing is all about timing. Once you have started the process, you must stick rigidly to a timetable for several weeks. So if you are unable for some reason to be around at the appropriate times, don't start.

QUEEN REARING: AN OUTLINE

Queen rearing is in four parts, as follows. First, you prepare the larvae for presentation to the queen-rearing units. This involves letting the bees choose their own larvae or grafting larvae about 24 hours old from your chosen colony into either plastic or homemade wax cells. Alternatively, you could use a queen-rearing kit whereby the queen is trapped in a cage on a comb where she lays her eggs into prepared plastic cells. These eggs are subsequently removed and presented to a queen-rearing unit.

The next stage comprises preparing queen-rearing units to receive the selected larvae. These units are strong colonies from which the queen has been removed or has been separated from the queen-rearing part of the hive by a queen excluder. Next, you transfer the resulting queens/queen cells to the receiving hives/nuclei, from where they fly and mate. Finally, the mated queen(s) are placed in a queenless nucleus or hive ready to begin work as the colony's queen.

PREPARING THE LARVAE

To take the first point, in most fully controlled, queen-rearing operations, the beekeeper selects larvae from their chosen colony, puts them into plastic or homemade wax cells and then places a frame bar hanging downwards (as nature intended) on them in a queenless colony that is rich in nurse bees. Because the bees are queenless they will recognize these cells as 'queen cups' and will draw them out into queen cells while, at the same time, feeding and nurturing the larvae within them. After a few days, you will find a neat row of queen cells hanging there. You know where they came from, and you know their exact age.

While there are excellent methods of rearing queens that do not require the larvae to be transferred from their original cells to small, artificial queen cups, should you decide to employ the swarm box system of queen rearing described later in this chapter, you will need to know the rules for transferring the larvae into queen cups.

Larval transfer

The term 'larval transfer' describes accurately this method of rearing queens, but the word 'grafting' is used colloquially and will therefore be employed here. Transferring small larvae from cell to cell requires excellent close-up vision and so, for many beekeepers, reading glasses and/or a magnifying glass may be necessary. If all the following looks a little complicated at first, persevere: it really is simple, is invariably successful and well worth the effort.

To transfer larvae, you will need some extra equipment:

- A bain-marie.

- Some wax, new or recycled.

- A wooden cell former (a piece of 8 mm (⅓ in) dowel with a rounded end).

- A frame with a cell bar(s).

- A 'grafting' tool. There are several different types of grafting tool, and most are available from bee-supply firms. The Chinese grafting tool is perhaps the easiest to use because it facilitates both the removal of the larvae and the placing of them in their prepared queen cells.

- A small, sharp scalpel.

- A magnifying glass, if necessary.

When you first start this process, you should prepare certain items in advance, and so the procedure starts off with a preparation phase.

First, prepare a frame fitted with two cell bars. Then make some artificial queen cells, as follows:

- Round off an 8 mm-diameter (⅓ in) piece of dowling as a cell former.

- Make a mark on the dowelling 5 mm (¼ in) from the rounded end.

- Place the rounded end in a glass of water for an hour or so.

- Melt some wax in the bain-marie and remove from the heat.

- Take the dowel rod from the water, shake the water off it and briefly dip it into the melted wax up to the mark.

- Remove from the wax and plunge into the water.

- Repeat this process about five or six times.

- Carefully rotate the wax off the dowel. You will now have a queen cup.

- Make about 30 of these.

- Run some molten wax along the underside of the cell bar(s).

- Place a blob of molten wax about 25–50 mm (1–2 in) along a cell bar and, before it dries, place a queen cell on this.

If you are using Langstroth frames, you can place 12 cells on each cell bar. If you use British Standard frames, you can place 8–10 cells. The more you space them out, the easier it is to remove them. You have now prepared your queen cells (see Figure 28).

Fig. 28. Cell bars with plastic cells (queen cups) hanging downwards. The yellow ones are used for Italian queens and the black ones for Carniolans.

Alternatively, having prepared your cell bars, place plastic queen cells (with their special mounts) on to the bars. There is no difference in acceptance rates between wax and plastic queen cells, but plastic cells are awkward to clean afterwards, whereas you simply re-melt wax ones.

MOVING THE LARVAE

You should now choose the colony from which you want to raise queens. In this colony, place a frame of newish comb in the centre of the brood nest. Eight days later, you will find eggs and newly hatched larvae ready for transfer. These small larvae will usually be situated around the edges of older larvae and capped cells. From this colony, take the comb of eggs and the very young larvae. (This is easier if the comb is of newish wax.)

Take this frame to your shed or car/lorry cab and inspect the larvae carefully. Look for those that are so small that you can hardly see them. The ones you want will resemble a small letter c or a comma sitting in the bottom of the cell in a bed of royal jelly. Use a magnifying glass if necessary.

With a scalpel, pare down the cell walls of a row of these larvae. This will make it easier to remove them. Using your favourite grafting tool, transfer each larvae you have chosen from its original cell to the artificial cell. If you roll a larvae or in any way damage it, discard it.

When you have transferred the required number of larvae, put the cell bar(s) into the down position and, for safety, place the cell frame in an empty nucleus hive. Next, return the rest of the brood frame to its brood chamber. Remember that, if you produce too many queen cells, you may not have enough colonies to provide the bees necessary to make up the number of nucs. If you need 20 queens, go for 30 queen cells to allow for failures and wastage.

Now put the cell bar(s) in the down position and place the frame into the rearing colony. Some 48 hours later, check the bars for acceptance. You will know if the cells have been accepted because the bees will have drawn out the cells and the larvae will be floating on a bed of royal jelly. You will now know how many nucs to prepare for the number of queen cells. Ten days after grafting, remove the queen cells with a scalpel (or unplug the plastic cells) and place each one into a prepared mating nucleus.

REARING QUEENS: METHODS

Before you start to rear queens, decide which method you are going to use and which method of larval presentation: some are incompatible. Have a plan ready and mark it out in your diary. Modern queen-rearing systems, such as the Jenter or Cupkit (which can be purchased from bee-supply companies) have removed a great deal of the fiddly work of grafting as described above. If you don't use one of these systems or a let-alone system, therefore, you will have to graft the larvae.

Before raising queen bees, make sure there are plenty of drones flying or at least plenty of drone larvae in your hive(s). When selecting a colony to provide the larvae, it is common sense to select a gentle colony. This will make it easier to handle and may even provide gentle daughter queens. Remember also that queen-rearing units do not have to be super-strong, so choose one of a size you can easily manage.

Whatever method you decide on, the colony that is to rear queens (or the part of the colony that is to rear queens) must be queenless. De-queen thoroughly, therefore, and then check to see if there is another queen lurking about. This happens. Treat the eggs and very young larvae carefully – neither should be exposed to too much direct sunlight. Use healthy colonies only and, finally, remember that timing is all important in queen rearing, so a failure to keep accurate records could be disastrous.

The following sections describe a few easy methods of rearing queens in the numbers you want. There are other very good ones, such as the Cooke and Cloake methods – both named after New Zealand beekeepers – and there are excellent texts on these, but these methods are beyond the scope of this book.

The easy, let-alone method

(Larval transfer not necessary.) Let-alone methods of queen rearing offer the beekeeper easy ways of producing queens but they are the least controllable. This method permits the colony to decide when new queen cells are to be produced. There are several variations on this method that allow the beekeeper a greater degree of control over certain aspects of the operation, and two of these are described below. Generally, let-alone methods are used only during the spring build-up time because they require the bees' swarming impulse to kick in to provide queen cells. Finally, this method (especially the basic method) corresponds most closely to the way colonies reproduce in nature, and a surprisingly large number of beekeepers rely on it both by accident and by design.

Additional equipment

You will need a sharp knife or scalpel and the required number of prepared nucleus boxes. (Nucs with a frame or two of brood and bees, and a frame of stores as a minimum.)

Procedure

The following is the procedure for the basic method:

- In the spring during colony build-up, do not carry out any swarm-control manipulations.

- As soon as you see queen cells during a hive inspection, study them carefully to decide if they are suitable and if they are ready to be moved.

- Carefully cut out any large, ripe cells and introduce them to the waiting nuclei immediately. Make sure you cut right under the queen cells and through the comb's midrib. This will ensure you do not cut into the queen cell.

- Check that the queen is still present and healthy, and then deal with any other queen cells as required. These superfluous cells could be destroyed as part of an integrated swarm-control programme.

Advantages: This method is easy – the bees do all the 'thinking'. The beekeeper can also assess and choose the best cells from a good selection, and very little extra equipment is needed.

Disadvantages: The beekeeper has no control over the timing of queen-cell production, and assessing the age of the cells can be difficult. Remember that, if the cells are cut out and moved too early, the queen may be damaged.

Note: If you find sealed queen cells, it is likely the colony has already swarmed. Look for the open queen cell, therefore, and for a virgin or young queen: the bees may have re-queened for you.

The let-alone method: variations
(Larval transfer not necessary.)

Variation 1
This method is based on the fact that queenless bees will try to raise another queen from young larvae. Again, it allows the bees to develop their own larvae into queens but, this time, the beekeeper has a greater say in the timings.

Procedure
The following is the procedure for variation 1:

- During the spring, check that the colony has plenty of drone larvae or that the drones are flying.

- Make sure the colony has eggs and young larvae. Remove the queen and place her in a prepared nucleus with a frame of brood and bees, and some honey frames. This is for safe keeping in case things go wrong and the bees don't develop another queen.

- Inspect the colony 48 hours later to see if queen cells have been started.

■ Remove the queen cells 10 days later and place them in prepared mating nuclei – four or five frame nuclei with a frame or two of capped and emerging brood, one empty comb and two frames of honey.

■ If you don't need her anymore, destroy the queen you have been keeping safe.

■ Check the mating nuclei after two weeks to see if the queen has mated and is laying. Leave her where she is to build the nuc into a colony or remove her to the queenless destination hive and put new, just-about-to-emerge queen cells in the mating nuclei.

Advantages: The beekeeper has more control over the timings: they know the queen cells' age and can therefore move them when ripe. The method also retains many of the 'easy' features of the basic method, and very little extra equipment is needed.

Disadvantages: The bees rear queens from worker cells, not from eggs laid in queen cups. This may mean that larvae of the wrong age are chosen, possibly leading to inferior queens.

Variation 2

Procedure

The following is the procedure for variation 2:

■ In the spring, as soon as drone larvae are plentiful or the drones are flying, split a colony in two, making sure that each half has both very young larvae and eggs. If possible, move one half to a different apiary.

■ Two days later, check both halves. One half – the half without the queen – should now have queen cells of a known age.

■ Ten days after splitting the hives, assess the cells and cut out those you find as suitable for placing in mating nuclei.

■ Leave two good queen cells in the still queenless part and keep it separate, or destroy them and reunite the colony.

Advantages: This method has several advantages. It can be used to produce queens and as a swarm-control method. Similarly, there is no need to find the queen although, after day two, you will know which half she is in. This method can also be employed to increase your stocks, if necessary.

Disadvantages: Although not essential, another apiary site is an advantage. More work, time and care are also involved. It is important to note that, in both variations, the beekeeper is forcing the colony to raise queens from what were originally worker cells under 'emergency' conditions. Research has shown that queens produced in this way may, on average, be inferior.

The Miller method

(Larval transfer not necessary.) This a very easy, controllable way of rearing queens. First, take a frame of foundation and trim this to form triangular shapes, as shown in Figure 29. Put this frame into a strong nucleus hive that contains a queen, plenty of bees and frames of brood and honey.

Fig. 29. The Miller frame: trimmed foundation

Making the hive

To make up this hive (a four-frame nuc, for example), just place the Miller frame with its zig-zag foundation into it, a frame of capped and emerging brood, and two frames of honey. Then place a queen from a colony you believe has good characteristics into the box and shake in several frames of bees. Shake the bees off the brood combs so that you get the nurse bees, and shake to overflowing. The queen will have very little room to lay eggs, and so the bees will quickly draw out the wax on the Miller frame into cells where the queen will lay her eggs. Even easier is to place the frame in the middle of the hive's brood box in which the favoured queen lives but, whichever way you do it, you are basically enticing the queen to lay eggs. So far, you have control of the bee and the timings.

After six days, you could prepare a good, full nucleus of bees with stores and emerging brood but no queen; you could de-queen a strong colony you were going to re-queen anyway; or you could place a queen excluder over a strong colony's brood box (ensuring that the queen is below the excluder) and lift a couple of frames of emerging brood and some stores to the top box. Whichever way you do it, you are making sure the colony that will develop your queen cells will be queenless for a day before introducing the cells.

Preparing the larvae

A day later, look at the edges of the triangles of comb. The larvae along the triangles' edges aren't, in fact, larvae but eggs. Trim these edges back until you can see the tiny, comma-shaped larvae. These will be about 24 hours old or younger. They really will look like a tiny c. Don't confuse these with the eggs. Once you've trimmed the eggs away, each cell on these edges will contain just the right type of larvae.

Now, following the edges of the triangles, with a matchstick destroy two out of three larvae. Once you've done this, place the frame into your queenless hive/nuc. Check there are no queen cells in this hive/nuc you may have missed and no open brood. If there are, the bees may not accept your Miller frame larvae.

The bees will now develop the larvae along the edges of the trimmed frame. They will automatically draw out queen cells along the bottom and slanting edges. After 10 days, these cells can be used for re-queening purposes. Very carefully cut them out with a sharp scalpel, ensuring you don't press or squeeze them and that you don't cut into the cells.

The main reason for cutting the foundation into triangular shapes is to give the bees plenty of 'edges' to construct queen cells, and the reason for destroying two out of three larvae is to give the bees more room to draw out uncrowded queen cells. This will make it easier for you when you come to cut them out.

Remember that you will have to have places to put these cells. De-queen your hives in readiness, therefore, or prepare good nucleus hives for the cells if you are building up new colonies.

Rearing queens

But what if you want queens, not cells? In this case you have to go a step further when you cut out your cells from the Miller frame. A day before cutting, prepare nucleus hives with a frame of capped and emerging brood, with loads of bees, frames of stores and an empty frame of comb. You make these nucs from bigger colonies, so once made it is best to move them to another apiary so that all the bees don't fly home. Or you could plug the entrance with grass so that they'll take a while to get out.

Another method of preventing the bees from flying home is to use frames of brood from just one hive. Place the nucs in a circle around the hive, with their entrances pointing towards the original hive. The bees in the nucs will now not go back to the main hive. This idea was developed by a New Zealand beekeeper, Vince Cook, and I've tried it. It works well although, to be honest, I'm not sure why!

A day later, cut out the cells from the Miller frame and place one cell on the frame of brood in each nuc. Gently push the cell into the wax on the brood frame, being careful not to damage it and positioning it so that it hangs downwards. The bees will now look after the cell until the queen emerges. After about two or three days, the queen will fly off to mate and, if all goes well and she isn't eaten or doesn't get lost, she will return to the hive. A few days later she will commence laying eggs, and you will have a mated queen to sell, to build the nuc into a colony or to re-queen another hive.

The Miller method: a summary

Before you begin, choose a colony with good characteristic (e.g. gentleness, low swarming, superseding, adequate honey yields, etc.):

- **Day 1**: make the Miller frame from good foundation wax and place this into a full and queen-right nuc.

- **Day 6**: prepare your queenless cell-building nucs or queenless hive.

- **Day 7**: remove your Miller frame, trim the edges back to the little comma-shaped larvae and place the frame into the centre of the queenless hive/nuc, which will act as the developer hive.

- **Day 16**: if you are going a step further to rear mated queens, prepare your queenless nucs ready to receive one queen cell. Move them to another apiary, block their entrances with grass or place them in a circle around the original hive.

- **Day 17**: carefully cut out the developed queen cells from the Miller frame and use these to re-queen your hives, sell them or place them in the prepared mating nucs described in the previous point.

The *advantages* of this method are that it is low tech and needs no equipment other than hives and/or nucs. You can also raise a good number of queens from it. Once you have removed the Miller frame full of eggs and young larvae from the starter hive, you can put in another frame to start the process again. In this way, you can keep on producing good queens according to a controlled plan, with no need to graft the larvae.

The swarm box method

(Larval transfer necessary.) This is probably the most extensively employed queen-rearing method, especially by serious queen rearers. It is not compatible with the let-alone method of larval presentation because you need to graft some larvae yourself or use a queen-rearing kit, such as the Jenter or Cupkit, to prepare the larvae. This method is, however, suitable for continuous production.

Additional equipment

You will need a well ventilated, three- or four-frame nucleus box and a frame feeder.

Procedure

The following is the procedure for the swarm box method:

- Take a well ventilated, three- or four-frame nucleus box. Into this shake the bees off three well covered combs of brood. If you shake off brood frames you will be more certain of obtaining nurse bees.

- Place into the box a full frame mainly of honey but with some pollen and a full frame of pollen. Do *not* put in any brood. Leave a gap between the frames.

- If the box takes four frames, put in a frame feeder filled with sugar syrup.

- Prepare the larvae by your chosen method and place this frame into the box between the two frames of stores.

- Close the nuc and place in a dark, cool room for about 24 hours. Note this in your diary.

- About one hour before opening the nuc, take a populous, healthy colony of at least two storeys and confine the queen to the lower chamber with a queen excluder.

- Put a frame of young larvae into the centre of the upper chamber (this will attract the nurse bees) and a frame of pollen. Make sure there is a gap between them.

- Fill the rest of the chamber with sealed brood or stores.

- An hour or two later, open the swarm box and transfer the started queen cells to the main colony above the queen excluder and close up. Note this in your diary.

- The cells stay here until they are transferred to the mating nuclei – i.e. just before the virgin queens emerge. Meanwhile, you can place another batch of prepared larvae into the swarm box.

Advantages: This method is fast and simple, can be used for continuous production and is very reliable.

Disadvantages: This method involves a larval transfer and two hives (a nuc and a full hive), and is not really the best method to use if you require only, say, 10–12 queens.

Note: If you are unable to transfer the started queen cells to a builder hive in the timeframe outlined above, don't worry. Just make sure you place the swarm box outside in a convenient position and let the bees fly. Transfer the frame of cells when you can. You must, however, remove the queen cells to mating nuclei (or an incubator) 10 days after introduction. Swarm boxes are not designed for this but, *in extremis*, they will produce queens.

Other methods

There are plenty of other methods of rearing queens but, because they are all based on the same biological principles, they differ mainly in the detail. Read up and experiment if you have the time because it is well worth the effort, but always remember two things. First, timing is all important and, once you've started the process, you can't stop it until the queens are finished. One year in Spain I had to move all my mating nucs at just the wrong moment and so I lost most of the queens. Another time, the weather was very cold and wet and so few, if any, of the queens mated successfully.

The second thing to remember is that any hive or nuc you want to develop queens in must be queenless or the queen must be kept away from the developing cells.

Queen-rearing kits

There are several queen-rearing kits on the market, but they all employ the same principle of inducing the queen to lay eggs in special, plastic, cell bases. These little plastic cells can be removed and set into special frames that hang downwards without touching the larvae. The frames are then placed into queenless cell-builder hives and developed into queen cells.

While these systems allow the beekeeper a large degree of control over their queen-rearing efforts, they are essentially for convenience: the same results can be achieved without them. I now use the Cupkit system whereas a colleague of mine employs a homemade system. Another favourite system is the Jenter kit. Full instructions are provided with all these kits.

INDUCING SUPERSEDURE

With care and an element of luck, supersedure can be induced or, rather, the bees can be 'tricked' into thinking that a virgin emerging from a queen cell placed there by you has come from a supersedure cell and so will accept it as such.

Procedure

The following is the procedure for inducing supersedure:

- Place a ripe, protected queen cell between two frames of a honey super. Make a small entrance in the super or between the two supers.

- Leave alone until the (hopefully) resulting queen can be seen laying.

- Mark the new queen to distinguish her from the old one.

- Now wait to see if the new queen is accepted as a supersedure queen.

As an added precaution, a queen excluder can be placed above the brood nest that contains the queen and taken away when the new queen is laying. When the excluder is removed, the bees and new queen can be smoked down.

Recognizing the supersedure cell

There is no easy way of distinguishing a supersedure cell from a swarm cell. There tend, however, to be fewer supersedure cells than swarm cells. Therefore if you find only one or two cells, these could well be supersedure cells.

The position of the queen cells may be important. Many beekeepers have reported that queen cells built along a frame's top edge are more likely to be supersedure cells.

MARKING YOUR QUEENS

Once you have produced your own queens, it might be a good idea to mark them. For various reasons (see below), queen bees are marked on the thorax. There is no evidence to suggest that marked queens have shorter lives, are superseded more quickly by workers or produce fewer eggs than unmarked queens, unless they are damaged in the marking process.

Advantages: A marked queen is more easily identified: if you mark a queen but later find an unmarked queen, you will know that either swarming or supersedure has taken place, or that your marked queen has died. If you employ the International Marking Code (see Table 7), you will be able to tell a queen's age. Marking queens with coloured discs or numbers can be of value in research and is helpful for identifying specific strains, lineages or other qualities.

Disadvantages: You could damage a queen while marking her, which could lead to her being rejected by the colony. Damage could also lead to a reduced egg-laying rate or even to a drone-laying queen. You may also become accustomed to looking for dots and not queens, and so you could miss a virgin queen without a mark. You might then assume you have a queenless colony and so make the wrong decisions.

Year	Colour
0 or 5	Blue
1 or 6	White
2 or 7	Yellow
3 or 8	Red
4 or 9	Green

Table 7. The International Marking Code
A queen for 2012, for example, would thus be colour-marked Yellow.

Methods
There are three basic ways to mark queens:

■ The queen can be picked up manually by placing your fingers on the sides of the thorax or by holding one of her hind legs. Once picked up, mark her thorax, allow the paint or glue to dry, and place her back in the colony. This takes some practice and is the method most likely to damage a queen. Try it on drones first. If you try it on workers, you will be stung.

- A small cage can be constructed or purchased that is held over the queen on the comb. The workers can escape through the cage, but the queen is too big. The cage is pressed onto the comb until the queen is trapped fast, and the paint is then applied. Wait until the paint is dry before removing the cage. This method is simple and is less likely to damage a queen.

- A queen catcher can be employed. You put the queen in a marking cage where she is pushed up to a screen a sponge plunger. Once trapped against the screen, apply paint to her thorax and allow this to dry before releasing her.

I personally find marking queens useful: it makes my colony inspections faster and easier. I never touch a queen by hand, however, when marking her. I always employ a queen catcher and a press-on cage, and I mark the queen through the grid with a marking pen (see Figure 30). This is a safe and easy method. I normally use white whatever year it is, mainly because I never seem to have the appropriate colour to hand and, if I can't find my pen, I use typewriting correction fluid (this comes with a handy little brush).

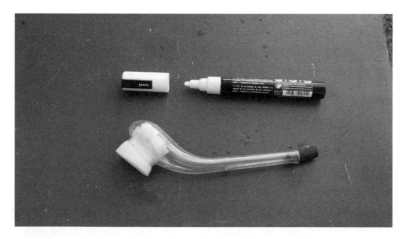

Fig. 30. A plastic queen catcher (with the openings blocked) and a marking pen

TROUBLESHOOTING QUEEN CELLS

This section deals specifically with the problems that may affect ripe queen cells in the rearing chamber or mating nuc.

Queen cell found on the floor of a mating nuc

The beekeeper did not fix the queen cell firmly enough to the brood comb. The cell must be securely attached. When you cut out the wax, leave a large flange of surplus wax to attach the cell to the comb. If necessary, add burr comb to the cell's base – the bees will have made it more secure by the next day.

Queen cell is ripped apart prior to emergence

This can happen if the cell, having been placed in the nuc's brood nest, extends too far above the comb's surface and is partly attached to the adjacent comb by the bees. Make sure you push the queen cell well into the comb when attaching it. You may have to make a largish depression or recess in the comb's face before you attach the cell.

A queen cell on a bar is empty even though it appears normal

Other cells may also have been destroyed. In such cases, a virgin has emerged and has destroyed the other cells. She has ignored the apparently healthy cell because the queen inside has died of other causes. Check that your timing is right and/or place protection cages over developing cells to prevent their destruction.

A queen cell in a mating nuc appears normal but no queen emerges

On inspection the queen cell is found to be empty. This usually means that the queen has emerged and the bees have resealed the cell. This happens. Look for the queen and/or eggs.

Queen cells on a bar have holes in their sides

The occupants are dead. Either one virgin has emerged earlier than the rest and destroyed her rivals, or a queen or virgin has beaten the queen excluder and entered the queen-rearing part of the hive (this is especially easy for virgins). Make sure you employ sound queen excluders and that there are no queen cells in the excluded part of the hive before the rearing takes place. Placing cell protectors around the queen cells can prevent these problems. These can be purchased from bee-supply shops, or hair curlers can be used with their open ends covered or drawn closed with thread.

ASSESSING QUEEN CELLS

One factor that has been stressed in this chapter is the necessity to choose good queen cells, but how do you ensure the queen cells are good? The following are some valuable pointers.

Regardless of how you have produced your queen cells, only the best should be used to head colonies. Queen cells do vary, partly because of their developmental environment. Some of the differences in this environment are reflected in both queen-cell size and appearance. When assessing queen cells, remember that size is important. Research has shown that larger queen cells generally produce better queens than smaller ones.

Highly sculptured cells have received more attention from the bees than smoother cells, and thus they usually produce larger and better queens. Sculpturing makes the cell resemble a peanut's shell. Size and sculpturing normally go together, so a larger queen cell will often be more highly sculptured.

The open cell test allows you to check the age and condition of the queen in her cell. It takes advantage of the fact that the cocoon – which is difficult to cut – surrounds the lower part of the cell only. The part near the base is, however, wax only and can easily be cut. Proceed as follows:

- With a very sharp scalpel, carefully cut round the cell wall.

- Gently fold over the cell wall and inspect the queen.

- Finally, fold the cell wall back to its original position so as to achieve a seamless closure.

ASSESSING QUEENS

Queen bees can be judged according to a multiplicity of criteria. For many beekeepers, the two most important are 'productivity' (the number of eggs produced on a daily basis) and the 'hatchability' of the brood (a measure of fertility).

If climatic conditions permit, the queen will fly and mate five or six days after emergence. She will begin to lay eggs 36 hours or more after her mating flight, but usually after three days. Therefore, when you check the nuc two weeks after placing the queen cell, look for the following:

- On one frame at least, a small, round patch of sealed brood surrounded by uncapped brood. The brood should become younger towards the edges.

- There should not be too many empty cells in the area of capped brood (the 'pepper pot' appearance).

- Eggs around the edges of the unsealed brood. At this time, make sure the queen is safe and well.

KEEPING RECORDS

It may sound tedious but, when you rear queens, it is essential to keep at least a note of what you did and when. If you don't, you will inevitably forget where you have got to, and so a great deal of preparation and hard work will go down the drain.

BREEDING QUEENS

Breeding queens is complex subject but one that many beekeepers like to become involved with for various reasons – perhaps they have dreams of developing a 'super-bee' resistant to disease and able to gather more honey than any other; perhaps they just want to improve their stock to obtain a bigger harvest; or even perhaps because they are just interested. Whatever the aim, queen breeding depends on you knowing about bee reproduction and genetics.

Bee production and genetics

Until very recently, we knew very little about bee reproduction and genetics, but with research agencies all over the world having to face an onslaught of new pathogens, a new interest in this subject has emerged. This, together with the mapping of the bee genome, has told us a great deal about the realities of bee genetics and breeding.

Most organisms function according to a certain set of basic principles, and now that many of the genomes of a variety of plants and animals have been decoded we can see just how much alike we all are. For example, humans share 99% of their genes with chimps and 25% with bananas! But what makes bees and some other organisms slightly different is the fact that the male bee has no father. He is born from an unfertilized egg (a process known as parthenogenesis), and this has enormous implications for breeding bees.

Another factor is that queen bees mate with many drones, all of which could be described as flying gametes because they are the offspring of one queen only (no father remember) and so bring the genes of another queen to the receiving queen. Confused? Probably, but the situation does explain much about the social make-up of a colony.

It was mentioned in Chapter 2 that a queen who mates with drones from a wide area will bring the benefits of genetic diversity to the hive. This means that the colony will be made up of different subfamilies, each with the same mother but different fathers. The next section of this chapter therefore explores basic bee genetics – something that should help you to understand better the nature of these subfamilies, and how and why a colony of bees is made up as it is.

Understanding basic bee genetics

Passing on genes

Chromosomes contain the genes that determine an organism's make-up. Humans have two sets of chromosomes, 23 from the female egg and 23 from the male sperm, which makes 46 in total. Queen and worker bees have 32 chromosomes, again in two sets – 16 from the queen's egg and 16 from the drone's sperm. Queen and worker bees are therefore *diploid*: *di* (two sets) and *ploid* (of chromosomes). Drones, which result from an unfertilized egg, have 16 chromosomes only. They receive these from the queen's egg (they have no father). They are therefore called *haploid*: *ha* (one set) and *ploid* (of chromosomes).

After a queen has mated with a drone, she will produce eggs. As in humans and most other animals, each egg will contain half her total chromosomes – in this case, 16. This means that she can pass on to her offspring only 50% of her genes, and her eggs will contain a random selection of these genes.

The drone contributes the other 16 chromosomes, which are 100% of his total genes. Each sperm from a drone is identical – i.e. it is a clone. A worker or queen thus receives 50% of her mother's genes and 100% of her father's genes. A sister worker or queen from the same drone and queen will hence have a 75% relationship. These sisters are called super-sisters and comprise definite groupings within a hive.

In humans and other animals, the offspring have only a 50% relationship (50% from the mother and 50% from the father). If a worker had her own offspring, she, too, would have only this 50% relationship with her offspring. By helping the queen to raise her super-sisters, however, she has increased this relationship to 75%. This close relationship probably explains why workers have given up reproducing in favour of helping the queen raise more super-sisters. This may satisfy a biological principle whereby organisms try to pass on to the next generation as many of their genes as possible. This is the first complication for bee breeders.

Controlling for sex

The next complication stems from the first: the sex of bees is controlled by what could be called a lethal gene, or sex allele. Despite a colony's fairly complicated family structure and despite the fact that a male bee emerges from an unfertilized egg, the basic principles of genetics still apply to bees. We must now, therefore, go beyond generalities and plunge into chromosomes, genes and alleles.

The specific place on a chromosome where particular genes are found is called a locus. All the forms of a gene that occur at a locus are called alleles. 'Allele' is simply a word that means a version of a gene. For example, genes for blue eyes and brown eyes are alleles of the eye-colour gene. Importantly in bees, there is a gene that controls a bee's sex, and this, of course, is called the sex allele. If two different sex alleles are present, the bee will develop into a female (worker or queen). If only one allele is present, the bee will develop into a drone.

There are two ways that only one sex allele can be present. First, as described above, the egg may be unfertilized and thus contain one sex allele only. Second, both the mother and father may contribute the same allele in a fertilized egg, and so this egg – even though fertilized – will also develop into a drone. The drone will therefore have two sets of chromosomes instead of the normal one set (i.e. a diploid drone) and will not be able to function as a normal drone. These diploid drones are always destroyed by the workers, who eat them on hatching. When inbreeding occurs – i.e. when the mother and father have the same allele – the queen lays her diploid drone eggs in worker cells, and these eggs are subsequently eaten. The brood pattern will therefore be holes alternating with normal larvae. Most beekeepers will have seen this shot brood pattern. The closer the relationship between the mating partners, therefore, the fewer the viable brood. A brother and sister who mate, for example, will produce only 50% viable brood, and the brood pattern will look terrible.

Genetic variability is, therefore, of paramount importance and queens flying to a drone congregation area (DCA) to breed with as many drones as possible from as many different colonies as possible now assumes greater validity. Scientists believe there are around 19 alleles of the sex gene and, the more such alleles present in the bee population, the more solid will be our brood patterns and so the more bees will be available to collect honey.

Genetic variability

While sex determination is, therefore, generally complicated, other characteristics can be even more complex. Different combinations of alleles at a locus can result in many different expressions of characteristics, and all these different factors result in complex genetic systems that produce a wide variety of character expressions in bees. Alleles at other loci can also affect a characteristic, but from this variety comes some of the raw material necessary for the genetic improvement of bee stocks.

So far we have looked at the genetic make-up of queens and drones and have explored how these genetic characteristics can affect colonies. A key factor in all this is the number of chromosomes in bees. To summarize so far, therefore (see also Figure 31):

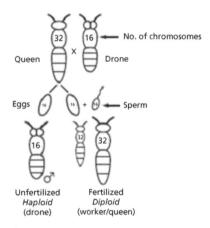

Fig. 31. The number of chromosomes in bees

- Drones result from unfertilized eggs by a process known as parthenogenesis. They have no father.

- Eggs and sperm carry 16 chromosomes each.

- Each egg contains a unique combination of 50% of the queen's genes, and sperm contains 100% of the drone's genes.

- Almost all the 10 million sperm produced by a drone are identical clones. As a drone results from a queen only, he inherits her characteristics, converting her egg into sperm and carrying this to another queen.

- Since each queen mates with 10–20 drones, colonies comprise subfamilies, each having the same mother but different fathers.

- Workers of the same subfamily are related by 75% of their genes.

- This 'extra' close relatedness may explain the co-operative and altruistic behaviours found in colonies.

- It may also explain why workers forgo their own reproduction in favour of helping their queen/mother raise more sisters. Their sisters are more closely related to them than their own offspring would be (75% v. 50%).

Mitochondrial DNA

As a small digression, it is worthwhile looking at how genetics can be employed as an investigative tool when tracing the lineage of bees. To track the lineage of bees – for example, to work out if a bee is of a European type or an African type – researchers look at the mitochondrial DNA.

Mitochondria are small organelles found in every living cell. Their job is to release energy by burning sugar with oxygen. In this way they make respiration possible. When a cell divides, the mitochondria divide as well, but the small amount of DNA they have remains separate from the nucleus. Also, when the sperm and egg unite at fertilization to create a new genetic composition, the mitochondrial DNA stays unchanged. Mitochondria thus pass through generations without their DNA ever being changed, except by occasional mutations. These changes slowly accumulate, and it is these accumulations that enable scientists to differentiate bee lineages.

PRACTICAL BEE BREEDING

So far we have looked at the theory of bee genetics. In this section we explore what we can do with this information. Can we breed better bees, just as farmers improve cows and other livestock, for instance? Given the knowledge we now possess about the subject, the answer to this must be yes. Remember, we can only skim the surface here, but the following should give you an idea of how bee breeders go about their work. For those interested in pursuing bee breeding further, there are many books on the subject (see the 'Further reading' section at the end of this book).

Improving bees' behaviour

Bee breeders have as their objective the improvement of one or more facets of bee behaviour: better honey collection, a better ability to overwinter, a tendency not to swarm, a better temper and so on. Many of these traits may be incompatible with one another, and so compromises have to be made but, generally, the idea is improvement.

Once the breeding goal has been established, the bee breeder must choose their stock from the on-site performance of colonies established in apiaries. These colonies are then tested and given numerical scores for the characteristics being evaluated. This procedure can take two years or more, and as many colonies as possible should be evaluated. This latter point is one of the most difficult to overcome for the hobbyist with only one or two colonies, but it is often equally as difficult for the professional beekeeper with thousands of colonies simply because of the time constraints.

Once all the colonies have been evaluated, breeder colonies can be chosen. To select the best colonies to breed from for a particular trait, the scores for certain characteristics are given more prominence than others. For example, if honey production was considered twice as important as temper, honey production would be scored on a scale of 0–20, whereas temper would be scored on a scale of 0–10.

Once the colonies have been evaluated, there are two main methods of breeding queens: line breeding (closed-population breeding) and hybrid breeding. Both methods have their merits and either may be employed, depending on which part of the world the bee breeder lives in.

Line breeding

Line breeding is the commoner of the two main methods, and this can be defined as breeding and selecting from within a relatively small, closed population. Queens are reared from the best colonies – i.e. those that produce the most honey, that have the best temper and so on. These queens are sold as production queens or are used to re-queen the breeder's test colonies. They are also allowed to mate with the drones in the breeder's apiary. Controlling the drone brood and the propagation of drones from exceptional colonies are, therefore, part-and-parcel of the line-breeding process. This improves the stock's male parentage but, obviously, this procedure can be employed effectively only in those areas where mating apiaries can be isolated.

The main problem with line breeding is that a fixed population of bees means that some inbreeding is inevitable. This reduces the stock's vigour, the result being a poor brood pattern. Inbreeding can, however, be minimized by rearing queens from as large a number of outstanding queens as possible and when possible, by re-queening all the colonies with queens from other breeders.

Is line breeding, therefore, worth the effort? The answer to this question must be yes. In the USA in the 1930s, for example, a four-year line-breeding selection project resulted in an increase in honey production from 67 to 181 kg (148 to 398 lb) per colony. Two important features of this project were the culling of poorer queens and grafting from the best queens.

Hybrid breeding

When inbred lines or races of bees are crossed, the progeny are often superior to either parent for one or more traits. This phenomenon is called hybrid vigour or heterosis, and little is known about it apart from its effects. Hybrid-breeding programmes are more complicated than line-breeding programmes and involve the use of artificial insemination. At the minimum, three inbred lines must be combined so that both their queens and worker daughters are hybrids.

According to John Harbo and Thomas Rinderer in the USA, comparative tests of bee-breeding programmes have demonstrated the superiority of hybrid over line-breeding techniques. For example, increased productivity of 34–50% over the average has been reported in hybrid as opposed to line-bred strains of bees. The one big problem with this type of improvement, however, is that you have to keep on crossing. Hybrids are an end product and, to make the best use of them, it is necessary to re-queen every year – you can't breed from them to continue a line of successful bees. Because of the complexity of this type of breeding programme, and because of its requirement for artificial insemination, few bee breeders have undertaken an entire hybrid-breeding programme.

Selecting traits

Hygienic behaviour is probably one of the bee breeder's most successful achievements. This trait benefits colonies in terms of disease resistance: hygienic bees will remove infected larvae within 24 hours of their appearance and so quickly prevent the build-up of harmful organisms. After a few generations of bees bred from colonies that express this trait, hygiene can become a fixed trait in a population of bees.

But how do you check for the existence of such a trait? In this case, the procedure was fairly simple. Blocks of around 100 capped brood were frozen, and each colony was timed to see how long it took the worker bees to clear away the dead brood. Those that accomplished this task the most quickly (i.e. in under 24 hours) were used to propagate from.

Other traits that have been successfully encouraged include, in the USA where they are a problem, a resistance to tracheal mites and, more recently, the SMR trait in the fight against the varroa mite discussed in Chapter 10. Other experiments in breeding and crossing bee lines have gone spectacularly wrong, such as the efforts associated with the extremely aggressive Africanized bees that are now causing such a problem as they advance into the USA.

The selection of high brood viability (i.e. a loss of sex alleles in the population, leading to inbreeding depression) can also be achieved by beekeepers fairly simply through programmes such as the one described below. If you cut out a parallelogram measuring 5.3 cm (2¹⁄₁₆ in) by 5.3 cm from a piece of card, you should find that there are 100 cells in this cut-out if you place it over a frame of brood. Position it over the most solidly sealed area of brood and count the number of empty cells. Subtract this number from 100. The result should give a percentage brood viability, and anything above 85% is acceptable. Once this trait – or any other trait – is elected, it can be propagated, as the example below shows.

A BEE BREEDING SYSTEM: AN EXAMPLE

Bee breeding and improvement are not something that can be undertaken in isolation by small-scale beekeepers. Evaluations of the results require large numbers of trial colonies, but progressive improvements to populations can be achieved on a smaller scale. The following is an example of such an improvement.

Closed-population line breeding is employed by breeders all over the world. In this system, instrumental insemination is used to improve the breeding population progressively and to maintain high brood viability (this minimizes the loss of sex alleles and so minimizes inbreeding depression).

The procedure for closed-population line breeding is as follows:

- Identify the superior-performing queens in your stock and select 35–50 of these. These are the breeder queens.

- Produce several virgins from each breeder queen.

- Mate the virgins with 10 drones selected at random from the population.

- Place these mated queens in hives and evaluate their performance. The more evaluations, the better.

- Select superior queens from among these queens and use them as breeder queens.

Researchers have estimated that 35–50 breeder colonies must be selected and maintained in each generation if there is to be a 95% probability of retaining sufficient sex alleles for at least 85% brood viability for 20 generations.

There are variations on this method. For example, the semen from a large, equal number of drones from each breeder queen can be pooled and homogenized. This is used to inseminate the daughters of the selected queens, thus ensuring that all the queens are effectively mated with the population's entire gene pool. If the breeder queens were selected for high brood viability, this would also maintain more sex alleles in the population. This system relies on advances in artificial insemination, which is now routine in the bee-breeding world.

BEE BREEDING: A SUMMARY

This chapter has only skimmed the surface of bee breeding. Bee breeding can, however, lead to a very interesting and even lucrative career as either a researcher or breeder. Even the hobbyist beekeeper can institute an improvement programme by rearing queens from their most productive, gentle colony. While this may not always work – the new virgin queens may mate with some not very nice drones – generally, if you keep trying, you should see improvements in your yields of honey or in your bees' temper.

I mentioned in Chapter 8 that I had a Cecropian queen called Rose. I tried propagating from her, but the results were awful. Obviously, her characteristics did not combine well with those of the local Iberian bees. If you recall the Africanized bee disaster where African bees were mated with European bees, you will appreciate just how far things can go wrong. But, by and large, in your own population you should be able to improve your bees – and, in doing so, you will gain a huge amount of knowledge about bees.

There are many good books on the subject, and the best of these are listed in the 'Further reading' section at the end of this book. As far as I am concerned, I need to remember just one thing about bee breeding and genetics: 'the drone doesn't have a father.' It is when I contemplate this that I can only admire those who go on to become successful bee breeders.

Chapter 12

Exploring products and career possibilities

This final chapter introduces you to the many possibilities of obtaining an income from beekeeping, from harvesting pollen, to becoming a research scientist, to working as a jobbing beekeeper on the world stage – beekeeping has immense possibilities for everyone.

We looked at the products of the hive in Chapter 3, and we dealt with the honey harvest in Chapter 7, but what about harvesting other products? But first, we explore here the main purpose of the bees – pollination – a big subject that can be a very good financial proposition for beekeepers.

POLLINATION

Bees and the farmer

Many fruit and other crops produce more and better fruit or more and better seeds if they are pollinated by bees. The percentages of increased fruit yield are, in particular, amazing. Many orchards farmers have thus, at one time or another, kept bees to perform this vital function for free. This isn't really for free, however, because beehives have to be managed well if the bees are to take advantage of the often very early-flowering fruit crops, and this management is usually needed when farmers are, themselves, busy with their fruit or crops. Farmers also often find that they need to spray insecticides on their crops at the pre- and post-flowering stage, and so they have to move the bees out of the way. When the flowers are out and the bees are needed, therefore, the colonies are often weak as a result of neglect. Thus many farmers eventually give up keeping bees, and the colonies are sold or are abandoned to form reservoirs of disease and varroa mites until the wax moth finally destroys them.

I've seen this scenario so often, and that is why you, as a dedicated beekeeper are needed. You take your bees in at the right moment and take them away again when the job is done. The farmers makes their money from apples/pears/plums, etc., and you make yours from your bees.

Why bees are good pollinators

Honey-bees are good at pollinating crops – indeed, they have been doing so for over 40 million years. They have hairy bodies that attract pollen with an electrostatic charge; they recruit others to the flowers very rapidly and in large numbers because of their communicative abilities; and they can be trucked in by beekeepers in their millions to pollination sites (see Photograph 20 in the colour photograph section of this book).

Pollination hives are at their best when they are stimulated to collect pollen, and that is when there are plenty of unsealed brood. Very populous hives are needed with at least two brood boxes, the bottom one of which should be full. There should also be slabs of brood on about six or seven frames or more. The upper box should be well stocked with brood, and there should be three or four combs of honey.

Consulting closely with the grower

Hives should be moved to the pollination site in close consultation with the grower, who will probably need them at about the 10% flowering stage. For some crops that give no nectar, such as kiwi fruit, it is best to move them in at this flowering stage in any case because, if you move them in sooner, they may well go after other flowers and it will be very difficult to re-orientate them to the crop you want pollinated. The grower will probably want your bees until the very last flower has been pollinated. It is as well, however, to move your bees out at the 95% flowering stage, well before any post-blossom insecticides are sprayed.

Avoiding spray poisoning

One of the main problems for beekeepers is pesticides, and these may not originate from the orchard where your bees are but from the one next door or downwind of you. If your bees suffer from spray poisoning, you may lose your livelihood. Dead colonies are expensive in time and cash to replace, so go for the sprayer. This may be a contractor who should know better but has a tight schedule to maintain, or a grower who hasn't thought to check on their neighbours. Whatever happens, take action. If someone's cows are stolen and killed, there is always trouble. The situation should be no different for bees.

Siting hives

The siting of your hives for pollination is critical because you want the most out of your bees. Bees tend to fly at temperatures above 14° C (57° F) and not when it is very windy. The hives, therefore, should be sited in sunny areas facing the sun and, if possible, near a wind-break. Some beekeepers place their hives in laagers, surrounded by bales of straw. For field crops, hives are often sited along the hedgerow. Although this may be convenient for the beekeeper and farmer, it may not be the best place because bees tend to go to the nearest flowers and may therefore miss the centre of a field – or at least not pollinate it so well.

Siting and timing differ between crops, and so it is essential to obtain the advice of a horticultural consultant who knows a particular crop and its requirements. The farmer may also be aware of this, and so their advice should be sought as well.

Calculating the number of hives needed

The number of hives per hectare or acre is a major consideration, and this depends on several factors, such as the attractiveness of the crop to the bees and any rivalry from nearby, more attractive or equally attractive plants. In parts of New Zealand, for example, clover flowering can overlap with manuka flowering, and in kiwi orchards it is a tricky business to keep the bees' minds on the job if attractive wild flowers are around. Kiwis give no nectar, and so feeding the bees with sugar syrup is an essential, added cost.

Table 8 gives the number of hives per hectare for some crops that benefit from bee pollination. It must be stressed, however, that these are average figures – other factors mentioned above must also be taken into account.

Crop	No. of hives per hectare
Apple	2
Avocado	6
Blackcurrant	4
Cherry	0.5
Citrus crops	1
Clover	0.3
Pear	1
Plum	0.5
Kiwi	10–12
Sunflower	1–2

Table 8. Number of hives per hectare for a selection of crops

Moving the hives

Bees should be moved to the crops at night and, if the hives are strapped down well on the truck or trailer, there should be no need to block the entrances. All the hives should be settled in their positions by dawn.

When I was involved in pollination, we took our bees to the roadside near to the entrance to the kiwi orchards and unloaded them on pallets of four hives (the pallets had a mesh covering that were the floors for the hives above). A contractor would then arrive with a forklift on the back of his small truck, and he would move the pallets to the correct positions in the orchard as designated on a map. Sometimes, the orchardist would do this job, especially if he had forks that could be fitted to his tractor. Another contractor would arrive at intervals to feed the bees with sugar syrup – or the farmer would do this if he had the means to do so.

So the orchardist could choose how many hives he wanted, when he wanted them, whether they needed placing and by whom, and who would feed them. He would pay for each service accordingly. Generally, the operation ran smoothly but there were the inevitable hiccups caused by working at night and becoming tired and miserable or being stuck in an orchard in the truck. One of the most difficult tasks was to find the right orchard at night when they all looked exactly the same. We had a system in place in the form of signs at the orchard's entrance, but these were often pulled off by small boys, resulting in many a load of bees ending up in the wrong place.

Making a profit

Generally speaking, pollination contracts will make you money, but at a cost. The main costs are fuel, sugar syrup (if the crop doesn't give nectar) and wages (if you have to employ people). It is hard work and always at night. And because bees won't fly at night – they crawl – this can make the situation worse. I have never been stung so much as when I was doing this work.

We eventually worked out that, if each hive could obtain just a few more kilos of active manuka honey (a very few kilos more), it would make more profit. This would also remove the need to reposition the bees so frequently, thus reducing the beekeepers' stress, saving fuel and truck wear and preventing the bees from being sprayed with insecticide (which always seemed to happen). This example, however, concerns kiwi (a non-nectar giving plant) and manuka honey (a very high-value crop). The same maths may not work for other crops. Before you decide to take up this potentially lucrative aspect of beekeeping, therefore, work out your maths and then, if all is well, go for it.

HARVESTING OTHER PRODUCTS OF THE HIVE

Before you decide whether to harvest other products, it's worthwhile finding out the value of them in your own country. In other words, will anyone buy them, and how much will they pay? Another factor to bear in mind are compliance issues. These apply to honey as well as to the other food items, such as pollen, royal jelly and, perhaps, propolis if it is to be used for internal consumption as a tincture, etc.

These compliance rules become tougher every year and, by and large, are dictated by the big consumer blocks, such as the EU and the USA. If you don't comply, they won't buy. It's as simple as that.

Compliance costs vary and will depend on your status in the chain. If, for example, you are supplying honey to a packer, then the rules will affect you less than if you decide to pack and sell to the public yourself. The packer would pick up most of the flak. In most states the compliance rules are enforced by inspectors who will come knocking on your door. So, before you take the plunge, work out how you are going to comply with all the legislation.

Producing royal jelly

Royal jelly is possibly the most valuable (in monetary terms) product of the hive, and numerous, fabulous claims have been made about it. It is the food of queen bee larvae and, by feeding a worker bee larva this substance, she will develop into a queen rather than a worker. She will be a female bee that can mate – a totally different being from the worker, despite the fact that they start out genetically the same.

How can you become involved?

There is always a market for royal jelly and, whether you are producing it for your own use as a health supplement or you want to go into royal jelly production for sale, it is well worthwhile adding royal jelly production to your beekeeping skills. Any beekeeper who has reared their own queens will know how to produce it.

Royal jelly production consists of the following:

- Ensuring the hives you use are bulging with bees.

- Making wax queen cells or using plastic ones.

- Grafting young larvae into these cells.

- Letting the nurse bees fill the cells with royal jelly to feed the larvae.

- Removing the royal jelly before the larvae eat too much and before the cells are capped.

The queen producer will omit the last part of this process, allowing the cells to be capped. Otherwise, everything else is the same.

Removing royal jelly

The jelly is best removed with a small suction device available from beekeeping-supply companies, although Chinese beekeepers (who produce the bulk of the world's supply) use tiny wooden spoons to extract the jelly at an incredibly fast rate. Once extracted, royal jelly must be frozen or at least kept in the fridge until it is sold or used.

Much royal jelly is freeze dried and sold in this form, but there is a discussion among scientists about how much of the goodness is removed during this process. One piece of research showed that feeding larvae on reconstituted freeze-dried jelly didn't work – the larvae didn't prosper or simply died. Others say there is no difference and that reconstituted royal jelly retains its properties. Clearly this is an aspect of royal jelly production and sale that needs further research.

Nowadays, the availability of plastic cell inserts and small suction devices makes the production of royal jelly an easier and more viable proposition for all beekeepers even if they have just one or two hives.

The one thing that doesn't change in either queen rearing or royal jelly production, however, is the need to adhere to a very strict timetable. Once you start the process, each manipulation must be carried out on time – otherwise the cells will be capped and you will be producing queens, or the larvae will eat too much jelly and it won't be worthwhile extracting what is left. This is a technical business but one that can bring in great rewards, not least that you will learn a huge amount about what goes on in the hive and what goes on among your bees.

Before you start, however, obtain guidance and an outline plan of the proceedings so that you will have something to follow that will increase your chances of success.

Collecting pollen

There is a large market for pollen, especially as a health-food product, and some people regard it as the perfect food. Certainly there are beekeepers in some countries such as

Spain who dedicate their hives to pollen rather than honey collection and who make an excellent living from it.

Pollen collection should, however, be considered only on good, strong hives during seasons when it abounds. Bees collect pollen avidly in the spring when the colony is expanding rapidly, but pollen may be abundant at other times of the year, depending on the local flora.

Beekeepers and scientists have long debated whether taking too much pollen affects a hive's performance, but it seems self-evident that the bees will step up their pollen foraging to counteract the loss at the expense of collecting honey. Further, the colony's pollen-store level could dip below that required for food, and so the colony could dwindle.

Trapping pollen

Pollen is harvested in pollen traps, which are placed on the hive for this purpose. A basic pollen trap is simply a screen through which the bees have to scramble to get into the hive. As they scramble through the screen, the small pollen loads many are carrying are pulled off, and these drop into a specially constructed drawer below the screen.

A pollen trap should catch between 60 and 80% of all the pollen bought into the hive. Some beekeepers believe that traps that retain 60% of the pollen may be kept on the hives throughout the active season, whereas others believe this places too much stress on the colony and that, after two weeks of use, the traps should be removed for at least a week before being replaced.

Traps should effectively exclude all debris (such as insect parts, wax moths, etc.), should be easy to operate and should protect the pollen from sunlight, moisture and any forms of adulteration.

Pollen traps are either front- or bottom-mounted. Front-mounted traps were the first to be used, and these are still employed by commercial beekeepers in many parts of the world. While front-mounted traps are easy to install and remove, bottom-mounted traps are perhaps more efficient and effective.

Bottom-mounted traps can be housed in a standard hive body (see Figure 32). These traps have a screen bottom of 6 × 6.5 mesh per inch (25 mm). The collection drawer slides out to the rear of the hive and, for ease of operation, this may have sloping sides and may also be protected by a sliding outer cover. The drawer's pollen-collecting area is fitted with a plastic-wire or stainless-steel mesh bottom to allow for good ventilation.

Fig. 32. A bottom-mounted trap removable from the side. This is easy to use and causes less disturbance to the bees

Both types of pollen trap can be purchased from bee-supply companies or they can be made by the more talented carpenters among us. Plans are available for this purpose at http://www.beesource.com.

Drying pollen

Before drying the pollen, it is a good idea to freeze it overnight to kill off any wax moths or wax moth eggs that may be in it. Fumigants should not be used for this because they will contaminate the pollen.

When first collected, pollen has a moisture content of between 7 and 21%. It therefore needs to be dried to prevent fermentation and deterioration. Large-scale pollen producers use huge ovens for this purpose that can dry racks of pollen to an exact degree, which should be between 2.5 and 6%. Dry air heated to a temperature of 45° C (113°F) is forced through the pollen.

I have never collected much pollen but, when I did have a go at a small-scale production for my own use, I employed a heating device that could be placed on a table (see Figure 33). The pollen was heated gently on several racks positioned above an element. This device could also be used for drying fruit. Such devices are easy to operate but it is essential that you keep checking the moisture content because on several occasions, I burnt all the pollen.

Fig. 33. A pollen drier heated by an element

Drying pollen outside will not normally dry it sufficiently for marketing. To air dry, the pollen is spread about 20 mm (¾ in) deep in shallow trays with wire bottoms. The pollen should not, however, be placed in direct sunlight, although this is exactly what I have seen done. It should also be protected from dust and debris, which it normally isn't. (It may also have to be protected from bees.)

The moisture content of pollen can be determined easily by a pollen-moisture meter (see Figure 34). These can be purchased from most bee-supply companies and, if you are going to produce pollen for sale, you will need one of these. For those who don't have access to a moisture meter, the following guidelines are often given to Australian beekeepers: attempt to break a pollen pellet between your fingernails. If it does not disintegrate and is difficult to break, the moisture content is between 2.5 and 5%.

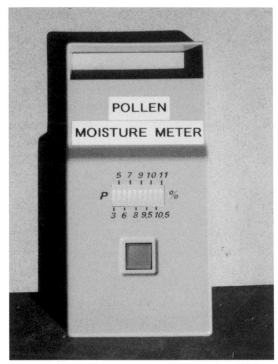

Fig. 34. A pollen-moisture meter

Cleaning pollen

When it has been dried to its optimum, the pollen should be cleaned of all debris. The amount of debris in the pollen is a reflection of the pollen trap's efficiency. Pollen is usually cleaned using a series of sieves of different calibers or by passing it through a series of differently sized screens. The dust is collected in a box below the lowest screen.

Post-harvest storage

Pollen should be packaged in clean, airtight containers immediately after drying and cleaning. If it is allowed to stand in the open air for any period of time, it will absorb moisture and subsequently deteriorate or go mouldy.

Pollen for human consumption should be sold (or used) as soon as possible to ensure its freshness. If it is going to be fed to the bees, it should be used within 12 months.

Extracting beeswax

Beeswax is essentially a side-product of beekeeping, although one that can provide a useful – if sporadic – income. Because of the following, beeswax is an ideal product:

- Processing beeswax is easy. Rendering it to a quality suitable for sale or export involves simple heating and filtering methods only.

- It can easily be moulded into blocks, using any suitably sized containers.

- The transport and storage of beeswax are straightforward because no special packaging is required.

- It does not deteriorate with age, so you can store small amounts until you have enough to sell. The wax moth tends to leave it alone because there is little, if any, sustenance in beeswax.

The value of beeswax varies according to its purity and colour. Light-coloured wax is more highly valued than dark-coloured wax because dark wax is likely to have been contaminated or overheated. The finest beeswax comes from wax cappings, which are the wax seals with which the bees cover ripe honeycombs. This new wax is pure and white – pollen and other impurities turn beeswax yellow.

Rendering beeswax

Most beekeepers produce surplus beeswax by rendering down old, dark comb, and this practice is to be encouraged. After about three or four years, the wax in the comb, especially brood comb, becomes almost black in colour. It is full of impurities in the form of old cocoons and other accumulated debris, and it should be rendered down and either recycled or sold. Also, any other wax scrapings from the hive should be collected and rendered. There are three fairly easy ways to do this.

Solar extractors

A solar extractor is merely a box with a glass lid and a couple of metal pans inside it (see Figure 35). The box is placed at a slant so that the glass lid faces the sun. If you paint the box black and double-glaze the lid, it will even operate in very feeble temperatures as long as the sun is out (for example, on a cool but sunny winter's day).

You place old wax in the upper pan, where it melts. The wax then passes down through a sieve or grating to a small collection pan. When this pan is full, you remove it and cool it, while placing another collection pan in the extractor. You then invert the cooled pan and a block of wax will fall out of it.

If this wax has been made from old black comb, it will be a darkish-brown colour (but nowhere near as black as the comb). If it came from cappings after the harvest, it will be clean and white (and so more valuable). These blocks of beeswax can then be stored until sold or employed to make new foundation using a hand foundation-maker that is available from most bee-supply companies.

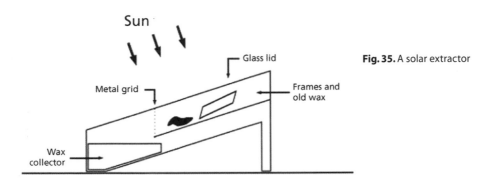

Fig. 35. A solar extractor

The only disadvantage of solar extractors is that, if they are used to render old wax comb that is full of cocoons, they will not extract all the wax from the cocoons. The remaining slum gum can, however, be steam rendered (see below) to extract the maximum amount of wax or, perhaps more practically for the hobbyist, it can be used as firelighters.

Steam extractors

A steam extractor will become a necessity if you build up your hives into a commercial operation of around 100 hives. Figure 36 explains the procedure. I use a portable gas ring below the extractor and a cylinder of butane to power it because I have access to solar power only, but an electric element could also be used if you have a mains supply.

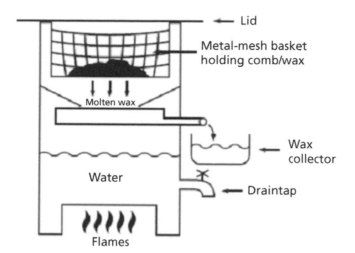

Fig. 36. A steam extractor

As you will see, you just need to place the old frames or the wax into the upper basket, close up, light up and wait for the wax to come pouring out. Make sure, however, that the container receiving the wax is pliable and large enough to hold a decent-sized block and, as soon as this is full, replace it with another one. You will need several of these containers on a good rendering day.

Boiling water

An even simpler way to render down old combs is to put them in a clean sack and then plunge this into a container of boiling water. As the sack boils away, press it down with a block and the molten wax will escape and rise to the surface. A spout near the container's top will enable you to pour the molten wax into a collection tray. In fact, because the spout on my container often blocked or because something else would stop the flow of wax, I usually just collected the wax as a cake at the top of the tank. Eventually I did away with the spout altogether. Because the cake was a large, circular lump of wax, I rendered it down in a solar extractor into smaller cakes that were easier to handle.

Reusing beeswax

If you want to reuse the wax, it is worth investing in a wax foundation mould. I use one that makes a single sheet of Langstroth-sized foundation. This is simply a press with hinges. Inside, on the upper and lower leaves, made of a rubber material are the imprints of foundation.

To make a sheet, you melt the wax in a bain-marie, spray some liquid lubricant over the rubber leaves, pour over the wax, close the press and wait a short while. Next, you trim off any excess wax, open the leaves and gently pull off the sheet of wax.

An even easier method is to take your wax to a bee-supply company to exchange this for wax foundation, or even just to sell it. There is always a demand for wax.

Harvesting propolis

Propolis is another side-line of beekeeping, and few, if any, commercial operators harvest propolis alone. With advances in our understanding of propolis and with advances in its uses in medicine, perhaps one day they will. In the meantime, however, propolis is a very saleable product.

There are two basic methods of harvesting propolis.

Scraping

First, propolis can be scraped off all the woodwork. The main problem with this method is the tiny wood shavings that get into the propolis. Not only that, but this also is a very time-consuming way of collecting propolis and so, if you have to pay someone to do it for you, it is probably not a cost-effective method.

Propolis screens

The main way to collect propolis is to employ propolis screens. These screens (or grids) can be purchased from any bee-supply shop, or you could make your own – but they must be flexible. The screens rely on the fact that the bees will propolize any small holes in the hive. If the screen is made of slots (holes) around 3–4 mm (⅛ in) in width, and if the screen is placed on top of the bars (where you would place a crown board if you used one), then the bees will propolize the slots. When these are full, you remove the screen, put it in a freezer and, when it is very cold or frozen, you take it out of the freezer, flex the screen and out will pop the propolis. In the commercial versions of this product, the slots have slightly sloping sides that aid in the extraction of the propolis.

Alternatively, polyethylene-yarn netting can be employed. The propolis is removed by scrunching up the netting after it has been frozen. Again, this netting can be purchased at bee-supply shops, but many beekeepers buy a similar material from DIY or garden stores that can do just as good a job but more cheaply. It always surprises me how many items of beekeeping equipment can be substituted by much cheaper items that do the job just as well.

Remember to keep the propolis well sealed to protect it from the wax moth. Propolis contains varying amounts of wax and, on one occasion, we sold two barrels of propolis heaving with wax moth larvae. We didn't receive much for them.

Collecting venom

To collect venom, a glass electric-shock plate is usually placed on the hive's alighting board. On receiving a shock, a bee will sting the thin membrane that covers this plate. Because it is able to withdraw its sting from this membrane, the bee then continues to enter the hive. The venom is captured between the membrane and the glass, where it dries. Once the venom has been scraped off this plate under hygienic conditions, the plate is placed on another hive's entrance – colonies can become very defensive if the plate is left on a hive for too long.

Interest in apitherapy (a branch of natural medicine using bee products) has increased in recent years, and so the value of bee venom has consequently grown. Unfortunately, there have been no double-blind, placebo-controlled studies validating the effectiveness of bee venom. A trial carried out in 2005 did not show any efficaciousness for bee venom in the treatment of multiple sclerosis. Another study done the same year did, however, show that bee venom may be effective as a treatment for arthritis.

Venom collecting is a very specialized branch of beekeeping, but it can be a lucrative sideline or mainstream activity. Advice should therefore be sought from bee-supply companies or from a specialist supplier, such as Apitronic Services in Canada (**http://www.beevenom.com**). Although difficult to collect, there is a demand for bee venom, and so beekeepers should not disregard this product of the hive.

Producing silk

No research I am aware of has looked into the commercial harvesting of honey-bee silk, and it will probably take a great deal of investigation before silk production is deemed viable on either a large or small scale. All that is known so far is that cocoon silk is tough and effective. Producing silk is, therefore, something to keep your eye on.

GOING ORGANIC

Producing organic products can be very rewarding. Not only are you ensuring purity of product but you are also assisting, in however small a way, in preserving the health of the planet. And, of course, you are charging a premium for this, so you can be satisfied and rich!

We decided to go organic in Spain partly because I incline that way (although not fanatically so) and partly because it was a good business proposition. Unfortunately we relied on natural flora (no crops) to give us the honey crop and, when a prolonged three-year drought hit us, we were unable to move the bees to cultivated and irrigated crops because we would have lost our hard-earned organic status. We had invested in organically-produced queen bees to head all our colonies and we did not use chemicals to treat diseases. This would all have been lost if we had moved the hives.

Organic beekeeping rules

The rules pertaining to organic food production, including honey, are set out in European legislation. This legislation is followed by most other states, so these regulations can be regarded as the norm. You can access them online (at **http://www.beekeeping.com/ databases/eu_organic_honey_standard.htm**). Have a look at Council Regulation (EC) No. 1804/1999, which supplements Regulation (EEC) No. 2092/91. This regulation covers livestock – from bison down to roasting geese and guinea fowl – and it sets out a whole series of definitions. The important part in terms of organic beekeeping is in Annex I, Part C. Of major concern here is paragraph 4.2, which pertains to the siting of apiaries and which determines whether you can produce organic honey or not. This paragraph states that the siting of apiaries must:

a. ensure enough natural nectar, honeydew and pollen sources for bees and access to water;

b. be such that, within a radius of 3 km from the apiary site, nectar and pollen sources consist *essentially* [my italics] of organically produced crops and/or spontaneous vegetation according to the requirements of Article 6 and Annex I* of this regulation, and crops not subject to the provisions of this Regulation, but treated with low environmental impact methods such as for example, those described in programs developed under Regulation (EEC) No 2078/92(5)* which cannot significantly affect the beekeeping production as being organic.

c. maintain enough distance from any non agricultural production sources possibly leading to contamination, for example, urban centres, motorways, industrial areas, waste dumps, waste incinerators etc. The inspection authorities or bodies shall establish measures to ensure this requirement.

(*These further references define organic agriculture and low environmental impact methods, respectively. The latter is, in my opinion, an excellent method of farming for those who cannot meet the organic regulations. You will find that all the regulations refer to other regulations *ad nauseam*. Although admittedly providing a comprehensive and logical regulation base, the regulations do, however, take some reading.)

The above requirements do not apply to areas where flowering is not taking place or to when the hives are dormant (for example, in southern or eastern Spain).

The important observation in these regulations is the 3 km (approximately 2 miles) limit. This really means 6 km (4 miles) without pollution of any kind and, even in the wild areas of Spain, this is not easy to comply with – there is always one little isolated household where the owners spray their cabbages or whatever. It is here, I think, that a sensible interpretation of the word 'essentially' comes into play: local certifying authorities will have to determine each site on its own merits.

Other regulations pertain, especially in the treatment of bee diseases, which, of course, must be organic (for example, varroa must be treated without the use of synthetic chemicals). Overall, however, the rules are designed to ensure a clean, pure, organic product.

Another point worth mentioning here is that, as every beekeeper knows, bees will forage as close to home as possible. Therefore if there is sufficient wild forage for them they will happily confine themselves to an area within a radius of 3 km (2 miles). While bees have been known to forage up to 13 km (8 miles) or more from a hive, this occurs only when there is nothing else nearer. If this is the case, you shouldn't be in the organic-honey production field, or even in beekeeping at all. In effect, therefore, a beekeeper can control the flowers or areas over which their bees forage only if they are lucky enough to have sufficient land with a known wild or organic crop on it.

My holding in Spain encompassed approximately 1,500 acres (600 ha) of wild land and was surrounded by vast areas of the same. It was populated by numerous wild flowers and trees, none of which were sprayed, and I doubt the bees went anywhere else. Whether this is achievable in more populated countries I'm unsure, but I firmly believe that, if you can do it, you should go for it.

MAKING A CAREER IN BEEKEEPING

Hobby beekeepers

Beekeeping as a hobby is large in scope but little known about. Many beekeepers – in fact most – remain hobbyists, and they enjoy their beekeeping immensely to their dying day. It is these beekeepers who add so much to the world of beekeeping because they have time: it is a hobby. Because they have time, they notice things, and many an idea put to commercial use in beekeeping has been dreamt up by a hobbyist.

Hobbyists are also experimenters. While the commercial operator simply hasn't got the time to experiment, the hobbyist will try things out and buy new-fangled devices from bee-supply shops they don't need but do want. They will use them and either debunk them or tell the world how well they work. Hobbyists are as essential to the beekeeping world as the largest of honey farmers.

Beekeeping for the disabled

I firmly believe that many disabled people could enjoy beekeeping. Obviously this would depend on the extent of their disability but, for those in wheelchairs, for example, low hives (such as the Dartington hive, in which the combs go horizontally rather than upwards in supers) or African long hives (which work on the same principle) may be used. One disabled gentleman asked me about the Spanish Layens hive, which he thought would be suitable for him. These are a single box with a hinged lid, and he found that, even in his wheelchair, he could manage them. I sent him the plans and he got on with it.

There are several very successful projects in developing countries that have targeted disabled people and introduced them to commercial beekeeping. The projects run by the Food and Agriculture Organization (FAO) have been very successful.

Beekeeping associations and courses

In most countries, hobby beekeepers are generally the life and soul of local associations. They are the ones who organize the social gatherings and talks, and many become involved in arranging beekeeping courses. For the beginner, these courses are well worth attending, not least because you may find that you don't really like beekeeping after all, and so you can leave the scene before committing any money.

Most associations offer courses at various levels and, because you can never stop learning about beekeeping, you can take courses to a very high level.

In the UK there is a qualification known as the NDB, or National Diploma in Beekeeping. I have seen the syllabus for this and have talked to several beekeepers who have passed the exam and, as a graduate and postgraduate myself, I can't understand why it isn't called a degree. The amount of knowledge needed to pass it is certainly more than that required by some of the degrees I have come across. In my opinion it is very typical of the UK not to do so.

Hobbyists are also the people who tend to define our thinking about beekeeping. At the time of writing I received an email from someone in the UK who wanted to know about the treatment of mason bees. I replied that I didn't know much about them but would put her in touch with a university department that might help. In her reply she said that she didn't realize bees could be studied in university departments: she thought they were 'kind of nice and rustic'. I was pleased to enlighten her but I know that this is the view of many. Beekeepers are perceived as elderly, pipe-smoking gents or dotty old dears who love their little craft and who keep themselves to themselves. It's a nice view but, of course, totally wrong. In Chapter 1 the immensity of the subject and the huge amounts of money pumped into beekeeping research, not just by governments but also by universities and other scientific institutions, were discussed. From all this there must be opportunities for careers. There are, and the following are some examples.

Jobbing beekeepers

There are opportunities throughout the world for jobbing beekeepers with some experience to work for commercial companies (see Photograph 21 in the colour photograph section of this book). These opportunities occur mainly in New Zealand, Australia, Canada and the USA and, when the beekeeping season approaches, there are plenty of adverts in local papers for experienced beekeepers. If you can demonstrate that you have also had some commercial experience, you are almost certain to be employed. How you obtain that commercial experience can be difficult, but many people attain this by working for a commercial beekeeper in their home country, just for the instruction.

Most beekeeping is hard, heavy lifting, and so most commercial beekeepers are happy to have someone help them, especially when the work involves humping bees around at night. Not only that, but the change from being a hobby beekeeper to working for a commercial operator can be traumatic for some. While the processes are all basically the same, a commercial beekeeper would probably pay you by the hour, and so speed is of the essence. The sheer numbers of hives to be dealt with in a day and the sheer scale of things can also be very daunting. Flying prepared hives into remote areas by helicopter; preparing hundreds of hives for a night move; or loading and unloading hives into orchards that all look the same and knowing you must finish the job before dawn can all be very stressful experiences. Being stuck in some remote, wet area with your truck tilting into a river (see Photograph 22 in the colour photograph section of this book) with no phone coverage, or your trailer has overturned, scattering fifty hives across the road that all need putting back together again before dawn – these are all actual examples. I can only stress again that, before venturing into this exciting and really interesting work, you should first obtain some experience of it close to home.

Obtaining a job

Unfortunately, there is no central, international agency that collates beekeeping jobs, and beekeepers tend to advertise in their local papers only. One way to find an overseas job, therefore, is to place an ad in a foreign magazine or newspaper. When I was involved with a large company in New Zealand, the company would scan the magazines and newspapers when it needed beekeepers to see what was on offer – usually around the July/August period.

Another way is to find out the names of the large and medium-sized beekeeping companies in the area of your choice and to write to them, offering your services and explaining your level of experience. Again, we used to take such letters seriously and, before the start of the season, would contact those we thought would do well. Obviously, if you knew someone in that country you could ask them to obtain the information for you and to keep a lookout in the local press, or even to go and ask at the beekeeping company. Companies need beekeepers because of the shortage of them, especially in such countries as New Zealand, and beekeepers want jobs. It is just a matter of ensuring that the twain meet, and you should be proactive in this. Remember, though, that large, industrial-scale beekeeping is not the same as hobby beekeeping, so be prepared for a vertical learning curve, both mentally and physically.

Many of the beekeepers who worked for us in New Zealand would complete their contracts and then move to Canada or the USA, if they could get in, to work the season there before returning to New Zealand at the end of that season. Many worked their way around the world in this fashion and then used their experience and earnings to set up their own beekeeping enterprises.

Running your own beekeeping business

You can approach running your own beekeeping business from two angles. First, you could gradually build up the number of hives you have as a hobbyist, gathering experience all the time, until you have sufficient hives to earn some side-money from. This is usually where most beekeepers stop, but some go on and suddenly find that not only are they earning money but also they now have the experience and contacts to earn more, if only they had the time. This is when you must decide whether to chuck in the safety of your main job at the office or take up the undoubtedly lucrative but riskier job of working for yourself in an activity that is dependent on the weather, like most farming activities. As I mentioned earlier, in Spain, we suffered several years of drought that, allied to a forest fire, so reduced our circumstances we had to flee.

This slow but sure method of building up a business is, nevertheless, sound, for two reasons. First, you gain a great deal of experience and many contacts so that little comes as a surprise and, second, by the time you make the decision or not to go full time, you at least know whether you like it or not!

If you go down this route there will be another decision you must make. At around the 400–500 hive mark you will need help, but you won't necessarily have enough money to pay someone to work for you. Unless you do, however, you won't be able to increase the number of your hives or be able to make the best of what you have. It is not, however, until you reach the 800–1,000 hive mark that you will be able to afford to employ someone, and so in the meantime you could run out of cash. This type of decision needs sound financial advice and input from your bank, but it has been done and there are many medium to large beekeeping companies that have been through this phase of development successfully.

The second way of starting your own business is to gain experience at home and abroad with commercial beekeeping companies and, after several years, form your own company with plenty of hives without going through the slow build-up process. You will already have experience and you will have the advantage of having seen different ideas and systems in action with various companies. This is a great way to start in beekeeping and has many advantages over the slow build-up method, not least the fact that you are already aware of all the costs involved and the experience levels required to run large numbers of commercial hives.

Funding for such enterprises can come from a variety of sources, and a friend of mine received his start-up funds from the Prince of Wales's Trust. He was not an experienced beekeeper but had been a hobbyist. The fund's discipline and support gave him an excellent start from which he has made a successful career as a commercial beekeeper. So look around at all the funding possibilities in your area, especially those organizations that deal with rural industries.

Scientific careers

A career in beekeeping doesn't necessarily mean being a beekeeper. The world of science is open to those who are suitably qualified, and the number of research possibilities is endless. We know comparatively little about the bees we use compared with, say, cattle or sheep, and the whole idea of insects as social animals can teach us a great deal.

I completed a postgraduate diploma in apiculture at Cardiff and really would have liked to have gone on to a Masters and a PhD, but I was then in my early forties and no one was going to sponsor me at that age. Had I been younger I would no doubt have been accepted onto a programme under some sort of sponsorship. I researched drone congregation areas, which is a very little known and studied area of bee research. It always amazes me that we still don't really know the parameters of these areas or how exactly queens and drones find their way to them, or how exactly their boundaries are defined. I would have loved to have carried on, but having to make a living got in the way. However, this should not stop you, and there are thousands of questions about bees and their products that would provide valid and useful research opportunities.

Entry to research is usually through a bachelors degree in science and then moving on to postgraduate study. A talk with your university adviser and a basic Internet search should show which research institutes are open to supervising this type of research, and don't forget the government laboratories that generally require scientists at this level. I first took honours from London in the geological sciences, but it was 20 years later that I used this degree to obtain a place on a postgraduate research programme. If you are heading in this direction, your reading list should include at least *The American Bee Journal, Apis UK, The Journal of Apicultural Research* and *Apidologie*. So my advice is if you can, go for it, and the earlier the better. We need you.

BEEKEEPING AROUND THE WORLD

Wherever bees can live, beekeeping is practised and has been for thousands of years. The western honey-bee was introduced to many areas of the world as the discovery of new lands gathered pace. The USA, South America, Australia, Canada and New Zealand didn't have *Apis mellifera* until colonization began, and these useful insects were taken there by the colonists. Wherever they went, the bees spread and became an indispensable addition to local agricultural operations.

Hives and other equipment – along with management methods – vary from the very advanced to the incredibly primitive, even within countries. Spain, for example, has advanced beekeeping operations that can compete with any in the world, but it also has some of the most primitive, with beekeepers using old cork hives with cross sticks in them for the bees to hang their combs on. Many beekeepers use the Layens hive, which is truly awful (I tried a couple of them) and, while they are easy to close and load up, the bees inside them are hot and crowded and swarm like crazy.

In Central America, prior to European honey arriving with the Spanish, the local 'honey' bee was the stingless melipona bee. These were kept in tubular log hives, gourds or cylindrical pot hives and were regarded as the messengers of the gods by the Mayan Indians. Special religious ceremonies were conducted at various times of the year, and the Mayan Honey God presided over everything. These bees were a source of great wealth, and the honey from them was used as a trading commodity. Each hive would produce only some 2 kg (4 lb) per year of honey, and so many hives had to be kept to ensure a good and plentiful harvest. The arrival of the more efficient *Apis mellifera* almost caused the abandonment of stingless beekeeping, but recently there have been concerted efforts to devise more efficient hives for these bees and to encourage their use, not least because their honey may well hold a host of medical secrets.

These bees also have ways of conducting their nest mates to food sources. They leave odour trails, and scientists have found that some of these bees use abbreviated odour trails to prevent competitors from following them. Stingless beekeeping is now a hobby practice in Australia and, hopefully, it will grow in tropical areas. There is really no end to the enjoyment and uses of bees, and their study will reap benefits for the future in the pollination of food in a more populous world.

Keeping bees all over the world – whether advanced or primitively managed – generates a sort of global community, and it doesn't matter where you go on holiday, if you are a beekeeper, you will end up talking to other beekeepers. The biannual Apimondia Expo also brings together thousands of beekeepers from this global community, or at least those who can afford to go.

FINALE

So ends this manual of beekeeping. It could go on for a thousand more pages because there is so much to tell, but its purpose is just to get you started – obtain your bees and learn as much about them as you can, either on your own or with others. Read the following information about beekeeping organizations, charities and supply companies and find out what they can offer. Finally, join your local beekeeping organization if only for their advice – especially if you are starting out. You should also find that they are a great bunch of people, as are most beekeepers I have met throughout the world. Good luck.

Weights and measures ready-reckoner

Many of the measurements in this and other beekeeping books may be in units you are unfamiliar with (e.g. metric, US or imperial). The following conversions may therefore assist.

Note: The quantities have been rounded up. For more exact measurements, you should consult a dedicated weights and measures ready-reckoner or one of the many online conversion sites.

Abbreviations

oz = ounce
lb = pound
cwt = hundredweight

in = inch
ft = foot (feet)
yd = yard
nm = nautical mile

g = gram
kg = kilogram

pt = pint
gal = gallon

ml = millilitre
l = litre

mm = millimetre
cm = centimetre
m = metre
km = kilometre

ha = hectare

fl = fluid   sq = square

Linear measurement
1 in = 25 mm   1 yard = 915 mm (0.9 m)
1 ft = 305 mm (0.3 m)   1 mile = 1.6 km

1 cm = ⅜ in   1 km = 0.6 mile
1 m = 3 ft 3 in   1 nm = 1.8 km (legally, but
                                               not by computation)

Area
1 sq in = 6.5 cm²   1 sq mile = 2.6 km²
1 sq ft = 0.09 m²   1 acre = 0.4 ha
1 sq yd = 0.8 m²

1 ha = 2.5 acres

Liquids
1 pt = 0.6 l   1 US gal = 0.8 UK gal = 3.8 l
1 UK gal = 1.2 US gal = 4.5 l

1 fl oz = 28 ml

1 l = 1.8 pt = 4.2 cups (US)

Liquid weights
1 pt water = 1.3 lb = 0.6 kg   1 gal water = 10 lb = 4.5 kg

1 pt = 20 fl oz = 570 ml

1 l water = 1 kg = 2.2 lb

Weights

1 oz = 28.4 g

1 lb = 0.5 kg

1 UK cwt = 1.1 US cwt = 50.8 kg = 112 lb

1 UK ton = 1 metric tonne = 1.12 US ton = 20 cwt

1 kg = 2.2 lb

Temperature

To convert Fahrenheit to centigrade (Celsius):

x °F = (x − 32) ÷ 1.8 (e.g. 60°F = (60 − 32) ÷ 1.8 = 15.5°C)

To convert centigrade (Celsius) to Fahrenheit:

y °C = (y × 1.8) + 32 (e.g. 60°C = (60 × 1.8) + 32 = 140°F)

Further reading

The following is by no means a comprehensive list of all the beekeeping books available, but it does give those I believe are the best of the bunch. Be careful about publication dates – beekeeping is a fast-moving subject, and so books become out of date very quickly. This is especially important in the area of pests and diseases.

Atkinson, J. (1999) *Background to Bee Breeding*. Mytholmroyd, West Yorks: Northern Bee Books. An up-to-date book on bee breeding, including a comprehensive introduction to bee genetics.

Bailey, L. and Ball, B.V. (1991) *Honey Bee Pathology* (2nd edn). London and San Diego, CA: Academic Press.

British Beekeepers' Association (n.d.) *Honeybee Anatomy*. Stoneleigh Park, Warwickshire: British Beekeepers' Association. A series of transparent illustrations (in sectional form) through a bee. Excellent.

Brother Adam (1975) *Bee-keeping at Buckfast Abbey*. Mytholmroyd, West Yorks: Northern Bee Books.

CAAPE (n.d.) *Enfermedades de las Abejas. Prevencion, Diagnostico y Tratamiento*. Cordoba: Centro Andaluz de Apicultura Ecologico, Cordoba University. This very comprehensive book on bee diseases is the ideal companion for those who speak Spanish. Written by the team from CAAPE, the Andalucian centre for organic beekeeping at Cordoba University, it gives excellent advice on organic treatments.

Cook, Vince (2004) *Queen Rearing Simplified*. Mytholmroyd, West Yorks: Northern Bee Books. A very simple and easy method of rearing your own queens explained step by step using the Cook method.

Cramp, David (2006) *The Beekeeper's Field Guide*. Tauranga, NZ: Bassdrum Books.

Not a starter guide but an aide-memoire to take to the apiary. Covers management, manipulations and diseases in a series of comprehensive fact sections.

Crane, Eva (1999) *The World History of Beekeeping and Honey Hunting*. London and New York: Routledge. A really comprehensive and up-to-date history of beekeeping by the founder of IBRA. A must read.

Dade, H.A. (1994) *Anatomy and Dissection of the Honeybee*. Cardiff: IBRA.

Free, J.B. (1982) *Bees and Mankind*. London: George Allen & Unwin.

Graham, Joe (ed.) (1992) *The Hive and the Honey Bee*. Hamilton, IL: Dadant & Sons. A very comprehensive text that needs updating, but it is still very useful.

Hansen, H. (n.d.) *Honey Bee Brood Diseases*. Danish State Bee Disease Committee (also available in Spanish). An essential read.

Howes, F.N. (1945, reprinted 2007) *Plants and Beekeeping*. Mytholmroyd, West Yorks: Northern Bee Books.

Jean-Prost, P. (1994) *Apiculture* (6th edn). Andover: Intercept. A French perspective. Written as a series of lessons, this offers a different and interesting angle on apiculture.

Kirk, W.D.J. (1994) *A Colour Guide to the Pollen Load of the Honey Bee*. Cardiff: IBRA.

MAF (n.d.) *Diagnosis of Common Honey Bee Brood Diseases and Parasitic Mite Syndrome*. MAF (available online at **www.hortresearch.co.nz/files/science/biosecurity/ 227525-Bee-Pamphletpths-small.pdf**).

Morse, R. and Flottum, K. (eds) (1997) *Honey Bee Pests, Predators and Diseases* (3rd edn). Medina, OH: A.I. Root Co.

Ortega, J.L. (1987) *Flora de Interes Apicola y Polinizacion de Cultivos*. Jaen: Libros Aula Magna. An excellent book on flowers, fruits and crops that are of interest to bees and therefore farmers and beekeepers (in Spanish).

Phipps, P. (ed.) (annually) *The Beekeeper's Annual*. Mytholmroyd, West Yorks: Northern Bee Books. Published annually in the UK, this is a complete guide to beekeeping and research organizations in Britain.

Seeley, D. (1985) *Honeybee Ecology*. Princeton, NJ: Princeton University Press.

Shimanuki, H., Flottum, K. and Harman, A. (eds) (2005) *The ABC & XYZ of Bee Culture* (41st edn). Medina, OH: A.I. Root Co. Similar to Joe Graham's (1992) book but in alphabetical order. Try to obtain the latest edition.

Storch, H. (1985) *At the Hive Entrance*. Brussels: European Apicultural Editions. This gives guidance on helping to determine a hive's health by looking at what is going on at the hive's entrance.

Van Toor, R.F. (2006) *Producing Royal Jelly: A Guide for the Commercial and Hobbyist Beekeeper*. Tauranga, NZ: Bassdrum Books. A step-by-step guide to making a profit from royal jelly – an extra dimension to beekeeping.

Von Frisch, K. (1954) *The Dancing Bees*. London: Methuen.

Von Frisch, K. (re-issued 1983) *Bees: Their Vision, Chemical Senses and Language*. London: Jonathan Cape. A classic. This and *The Dancing Bees* describe how Von Frisch discovered the secrets of honeybee communication.

Whynott, D. (1991) *Following the Bloom*. Harrisberg, PA: Stackpole Books. An excellent book about the world's last cowboys – the migratory beekeepers of the USA.

Winston, M.L. (1987) *The Biology of the Honey Bee*. Cambridge, MA: Harvard University Press.

References

Burdock, G.A. (1998) 'Review of the biological properties and toxicity of bee propolis', *Food and Chemical Toxicology*, 36: 347–63.

Goodwin, R.M. and Van Eaton, C. (1999) *Elimination of AFB without the Use of Drugs*. Tauranga: National Beekeepers' Association of New Zealand.

White, J.W. Jr, Kushnir, I. and Subers, M.H. (1964) 'Effect of storage and processing temperatures on honey quality', *Food Technology*, 18: 153–6.

International beekeeping organizations

The following is a list of beekeeping organizations and websites that have a global interest. Organizations tend to come and go, but the following have proved to be robust.

ANERCEA (Association Nationale des Eleveurs de Reines et des Centres d'Elevages Apicoles): the French association of queen rearers (**www.apiculture.com/anercea/**).

Apidologie: not an association but a major bimonthly international journal that publishes original research articles and scientific notes concerning bee science and Apoidea (**www.edpsciences.org**).

Apimondia (International Federation of Beekeeping Associations): promotes scientific, ecological, social and economic apicultural development in all countries and the co-operation of beekeepers' associations, scientific bodies and individuals involved in apiculture worldwide. Apimondia also aims to put into practice every initiative that can contribute to improving apiculture practice and to rendering the obtained products profitable. One of its major objectives is to facilitate the exchange of information and discussion. This is done by organizing congresses, conferences and seminars where beekecpers, scientist, honey-traders and legislators meet to listen, discuss and learn from one another (**www.beekeeping.com/apimondia**).

Bees for Development: an information service at the centre of an international network of people and organizations involved with apiculture in developing countries. It aims to provide information to alleviate poverty and to maintain biodiversity. It is financed from donations, sponsorship, journal subscriptions, training courses, project management, consultancies and information services (**www.beesfordevelopment.org**).

CAAPE (Centro Andaluz de Apicultura Ecologico): based at the University of Cordoba in Spain. Specializes in solutions for organic beekeepers or those trying to limit their use of chemicals.

IBRA (International Bee Research Association): a not-for-profit organization that 'aims to increase awareness of the vital role of bees in the environment and [to] encourage the use of bees as wealth creators'. Its website gives information about the association's mission, members, library services and publications – including the *Journal of Apicultural Research* (incorporating *Bee World*) – a major bee science journal. Information is also provided on conferences and other meetings, and there is a useful page of links to relevant websites (**www.ibra.org.uk**).

Finally, of interest to beekeepers the world over, **www.beekeeping.com** – the international beekeeping virtual gallery that covers just about everything in the beekeeping world (in English, Spanish, French and German).

Beekeeping charities

Beekeeping charities play an important role in helping people in poorer countries to earn a sustainable living from honeybees.

Bees Abroad: a UK charity that raises funds to alleviate poverty in developing countries by funding and running beekeeping projects (**www.beesabroad.org.uk**).

Bees for Development: see 'International beekeeping organizations'.

Hives Save Lives: based in the UK, this charity works for the alleviation of poverty in Africa by helping people to help themselves through beekeeping (**www.hivessavelives.com**).

IBRA: see 'International beekeeping organizations'.

Beekeeping journals

In most countries of the world there is a multitude of beekeeping journals. The following are some of the most popular, enduring magazines in English and Spanish.

American Bee Journal: a monthly that contains a wealth of interesting articles and news applicable not only to US beekeeping but also to beekeeping in general.

Apis UK: a free monthly, online magazine that brings to beekeepers worldwide the science of beekeeping and the latest advances (**www.beedata.com/apis-uk/index.htm**).

Bee Craft: a UK, full-colour monthly covering all aspects of beekeeping but aimed mainly at a hobbyist audience. Provides information from expert correspondents and keeps readers up to date with legislation.

Bee Culture: an American magazine that is aimed more at the hobbyist than the *American Bee Journal*.

Beekeeper's Quarterly: a glossy UK magazine covering all aspects of beekeeping aimed at an international audience. Many articles from a range of global correspondents.

El Colmenar (in Spanish): the following information comes from the magazine's website (**www.elcolmenar.org/**): *Colmenar* (the magazine of the Association of Beekeeping of Colmenar) contains articles, news about beekeeping, the environment and fairs, guides to important suppliers at both a national and international level and an online beekeeping course.

Journal of Apicultural Research (incorporating *Bee World*): a research-based journal that now incorporates *Bee World*. A truly international beekeeping magazine.

New Zealand Beekeeper: the official journal of the national Beekeeper's Association of New Zealand. Always up to date with its news and articles. Provides first-rate information to both commercial and hobby beekeepers.

Vida Apicola (Apicultural Life) (in Spanish): the following information comes from the magazine's website (**www.vidaapicola.com**): *Vida Apicola* (Apicultural Life) was first published in Barcelona in 1982 by a group of beekeepers and lovers of honey. It is now the most read beekeeping magazine in Spain and one of the best technical beekeeping magazines in the world.

Beekeeping supply companies

Beekeeping supply companies come and go, but the following details are current at the time of writing and are likely to last the course. There are many suppliers, and so I have included here the larger companies only. For those outside the UK I have included online companies.

UK

E.H. Thorne (Beehives) Ltd
Beehive Works
Wragby
Market Rasen
Lincolnshire LN8 5LA
www.thorne.co.uk
Tel: 01673 857004

Maisemore Apiaries
Old Road
Maisemore
Gloucestershire GL2 8HT
www.bees-online.co.uk
Tel: 01452 700289

National Bee Supplies
Exeter Industrial Estate
Merrivale Road

Okehampton
Devon EX20 1UD
www.beekeeping.co.uk
Tel: 01837 54084

Park Beekeeping Supplies
17 Blackheath Business Centre
78b Blackheath Hill
London SE10 8BA
www.parkbeekeeping.com
Tel: 020 8694 9960

Sherriff (beekeeping clothing and gifts)
Carclew Road
Mylor
Falmouth
Cornwall TR11 5UN
www.bjsherriff.com or **www.beesuits.com** or **www.beegifts.com**

Stamfordham Ltd
Heugh House
Heugh
Newcastle upon Tyne
NE18 0NH
www.stamfordham.biz
Tel: 01661 886219

Australia

For a comprehensive list of supply companies,
see **http://www.australiadirectory.com.au/ca705-beekeeping-supplies/
c1-australia-beekeeping-supplies.html.**

Canada

For a comprehensive list of supply companies,
see **http://www.canadianbusinessdirectory.ca/category.php?cat=309.**

New Zealand

For a comprehensive list of supply companies,
see **http://www.finda.co.nz/business/c/beekeeping/.**

USA

For a comprehensive list of supply companies with location maps,
see **http://members.aol.com/queenb95/bee_supply_companies.html.**

Europe and rest of world

The following website provides an important list of beekeeping supply companies in many countries of the world:

http://www.beekeeping.com/_menus_us/index.htm?menu.htm&0.

Index